Date: 2/11/22

BIO RAEKWON
Raekwon
From staircase to stage : the
story of Raekwon and the

FROM
STAIRCASE
TO
STAGE

FROM
STAIRCASE
TO
STAGE

The Story of Raekwon and the Wu-Tang Clan

RAEKWON

WITH ANTHONY BOZZA

GALLERY BOOKS

NEW YORK LONDON TORONTO SYDNEY NEW DELHI

G

Gallery Books
An Imprint of Simon & Schuster, Inc.
1230 Avenue of the Americas
New York, NY 10020

Note to readers: Certain names and identifying details of people
portrayed in this book have been changed to protect their identities.

First Gallery Books hardcover edition November 2021

GALLERY BOOKS and colophon are registered trademarks of Simon & Schuster, Inc.

For information about special discounts for bulk purchases, please contact Simon &
Schuster Special Sales at 1-866-506-1949 or business@simonandschuster.com.

The Simon & Schuster Speakers Bureau can bring authors to your live event.
For more information or to book an event, contact the Simon & Schuster Speakers
Bureau at 1-866-248-3049 or visit our website at www.simonspeakers.com.

Interior design by Michelle Marchese

Manufactured in the United States of America

10 9 8 7 6 5 4 3 2 1

Library of Congress Cataloging-in-Publication Data

Names: Raekwon (Musician) author. | Bozza, Michael, author.
Title: From staircase to stage : the story of Raekwon and the Wu-Tang Clan
/ Raekwon with Michael Bozza.
Description: New York : Gallery Books, 2021.
Identifiers: LCCN 2021013197 (print) | LCCN 2021013198 (ebook) | ISBN
9781982168728 (hardcover) | ISBN 9781982168735 (trade paperback) | ISBN
9781982168742 (ebook)
Subjects: LCSH: Raekwon (Musician) | Rap musicians—United
States—Biography. | Wu-Tang Clan (Musical group) | LCGFT:
Autobiographies.
Classification: LCC ML420.R235 A3 2021 (print) | LCC ML420.R235 (ebook) |
DDC 782.421649092 [B]—dc23
LC record available at https://lccn.loc.gov/2021013197
LC ebook record available at https://lccn.loc.gov/2021013198

ISBN 978-1-9821-6872-8
ISBN 978-1-9821-6874-2 (ebook)

Dedicated to my loving mother, Andrea Woods.
Love you, Mommy.

CONTENTS

FROM
STAIRCASE
TO
STAGE

CHAPTER 1

A CHILD IS BORN

I met my father once. I was six years old, living in Brownsville, New York, with my mother, just a street away from her sisters and my cousins. My father had been living in East New York where his mother and a number of his family members lived. Those two neighborhoods are next to each other, just down the road, but he never visited us. He left when I was a baby; I never knew him at all. My older cousins, who were about eleven at the time, knew where he lived though. They knew who he was and they told me about him and promised I'd meet him someday. One day when we were playing, they said, "Know what we doing today? We taking you to see your father." I didn't know what to think, I just followed them to a small house about fifteen minutes away, not really sure if this was real or a game.

What I remember most about him was that he was red. He had red skin, red hair, a face full of red beard. He had Cherokee in his blood and I'd never seen a man who looked like that. He came out of the house, he embraced me, gave me a hug and talked with my cousins and me for a little while. Then he asked if I wanted to meet his mother, my grandmother. We walked over to her house, which was just around the way, and sat in her kitchen. My father left the room for a minute to go to the bathroom and I never saw him again. He slipped out a back door or upstairs window and out of my life forever.

Moms and him met in the late sixties, when she was just nineteen. She told me my father was a nice guy, a snappy dresser, and a great dancer. She said he was a good person and she fell for him. But he was already getting into trouble in the streets, living that gangster life, robbing and stealing. She said he had respect in the streets, and that meant something. In the 'hood, respect is a tangible commodity. It determines how you are treated by your extended family and your neighbors. And that respect is passed down. Like my mom always said when she talked about my dad, "Son, the only thing your father ever gave you was your name and your respect in the neighborhood." And she was right.

Moms loved him. She was a good girl growing up, and when they met she was still going to school, trying to find herself, and staying out of trouble. But she fell for him. She used to say that he cared, he'd come and talk to her and spend time with her. But as nice a guy as she said he was, she never brought him around my grandmother, because I have a feeling Grandma would have sorted him out. Even after my father was gone, I could tell by the way my mother spoke to me about him that she still cared for him—even though he did nothing to help us, leaving her struggling to make ends meet, with a baby, when she was still in her teens.

My mom wasn't naïve. She knew he was up to no good in the streets, but that wasn't why she kicked him out. She dismissed him and forbade him from being around me when she found out he was on heroin. He'd managed to hide it from her for a while, but like any addict, eventually he slipped up. She had no problem with street life and violence: her sister and her friends ran wild in the neighborhood, acting tough, getting into fights, and making trouble. But she wasn't going to let an addict be around her baby. It fucked her up emotionally to do it, but she closed the door on him. She could tell he wasn't going to quit.

Mom was brokenhearted, so she cut him out of her life completely: she got rid of pictures, mementos, anything to remind her. To this day I don't have a picture of my father. He had a brother and a sister, but I've never met them. I remember his face, but as the years go by, it fades in my memory. Some days I wish I had a photo, just a way to make a connection to the man that lives inside me that I never knew.

My situation wasn't unusual; my whole neighborhood was father-less. All of my friends' fathers weren't around. The ones that were, which was maybe 3 percent, didn't interact with their kids because they were lost in one way or another or caught up in street life. In those days, in the late seventies, it was all about pimpin' and having women and doing drugs, and gangs of various sizes ran shit all through the communities of Brooklyn. People would be gambling in the streets, shooting dice, playing craps, with music by Sam Cooke, Al Green, Marvin Gaye, the O'Jays, Donny Hathaway, the Gap Band, Teena Marie, and the Spinners coming out of the radio.

One of my mother's sisters, my aunt Priscilla, was very involved in that life when she was young. My mother and her sisters were all brown-skinned girls, but Priscilla was different in every way: she was light-skinned and wild. Mind you, her crew wasn't like the Bloods and Crips, it was more like the Warriors. These were loose coalitions of street crews, and her particular group was out there to protect their friends and certain businesses in the neighborhood. They got into fights, I'm sure they stuck people up here and there, and it got to the point that my aunt was getting into serious shit. Tough as she was, she was the first in the family to move out of Brownsville to Staten Island, where she said it was safer.

Even though my mom was younger than her, I always felt like Aunt Priscilla was closer to my age. I felt like she understood me and I understood her. Even though Priscilla became a responsible working woman after her wild younger years, my mom came off as older because she was more serious, even when she was cutting loose. I get it, she had a hard life and she worked hard to support me and be a good parent. My aunt did what she had to do too, she just seemed to enjoy life a bit more. They were different, but they were closer to each other than they were to any of their other sisters. When we came home one day to find our door kicked in and all of our valuables gone, it made sense for us to follow my aunt to Staten Island.

Looking back on things, Brownsville was a war zone then. The violence became as ruthless as what goes on between drug cartels in Mexico today. As a child, I saw bodies hung from poles, throats slit, laid out in the street for the neighborhood to see, sending a message to everybody that the gang who did it was not fucking around. When gangs in Brownsville did shit in the seventies, they did it nasty. I remember riding in the car with my grandmother one day, and when we were stopped at a light, I saw a man get hit in the head with a car jack. Not just the iron, the entire device that you put under your car to lift it when you needed to change a tire. Those seventies cars were heavy as hell, so the jacks that came with them were heavy-duty. I was looking out the back window daydreaming when this dude ran out of nowhere and crowned this bigger dude. The guy on the receiving end was bald, so I saw it all in detail when his shit got cracked wide open. Brooklyn was serious.

I was about eight when we moved to Staten Island. Moms wanted a new life, and by then two of her sisters had relocated so it made sense. I was in school and didn't see her a lot because she worked so much just to keep us afloat. I went back and forth to Queens to live with my grandmother during the summer and whenever my mom couldn't support me. That was my life, going from one place to the other. I didn't get to spend too much time with my mom, but when I did, she made it count. Every year for my birthday she'd take me into Manhattan to see a movie. The year I'll never forget is when she took me to see *The Wiz* in Times Square. Diana Ross as Dorothy, Michael Jackson as the Scarecrow, coproduced by Berry Gordy—that film is a masterpiece. It was like a dream to me, sitting there watching it on the big screen and today, at fifty, I still remember it clear as day.

I loved the time I got to spend with my mom, but I felt at home living with my grandmother, Prince, who was always Nana to me. When you're a kid, your grandmother seems like she's so old, though mine was probably fifty-five at the time. I remember when she'd come to get me, all the way from Far Rockaway, Queens, to Staten Island on the A train and then the ferry, and that ride back by her side, seemed like it took an entire day. But I didn't mind, because when the train emerged from underground in Queens it seemed like we had entered another world. Eventually she got this big green Chevy, and she'd ride out to get me and let me sit in the big back seat with my face up against the glass, watching everything that passed before my eyes.

My mother has four sisters and two brothers, so my first father figures of any kind were my uncles, Orrie and Lenny. Orrie joined the army and made a life of it and was rarely around. He traveled the world and ended up settling in North Carolina, near Fort Bragg, where he'd been stationed. He'd come through and drop off money for Nana. He brought her plates from the faraway places he visited for her to display in her china case. G.I. Joe was the shit when I was a kid, so I looked up to him with that army suit on. My other uncle was more of an introvert and he was cool and really into music. When he'd come to visit, I'd share a room with him, but he didn't trust me or interact with me much. I don't remember what he did to get money, but he had enough to buy himself a stereo rack system that he left in the house and forbade me from ever touching. You might as well know this about me now: I'm a hardhead and already was at ten years old, so when he went out, of course I started pushing buttons and turned something on that I couldn't turn off. I had to get Nana to come fix it, and when Lenny got back he flipped out on me.

My grandmother used to take me to Rockaways' Playland every other month. We'd walk there from where we lived in the Hammels project in Queens, which was about six miles. Nana was in her late fifties doing that just to let me have some fun—she was a strong and loving woman. She kept me close because her neighborhood was so crime-infested; she wasn't going to let me run in the streets with the other kids. I had to stay in the back or the front of the building where she could see me. That didn't matter to me. Rockaways' Playland was the highlight of my life. The summers I was there, my mom would send whatever money she could. It wasn't much, just pennies and quarters and dimes. At the end of the day it was probably eighteen dollars, but when you're a kid, that's a lot. Nana used to let me go in the store and get snacks and that was the greatest. I'd take my fifty cents and feel good about it and get some chips, always the spicy ones in the red bag, or onion rings, and a twenty-five-cent juice. Wise Onion Rings, Bon Ton Bar-B-Q chips and a juice, that was all I needed. I was big on cookies too.

About this time, I was eleven and hip-hop was starting to bloom. It was music in the parks, it was turntables and people dancing. I wasn't allowed out there, but my bedroom window at Nana's faced the park so I'd see guys setting up and jamming. They'd be wearing Kangols and mock neck shirts with Lee jeans or French-cut slacks. Looking out that window I saw Adidas hard shells for the first time. All of it was mad cool. I wanted those sneakers, and I wanted to be like those guys. At that time Adidas were thirty-two dollars and Pro-Keds were eighteen, so you know which ones I had. That was the year I realized that music was dope. I'd stay up as late as I could watching these block parties from my window. Nana would close the window and lower the shade and put me to sleep before something happened—a robbery, a shooting, a stabbing. Something always happened later in the night when those parties took off.

My grandmother got it, though, because she loved music. She also loved baseball. We sat around watching Mets games all summer long, and I remember one time she took me to a game. For the rest of her days she used to laugh about it, because for some reason when the crowd would chant "Let's go Mets!" I kept saying "Let's go Rets!" She kept turning to me and saying, "Boy? That ain't the name of it. It's Mets!" I'd say, "Okay, it's Mets." Then I'd start chanting "Rets" again. Don't ask me why, I don't know.

I should mention that at the time, after a series of relationships, my grandmother was married to my step-grandfather Charles, who everyone called Cheese. He was good guy, but kept to himself. He just drank his Bacardi and smoked his Pall Mall reds, which was the cigarette of choice for the OGs back then. He loved baseball too and would talk to me about the game while we watched it together. So because of them I got into baseball. After Nana got me a glove for my birthday, she let me start hanging out with the kids in the building who were into sports. We started out throwing rocks at an X on the wall, then we started playing stickball. I discovered that I had a good arm and could pitch. Between watching music develop beneath my window every night and becoming obsessed with baseball, I had some serious interests.

But then I got hurt playing ball when I dove to make a catch and landed on a jagged tin can. I had to go to the hospital and get stitches. My knee was never really the same, so I began to just stay inside and watch ball games instead of playing with my friends. That was when music took over, and I began to sneak out at night to see what was going on. I was seeing too many dope things going on: parents who I'd see during the day, now out there dancing, smoking, and not acting like parents. There was a crazy lady that lived in the building who I liked to observe too. She was always up to something. She'd have a pile of discarded items and trash she'd try to sell people; she'd have entire conversations with herself or start yelling at someone walking by about something they had nothing to do with, and follow them all the way down the block like a protester. Pretty soon, my friends and I started doing bad shit like hanging out in the elevator shaft above the elevator as it went up and down or kicking people's doors and running away.

My Nana was no dummy. She saw that I was getting into shit and gave me a few ass whoopings around that time. By then, my mom was set up in Staten Island, and she'd managed to get her life a bit more stable in every way. She'd started a new relationship and felt it was time for me to quit bouncing back and forth—as I'd done from eight to eleven—and come be with her on a more permanent basis. It was time to put down roots.

OF her four sisters and two brothers, my mom, Andrea, was the responsible baby sister, the one who did well in school and planned to hold down a good job, the one they sheltered from the streets. She worked in the Twin Towers, for Bankers Trust, for years, some of them with my aunt Priscilla. Regardless, gangster blood was in my mom's DNA. Later in life my mom told me that my Nana had been in a gang when she was young. It blew my mind, because I saw her as nothing but a nice, sweet lady, but that wasn't always the case. In Nana's day, guns weren't the thing, it was knives, and she was no stranger to stabbing people. My mom told me that one time my grandmother found out my grandfather (this was not Cheese, he was my step-grandfather) had cheated on her with some female in their building and she wasn't having that. So one day as she was cooking him breakfast, making him fish and grits, she brought it up. They started arguing and one thing led to another until she burnt the fuck out of him by throwing the hot pot of grits on him.

Before I go on, I have to tell you that fish and grits is a big meal in our family, and it's one of my favorite meals to this day. You line the bottom of your plate in hot grits with cheese, drop your fried fish on there, sprinkle some black pepper over everything, and crack a raw egg on top, letting it cook until it's a perfect sunny-side up. You stir it all together and that's how my family makes grits. You should try it, you will not be disappointed.

The point of the story though is that, as a child, my mother was subjected to a lot of fights and saw violence all around, both in and out of the house. Even though she didn't fight in the streets, my mom was a fighter. I saw this firsthand when I moved back in with her full-time in Staten Island. She had begun a new relationship with a guy named Glen, who she eventually married, and they had my little brother Kareem, whose middle name, Kente, was inspired by the TV show *Roots*. Glen was a cool dude—he was nice enough, kind of humble, with a great smile. He wasn't out there in the streets, he had a job with the Transit Authority, which was good. I never got to know him because from the start he never paid any attention to me. He was a bit of a smooth type; he had a black motorcycle, and he'd pull up real slick and smile at me like, "That's right, I'm fucking your mom."

They were both still young and they were listening to all kinds of disco, like Junior's "Mama Used to Say," Kool & the Gang's "Ladies Night," Diana Ross's "Love Hangover," Gloria Gaynor's "I Will Survive," everything by the Jackson Five, and Michael's early solo stuff. These were big records at the time, and my mom loved them and played them constantly. After a little while I found myself singing along, loving all that music too. My mom was very social, she was a hangout chick, while Glen was more reserved—and that became a problem. She'd throw parties at the house and make fried fish and invite all her friends to come play cards, smoke joints, and probably sniff coke here and there. That's what was going on in the days of disco, when hip-hop was just starting out. My mom wanted to be a part of that as much as she could, while still being a good mother to her two boys.

My mom and Glen started having big arguments, and those were also my soundtrack. At first when I'd hear the yelling, I'd go to see what was happening. She'd tell me to get back in my fucking room and close the door—and that's when it would get bad. When the yelling and banging finally stopped, once Glen would leave, slamming the door behind him, I'd come out to ask if she was all right. She'd have bruises, or her hand would be bleeding, but she'd always say she was fine. "Don't worry about it, son," she'd say. "Just take your ass to bed and get to sleep." I could tell she wasn't all right, she was still angry and hurt. But I had no other choice, so I'd go back to my room.

Back then dudes was ruthless. They'd punch a lady in the face without a thought. Like I told you, Moms was a fighter, so she'd hit right back. And she had a big mouth and wasn't afraid to stand up for herself in every way. She was the type to tell her man exactly what he needed to bring to the table. From what I overheard of their conversations, this is what started the fights. It was a cycle that ended in continuous abuse. It would start when they were drinking Bacardi or Smirnoff and smoking weed and going through whatever they was going through until the conversation turned to how she needed him to help her out more financially. And if that talk didn't go the way she wanted, my mom was the type to say, "If you ain't helping me, motherfucker, then what the fuck is you here for?"

When some people drink hard liquor and smoke weed, they get angry, they argue, and they start shit. My mom was living that life. She never started the beatings, but she was the agitator. I'd hear it all develop from my room, and as time went on, these episodes escalated the way things do when you keep having the same argument and don't resolve it. Plates were broken, punches were thrown, and this became normal to me. All I could do was watch the little TV my mom had put in my room, sitting as close to the screen as I could with the volume turned up, trying to ignore what I still heard anyway. The fighting kept getting worse, so not long after my brother's first birthday, when my mom told Glen once more to get out of her motherfucking house and never come back, he listened. After that they divorced and my mom started doing it all on her own, raising twelve-year-old me and my eighteen-month-old little brother.

I wish I could say that was the end of her abusive relationships, but it wasn't. My mom continued to have boyfriends who were too quick with a fist, and she was right there to answer back. It was tough on me, because I wanted to protect her and help her, but she was the first to tell me to stay out of it because she didn't want to see me get hurt. I loved that my mom handled herself, but I felt helpless and weak every single time.

After my brother was born, my mother went back to work for a while. It was hard for her to keep it all together, even with the help of her sisters and me as her main babysitter. Every day after school I'd sit with my little brother and watch cartoons, mostly Tom and Jerry, Scooby-Doo, the Flintstones, and Woody Woodpecker. I've always loved Tom and Jerry, they were the shit.

My mom chilled for a little bit after Glen, but soon she started having boyfriends again. She would start fighting with them if they weren't willing to help her support our family. I hated to hear all the fights, but I got it—if the dude was going to be an extra burden financially she didn't need him. She was barely getting by as it was. My mother's next real relationship was with a guy she met at a bar named Pete, who was the opposite of Glen. He was a hangout guy, a real groovy dude who looked like a member of Kool & the Gang.

She fell for him because they shared the same spirit: both of them loved music, they loved to dance and party, and they loved to be social. They'd go out to bars or just have a party at home. Looking back now, I bet they were both sniffing blow. Soon enough my mom got pregnant and my sister Simoné was born, right around the time my mom turned thirty-two. Now, Pete was a good guy, and they had a nice relationship, but he was cocky. And now that I'm a man, I recognize that Pete was the type of guy who was running around fucking other girls while fucking the missus too. Knowing my mom, she definitely caught his ass out there.

One thing about Pete was that when he got upset and started yelling, his voice got so fucking loud. My mom never backed down, so they would be yelling and fighting and you couldn't hear anything else. That became the normal for them. What I never understood was how they'd go to sleep and the next morning wake up and act like nothing happened. There was one time they couldn't do that though. One night they got so bad that my mom hit Pete with something and broke his fucking arm. That wasn't the end of things, because as crazy as it might seem, these two really loved each other. Pete was a ladies' man, but he loved my mother. He also loved that they had a daughter together, so he stuck it out with her for five years.

They had the kind of relationship that is so wrong but was normal back then, the kind where men were quick to beat the shit out of their women. Men didn't look at that behavior as wrong, they saw it as "checkin' my bitch." And my mother grew up seeing her siblings live that kind of life, so they were on the same page, even though it wasn't the right page to be on. She definitely didn't get that from my grandmother and step-grandfather. There was no abuse there that I know of, but I can tell you that they argued. My grandmother put up with it because he was putting meals on the table and paying the bills. So I think my mother had both of those realities stuck in her head. She was used to the type of violence that defined men and women in her world back then, and she felt like a bit of arguing and fighting wasn't bad if he was putting food on the table. To her, you stuck with him no matter what if he was paying the bills, but if he wasn't, he got to go.

Once my sister was born, my mom didn't work anymore and felt like whoever was in her life was going to take care of her. And Pete did that: when he had a couple of dollars, he'd take all of us out to eat. We'd go to Beefsteak Charlie's on 42nd Street, and I thought that was just the shit. We'd also go to Tad's Steaks, where you could get a steak for ten dollars, and then see a movie. Those were the good times—the closest we had to what people consider normal family shit—and they didn't happen often.

Pete was the closest thing I had to a father figure, but he never acted like a father when it came to me. He had his own child in our little family, so that's where his focus was. And that was fine by me, because like I told you, I never knew what I was missing. My biological father was a ghost to me, a mystery in life and in death. I used to hear stories about him from people in the neighborhood as I grew into a man: that he overdosed, that he died of AIDS, that he left town, that he was in jail. The real truth is that he got stabbed up out in Brooklyn. He owed some gangster money, and when he didn't pay up, they collected it another way. That street life caught up to my father the way it does to anyone who stays in it long enough.

CHAPTER 2

BOYHOOD

When I moved back with my mom on a more permanent basis in Staten Island, it was still nice but getting ghetto real fast. Now, what I mean by nice is that you'd come to our building, you'd press the intercom for the apartment you'd want to visit, and someone would say, "Who is it?" You'd announce yourself, they'd press a button, a buzzer would go off, the door would open, and you'd go upstairs. There was a security guard in the building then, who would watch the lobby and the exits and patrol the stairwells and roof. The neighborhood was fucked up, but the project buildings were looked after like that.

By the time I turned thirteen just two years later, the drugs had flooded our project, and they took the good times with them. The intercoms didn't work because someone had broken them, and the buzzer system was busted too, so the addicts and dealers came and went as they pleased. And the security guards? If they weren't long gone already they'd have been eliminated in a permanent way.

Poverty was serious all around us, but by then my mom had gotten into her relationship with Pete. Things were stable enough that she was able to take me back full-time. Like I told you, Pete didn't pay me or my brother no mind as a father figure, he was focused on my half sister Simoné. His attitude was that I was a boy and I was going to do what I was going to do, so I started hanging out. I had to be in the front or the back of the building where my mom and Pete could find me, and I started becoming cool with the dudes who were out there every day.

Even though I'd hurt my knee pretty bad, at thirteen I had a fetish for baseball that kept me out of trouble, and I started playing with a few guys in my little building crew who were dope at sports. There were two wings to our six-floor building, doors with numbers from A–L on one side, and M–Z on the other. I had friends in both, all of us around the same age, united by sports. I had one best friend who was Italian and two who were Puerto Rican. My man Fats had three brothers and two sisters. One of his brothers, Dee, was full-blown gay. He dressed like a girl, prostituted himself, was just out there and wild. Fats being thirteen, just becoming a man and wanting to be a macho Italian guy, hated that shit. Fats's other brother Tommy was nuts and just a bad kid in every way. But Fats looked up to his brother Jerome, who was very into sports and who got us into them too. There are only two positions in baseball a fat kid can play, catcher or first base, and since Fats was a fat kid, he was our catcher. I was second base and Jerome was our pitcher, and he used to throw side arm. When you're thirteen and someone is throwing side arm real good, that is the flyest shit you've ever seen. I was infatuated with his pitching style. He was hard as hell to get a hit off, no matter how much I studied his technique.

That was my life as I started to emerge from my family and create my own world. We'd play stickball, and we'd watch the older guys play and pick up some moves from them. There was a group of older guys that were good role models for us. They were working dudes, not running around in the drug game, and they were athletes. They would cool out and play when they weren't at their jobs. That's how we would spend our days in the summer and after school when the weather was nice.

At night, though, we'd hang out with Fats's brother Tommy, which was a different story. Like I told you, he was bad. He'd light fires in the fucking woods and watch them burn, waiting for the fire department to come. He'd go up and down the staircases smashing out all the lights, leaving everyone in the dark. So I was seeing both sides of how people could turn out in my neighborhood.

Fats's father was never around, but we assumed he was in the Mafia at some level. We knew because Fats bragged about it every time he opened his mouth. That is, until the day he got checked. Fats's dad sent a few associates over to smack the kid up in front of the whole neighborhood. This fucking Cadillac pulled up in front of our building and three Italian dudes jumped out and grabbed Fats right up off the fence poles we used to sit on out front. They started smacking him up good. His mother leaned out the window and started yelling, and one of them said, "Get back in the window, Bernice, don't worry about it."

Fats's father might not have come around much or been involved in his life or the neighborhood, but Bernice and the kids never lacked for anything. She had everything but a car, which was the real sign that you were living large in the 'hood. His family always had plenty of food and the kids always had new clothes. Bernice was such a nice lady, she always cooked for us and fed us. She'd make us ham sandwiches after we'd been playing stickball. Back then my favorite shit was ham with cheese and mustard—I used to eat it every chance I got. After a game we'd go to Fats's and Bernice would have it all laid out, because Italians know their shit and always have food on the table. It meant a lot to me because I never had money and my family was barely getting by. So Fats's dad took care of them, but by the same token, he didn't appreciate his son running his mouth to the world about his business.

My other best friend in the building was Michael, who was Puerto Rican. He had a real pretty mom whose partner was a black lady named Deborah. Now Deborah, she was a hustler, a female in body, but a man in mindset. She was up to no good, and Michael learned from her and became a real bad kid. He was my boy so that rubbed off on me, no doubt. Michael's mom and her partner literally had a candy shop in the first floor of the building that was a front for selling drugs. They'd be selling candy to moms for their kids over the counter and selling coke and whatever else for the grown-ups out of the storage room in back. They were hustling, and doing well too. They bought a van and had the side painted in script that said "Lady's Night," which was a popular thing to do back then. When motherfuckers got a car they were proud of it, so you better know they were spraying something on it, customizing it every which way. Those ladies were doing their thing discreetly, but looking back now, I can tell you they were getting money. Cocaine was the thing, disco was king, and everybody was buying. Michael wasn't my only friend whose mom was hustling either: I had a friend named Space, at the end of my hallway, whose mom also happened to be a lesbian, and she and her partner were straight up dealing out of their apartment.

First time I smoked weed was with Michael, after he stole a joint from his mom and we went to the top of the stairwell to smoke it inside the door to the roof. We lit it up, and holy shit, we were like, "This is crazy." Next thing you know we're laughing and snapping on Fats, calling him a fat fucking pig. Fats spat on us, because we used to spit on each other and shit. Fats, by the way, was really good at doing that thing where you let your spit drip as far as you can toward the floor before you slurp it back up. When you're ten to twelve, that skill is impressive.

Michael, Tommy, Fats, and I became a little no-good crew. We'd bang on people's doors and run away. We'd get in the elevator, break the lightbulb, then start karate fighting in the dark, just kicking into space, hitting whoever we hit. We fucked with each other all the time, but Fats got it the worst because he was a butterball, just fat and short. Everybody loved him, because he had a good heart and he was the man, but he was so easily provoked that none of us could keep ourselves from snapping on him.

We were punks and shit, but by the same token we loved baseball and sports so much. We joined the community baseball team, the Park Hill Cubs, and for the three years we were on the team we were some of the best players. We learned a lot from this guy Darnell who lived in the other side of the building. His parents were Jehovah's Witnesses and he was a lot like Jerome—just a teacher and a leader type when it came to athletics. He was also the guy who taught me about fashion, because he was early into hip-hop. He was wearing Lee jeans and Kangol hats, looking cool as hell before it was ever a thing. We had some good times playing on that baseball team: we won championships and we were really passionate about it. I had big dreams then, thinking that if I worked hard enough I could make it into a professional league or at least be a starter for my high school team one day. But the fact was, my family didn't have money for that and never would. It just wasn't going to happen. I'd never be able to join a summer league or afford the equipment I'd need to grow and progress as a young player. So I stayed in the neighborhood YMCA circuit, but all that changed when some volunteer coaches got deep into drugs. This was the early eighties, and these guys were strung out so bad that it was obvious to me and my friends, even at our age. It ruined the fun of playing sports, that's for damn sure.

In my early teens, it was all sports all day and mischief all night. There was a wild individuality that defined me, my friends, and some of the other kids we knew. The combination of influences, both bad and good, that we were exposed to in our households and all around us in the projects caused us to grow up differently than any other people that age I've ever met.

I loved baseball more than anything else, but two years later, I didn't care about it or any sports no more. It wasn't just because our coaches were on drugs; it was puberty, it was culture, and as they say, the times they were a-changin'. Once the movie *Scarface* came out, in 1983, everything was different in my universe. Everyone wanted to be a drug dealer and live glamorously. At the same time, hip-hop was starting to develop, make an impact, and become a movement. I first saw that up at Fats's house, where we would watch *Hot Tracks* on WABC every week. For us in the projects, that show was our MTV. All I wanted to do was watch videos because music was everything. Back then Michael Jackson was in his prime, Prince was kicking off, and out on the streets people were playing hip-hop. They were dressing different too. The disco look was still going, but it wasn't as cool as what was coming up behind: sheepskin coats, leather bombers, Kangols, and of course Adidas sneakers.

One thing that hasn't changed is how important sneakers are to teenage boys. Back then I was lucky to get a pair of sneakers every four months. The best my mom could afford for me was Pro-Keds, but damn I wanted a pair of Adidas so bad. If you were cool you either wore Converse or Adidas; and I was stuck with Pro-Keds. When I did get a new pair, I tried to take care of them as much as I could. But when you're wearing them every day doing everything you do, next thing you know, they're run down, they've got holes. I remember one summer I had a pair with a hole, and my mom told me straight up I had to make them last until it was time to go back to school, no matter how dirty that one foot got from playing outside all day. I'd press my mom to sponsor my sneaker game and she'd just say, "You should be happy you even got clothes."

What she'd do was throw my sneakers in the washing machine and leave them on the windowsill to dry, and every day I'd put them on, until I just got used to wearing those fucked-up shits. Fuck it, what was I gonna do? When it got real hot outside, I wouldn't wear socks, so I'd come in with my feet stinking so bad my mom would make me leave my sneakers at the door. She sure as hell wasn't worried about someone stealing them. Ain't nobody wanted them, not even me.

What all the kids did want was a sheepskin coat or a leather bomber. The only kid we knew who had a sheepskin way before any of us was fat Fats. He also had Cazals, the square glasses everyone started wearing after Run-D.M.C. made them cool. You would have thought that getting smacked up that day on the block would have broken Fats. Not at all, it made him even more of a tyrant and a hustler. He got himself the gear and before you knew it, Fats—the most vulnerable to the criminal life out of all of us—started to sell coke. He was sniffing it too, and running around doing his thing with the older crowd while the rest of us were still acting like the kids we were.

I never had the luxury of willin' out like that. My mother gave birth to another kid, my brother Donperrion, and I was stuck being a babysitter every night so she could go out. I hated that, so I took it out physically on my younger brother Kareem every chance I got. We were into wrestling—Randy Savage and Andre the Giant and Bob Backlund—so we would tear the house up. We were jumping off furniture, fucking everything up, and I got blamed when something got broken. I'd get the ass whooping, but that didn't matter because I knew I was going to make him pay for that next time. I realized later that all of my beatings made Kareem a beast and a madman for years after I had left the house for good. I saw the start of it the time he got a knife from the kitchen and came at me saying, "You've got to stop fucking hitting me." I didn't flinch. I grabbed the knife and said, "What the fuck you going to do with this?" And then I started beating him up harder than before. In our neighborhood, this was a typical, normal household.

MY boys Fats and Michael were starting to do the things the older kids were doing. When I got the chance, I tried to dip into that pool too.

I started to hang out with my two girl cousins Dorinda and Brenda, who were off the hook. They were my first cousins on my mom's side, the daughters of my mom's sister Joyce. Dorinda was the oldest; she was a loudmouth who would snap on you, curse you out, and who just didn't give a fuck. Brenda was more the troublemaker who went outside and started shit in the streets and got into fights. I hung out with Dorinda more because she had her own apartment. One time when I was up there, I saw that she had left some weed on an album cover. She was passed the fuck out, so I took some of it and ran down to Space's house all proud of myself. But I hadn't taken enough weed to roll into a joint, so we got some oregano and filled it out and rolled it up and smoked it. And you know what? It tasted pretty good.

Those two cousins I called aunties because they were so cool. They were so down for me in their way, just guides through my life. They let me be around them while they did everything they did. They weren't much older than me, but they felt like adults who were looking out for me. I used to see them sniffing coke, rolling joints, bagging shit up. One day one of them handed me a joint and told me to light it up. "Go ahead," she said. I thought they would tell my mom on me. "Listen, I ain't going to tell on you, you probably going to tell on me."

Next thing you know, she punched me in the chest and told me to smoke it, so I did. I hadn't been inhaling to her satisfaction, she wasn't having no baby pulls. So I did what she instructed, and two minutes later I was high as fuck. Soon enough I'm falling out laughing, rolling around on the couch, eyes all red. I'd had some weed here and there with my friends, but I count that as the first day I got high. I got a taste for it, so next thing you know, I was hanging out there all the time, looking for crumbs.

Drugs got my friends starting to do some stupid shit around the building. We used to open the vent at the top of the elevator car and climb on top of it and ride up and down. We'd have a broomstick that we'd use to push open the door and climb out the floor above to get out. And we'd push a button in the shaft that would make the elevator skip the floor it was about to stop on. We'd watch the people inside push the button for their floor and then as it got there, we'd push the button that made the elevator skip that floor. It would stop at the wrong floor, so they'd push it again and we'd make it skip their floor again. The whole time we were looking at them through the vent, laughing our asses off but also trying to keep quiet so they wouldn't catch us. Doing that high was just so fucking funny. Around that time we started drinking forties of Old English too. You only needed one of them to get a couple of twelve- and thirteen-year-olds feeling nice. I got real good at coming into my house quiet and going straight to my room. I knew if my mom saw my eyes and smelled my breath she'd know the score and I'd get a beating.

Up at Dorinda's I really saw everything. She was a very pretty girl, about nineteen at the time, and for a while she was dating this real gangster dude from Queens. Back then he was already wearing Timberlands and Kangols and Cazals—he was really fly. He definitely brought all kinds of drugs around her and she got caught up in it, because that was the thing to do. Anyway, I went up there one day, and as usual Dorinda had left her door open (I don't know why she always did). I went in and it was clear to me that it had been a long night because shit was all over the place. Her bedroom door was wide open and I saw her and her dude on the bed, that nigga buck ass naked and shit. I closed the door and started looking for weed, and that's when I found the coke.

I snatched a little bit of it up and got out of there. I wanted to sniff it, but I was too scared, so I just put my thumb to it and tasted it. My tongue numbed up real quick and I figured that's all it does. I did think it was cool though, because everyone thought it was cool. I thought all the drugs were cool, I thought the parties they were having were cool, and I thought the music they listened to was cool—so I hung around there as much as I could.

To remind you, this was before Run-D.M.C. It was back in that time when hip-hop still had that disco flavor to it and a lot of it was more like R&B with early forms of rapping. The music was evolving from disco to break dancing; it was still party music but with a new edge. It had the same groove that kept people moving all night at Studio 54, but it was now speaking more to the street. It went from all that orchestration with strings and horns to nothing but drums and breaks being thrown back and forth between turntables. This was the time of Crash Crew's "High Power Rap," Sugarhill Gang's "8th Wonder," and of course Grand Master Flash's "The Message." Those records were the soundtrack to me wilding out as a young reckless teenager.

The staircase in my building became a clubhouse for me and my friends. When I snatched weed from Dorinda's, I'd find my boys wherever they were hanging. All I had to say was, "Yo . . . Staircase." We all knew what that meant. We'd be in there smoking our crumbs, and other kids our age would come in like, "Yo, I got this forty ounce," and that's all it took. That was our hideout, and just like outlaws, when anyone came up the stairs, we'd scatter. When we were in the staircase, we weren't trying to run into the mothers or fathers or aunties or uncles of anyone we knew. If we heard unfamiliar steps, we'd be gone until the coast was clear. Then we'd all come back like nothing happened.

Kids brought radios in there, sometimes a portable record player if they had one. Next thing you knew it evolved and dudes were beatboxing. In 1984, thanks to the Fat Boys, everyone in our building wanted to make those crazy sounds with their mouths. My boy Wise, whose real name was Sean, was real good and he'd just go all day. This brings me to the point that by now we had all started writing graffiti and no one was calling each other by their government names no more. Anyway, Wise was a little dark-skinned kid who was great at beatboxing, but that didn't keep us from beating on him. It wasn't nice that we fucked him up more than anyone else but that's the way it was. He was the poorest out of all of us, and I don't expect anyone who hasn't grown up in the projects to understand this, but when you're the poorest in that environment you get beat up the most. That's just the way it is. Nobody was trying to hurt him, it was just constant funny shit like giving him a wedgie or kicking him in the ass while he was walking. Wise wasn't a sucker, though, he'd fight back.

There's no two ways about it, me and my crew were nasty little kids. We'd put spit in our hands and throw it at each other, we'd slap box. There was this one Puerto Rican kid, Eddie, who went by the name of Man and he was the worst. He'd take a piece of gum out of his mouth and throw it in the middle of the street, let a truck run over it, then go pick it up and put it back in his mouth. He was a nasty motherfucker like that. But that's the type of shit that we got a kick out of. We'd go up to the roof and hang off the side like we were going to let go. We'd take the garbage cans up there, throw them off, and watch them land on cars then run into our houses before we got caught. We'd be high, running around drinking beers, not realizing we were playing with death on a serious level, all of us between twelve and fourteen.

One time we got our hands on a drug called Rush, which is amyl nitrate. In that era people would sniff it and get crazy. It was some disco dance floor shit. We would dip cigarettes in it and then toke on them without lighting them, which made you so dizzy I don't even know what would have happened if we lit it up. You would take a long toke off of that until you couldn't see straight, and then you'd hold your breath and then breathe in and out real hard while you were bent over, then you'd stand up and your friend would press on your chest, and usually you'd pass out. We called that the Dew Drop. We started making all our friends in the neighborhood do it; we just took it to the street. This girl we knew from school tried it because she thought we were just fucking around until she fell out. Then we saw this dude Cab that we knew from school walking down the street. Cab was from a church family but he was a real wild dude. It's funny how that happens sometimes. This guy would come visit your house and quietly steal something, then when you left to go somewhere, on your way to the elevator he'd hand it to you and tell you how he stole it from your mama's room and shit. He was fucked up, and you never would have thought he went to church three times a week.

So we had Cab try our pass out game, the Dew Drop, and it worked. When he fell, he fell hard, right into this stucco wall that scraped his face up. He was a really dark black dude, so when it happened you could really see how the stucco cut up his face. It was fucked up, but we died laughing at the dude lying there with these white lines like pinstripes up his face. That was our way of having fun, and all the while we were starting to listen to hip-hop.

The easiest way I can think to give you an idea of what my little crew of hooligans was like is to say that we were the Park Hill projects version of the Fat Albert Gang. We were a bunch of misfits, but each one different in his own way: one guy was a major thief, one guy was a bum, one guy was nasty, and on like that. And then there was me; I was the fly on the wall, but a quiet instigator at the same time. I'd never start shit directly, just make suggestions, then follow along to see where it ended up. I didn't know nothing else, so to me, at that time, all the fucked-up shit we were doing was real cool.

Some days when we'd be in the staircase smoking we'd run into some of the older guys. They were there for the same reason: to smoke and hang out off the street so no one would see them. We'd watch what they were doing and talk to them sometimes, and the coolest of them was a group who called themselves the Blif Brothers. Blif was an early term for a blunt, so you know exactly what they were all about. They were the first guys I saw rolling blunts at all, because back then nobody was doing that yet. They'd have a White Owl cigar and they'd lick it up, take a key from their pocket and cut it down the middle. Me and my friends didn't know what the fuck was going on, so to us they were like scientists with access to knowledge we didn't understand.

We were fourteen and they were nineteen or twenty, always with so much weed on them. They'd set up in the staircase, their radio blasting, not giving a fuck, drinking a bunch of Old English forties all afternoon. We observed and respected them from afar because we knew better. We had all learned the hard way that if you hung around too long with older kids like them, they would eventually start fucking you up. They'd start talking about making you tough, and before you knew it they'd start some shit. They'd be kicking you in the ass, then they'd be punching you and chasing you and hitting you because they didn't have nothing better to do. Mind you, they wouldn't be out there punching you in the face, but they'd bust your body up pretty good. It was always a fine line with the older kids we respected. We stayed close enough to see what they were doing because we looked up to them, but we made sure to stay far enough away that they wouldn't turn that corner on us.

On top of their affinity for weed, the Blif Brothers were a proper hip-hop crew: Pee Wee and Carnell, who were brothers, were DJs, and Scotty Watty, who was their cousin, was the MC. They used to hang on the fifth floor in the stairwell, and we would gather down on the fourth floor in the stairs just so we could listen to them. They'd be playing their music on a radio, and next thing you know Scotty Watty would start rhyming and Pee Wee would use Scotty's jacket to make cut sounds while Carnell would beatbox. Scotty always wore a nylon windbreaker so Pee Wee would scratch him on the shoulder with his nails, acting like he was a turntable, and it would sound like he was scratching a record. From there, using a jacket and beatboxing, they'd have a song going. We fell in love with them niggas for that.

These guys didn't have no money but they had musical qualities, and Scotty had a couple of rhymes and was good enough at freestyling, so the neighborhood loved them. Soon they were throwing parties in the buildings around the way, usually in the laundry rooms or rec rooms in the basement. For some reason these guys had relationships with the janitors who let them do this. Pee Wee had a set of turntables, and he and Carnell would both spin records while Scotty Watty got the party started. These dudes would charge five dollars to come down to the laundry room and get wild. They would do this in all the buildings around the way where people were open to it.

Of course me and my friends wanted in, and because we were cool with them, we could usually make that happen. At first we didn't, because they weren't trying to have a Fat Albert crew of fourteen- and fifteen-year-olds at their parties, but we earned their respect. One day we ran into Scotty Watty walking down the street after we had just snatched a few forties from the corner store. That was our thing: we used to steal Li'l Debbies, Suzy Q's, Hostess Apple Pies, and shit, plus as many forties of Old English as we could hide down our pants. We had just made off with a stash of five of them, so we gave him two and kept three for ourselves. We told Scotty how much we liked his rhyming, and honestly, the dude was amazed to hear it. He was touched that we were really listening to what he was laying down. How could we not? He was the closest thing to a superstar we'd ever known.

From then on, he was cool with us. He'd tell us when they were having a party and he'd make sure we got in. It was usually through the back door because no one wanted kids in there, plus I didn't have five dollars to spare if they'd let us in the front. It was usually me, Fats, and our friend Stevie. We became the crew who went to every Blif Brothers party we could.

That first one blew my mind. This was around the time that Whodini was blowing up, and Mary Jane Girls with "All Night Long," Taana Gardner's "Heartbeat," and so many R&B records like that. Those parties were rocking; everybody was in there smoking everything, just getting roasted. That's when I realized that my life was going to get out of control. Back home my mom was making me babysit so she could go out with her friends, but I wasn't doing that: I made them motherfuckers go to sleep so I could leave the house and party. We lived on the second floor, so when I came home late I'd sneak in by climbing the fire escape using a hook that I'd leave in the alleyway to pull the ladder down. A couple of times my mom caught me out there, coming in late after she was already home. She gave me a beating that was as bad as any I'd ever gotten. A funny thing happened, though. After two of those beatings I wasn't scared of them no more. I knew the consequences before I committed the crime, and after I'd survived it a couple times, I knew I could take the punishment. So in my mind, I was free to do what I wanted to do.

The Blif Brothers were my firsthand introduction into the environment that comes with music and the life that would soon be known as hip-hop. It was a movement that didn't have a name, but my friends and I knew that whatever it was, we wanted to be a part of it. We felt connected to that growing energy more than we did to anything else in our lives. We wanted to emulate those guys and what they were doing in every way possible. The Blif Brothers were the trendsetters; they were the ones who made us want to rhyme and be fly.

We started to branch out a little bit, because the Blif parties took us to new buildings where we started to make friends down the block. One of the first guys I got to know around the way was Cappadonna, whose name back then was OG. Like I told you, we all used to write graffiti, and that was his tag. Now, Cap was already something else. He was my same age, but he was able to get away with a lot of shit because he had older siblings hanging out and looking out for him. He had one older brother who was a dancer, and boy that motherfucker danced his ass off. He was a professional—he was on *Soul Train*, he could do the Hustle and all that shit like it was nothing. That dude was the life of any party he was at, which is how I met Cap. His brother used to hang out and dance with my cousins Dorinda and Brenda.

I've got to give it up to Cap, he was just cool from the start, and he was one of the dudes who got me writing rhymes. He was already into it, and he inspired me to start putting things together in that way. He was pretty much one of the first guys my age on our block to begin seriously rapping. He had a style about him from the start: he was a slim dude and he knew how to dress, looking a little bit like a young LL, with a Slick Rick vibe when he got dressed up. That was pretty fly for a fifteen-, sixteen-year-old back in the day.

Cap was into everything my crew and I were into, but he was more sophisticated. At the same time he was more of a loner who didn't run with a lot of people. He had his homies, but he never did gang shit, he didn't follow crowds, he just stayed with the same few dudes around him every day. That was different from how it was where I was at and the way most other kids our age were too. But I connected with him because he was an inspiration when it came to writing. I made sure to keep that connection because it opened something up in my mind. Cap was the first friend I had to start dropping rhymes in front of people, and when he did he caught the attention of Scotty Watty. The Blif Brothers loved Cap and kind of crowned him, saying, "Yo, he's the best of all of y'all."

Cap really was the first guy of my age group and era to take rapping seriously. It was all fun and games, just party music to the rest of us, but he wrote and focused his writing to the point of putting bars on tape. Next thing I knew, he came down the block with a tape of him spitting playing on his radio. Once me and my homeboys heard that, of course we wanted to do it. Because the truth is, all of us rapped—but when I say rap, I'm not talking about writing lyrics, creating bars and songs. I'm talking about being fresh, dropping rhymes, and spitting phrases that sounded dope. We did that on the fly, just hanging out, each and every day.

Cap inspired us. When we hung out, we started more serious cyphers, sharing a few bars that we'd memorized before passing it off to the next man, like a baton in a relay race. And while I was doing that shit at school between classes one day, I met U-God. He was a beatboxer and he was nice at it too. This was when hip-hop was growing fast, when *Beat Street* and *Krush Groove* were out, when Doug E. Fresh and Biz Markie were making their debuts. U-God knew how to do all the sounds that Doug E. Fresh did with his voice, so he was fly as hell. All of us were hip-hop heads. We devoted ourselves to every single thing we saw in those movies and heard on those albums. U-God was able to make that shit come alive for us in some kind of way, right there in our school lunchroom.

All of that changed everything for me. I was fourteen and I wasn't thinking about school, I wasn't thinking about a job. I was thinking about the culture rising up all around me, all of it getting bigger and better every day. I was in it but that wasn't enough. I wanted more. I didn't want to watch this shit in the movies, because I didn't need to. What I saw on the screen already looked a hell of a lot like what I saw in my neighborhood each and every day. It wasn't a musical fantasyland like the one I saw in *The Wiz*, somewhere over the rainbow where I didn't belong. This was an Oz right here where I already lived.

CHAPTER 3

NO HALF-STEPPIN'

I remember when things really changed in my neighborhood, because clear as day there was life before and after the Jamaicans moved in. Some came straight from the Caribbean, others moved in from the established Jamaican community out in Brooklyn, and they started selling weed—a lot of weed—plus coke and heroin too, because that's all people wanted before crack jumped off. The Jamaicans brought a hustle system that was smarter and more bulletproof than any operation anybody had ever seen. They let it be known what apartment in what building was the spot, and when you'd roll up there and knock on the door, thinking they'd open it up to do the deal, they didn't do nothing like that. They'd busted the lock out of the door and replaced it with a latch they'd swing open from the inside, uncovering a little hole for you to stick money through. You'd do that, the latch would snap shut, and then a minute later it would open and your bag of weed or whatever you were there for would slide out. The door was deadbolted from the inside, so nobody doing the deal saw each other or touched hands. It was a clean, efficient transaction, and some real clever shit to us. The Jamaicans were cool with me and my friends, so we were up there buying five-dollar bags whenever we needed them. They also had rented this storefront on the ground floor of a building nearby that was just that—a front—that they filled with music posters, which was the sign to us that something was going on because we knew they weren't selling records. It was around 1985 and they had a Michael Jackson *Thriller* poster in the window, so we started calling it the Michael Jackson spot. We'd be like, "Yo, I'm stopping by Michael Jackson house, you good?"

I was fifteen and I was at the point in my home life where I felt like a man even though I wasn't, because my mom was through trying to force me to come upstairs for dinner or come home at a decent hour. She was involved in her own life, her own relationship, and remember, I'm five years older than my oldest sibling, so she was too busy with all of them to chase after me. So long as I made it to school in the morning, I was able to get away with a lot of shit.

It was around this time that I started hanging out with my cousin Unique, Brenda and Dorinda's older brother. He is someone that I truly love and respect and who was a father figure not only to me but to my extended family in general. He was the one everyone turned to when they needed help because he was a street dude with a big heart who, at seventeen, was wise beyond his years. Unique had a motorcycle, and one day he invited me to take a ride. "Yo, I'm about to go uptown and shit," he said. "Let's roll." Unique was hustling, and I had enough of an idea of what that meant to know what he was about to go do.

It was my first time on a motorcycle, and next thing I knew, we were flying over the Verrazzano Bridge, heading up the BQE all the way through Brooklyn and Queens, over Randall's Island, straight up to the Bronx. That's a long fucking ride when you've never been on a bike before. At the time I had no idea why we were going so far, but as I soon learned from Unique, you got the best product if you went the extra mile, all the way uptown to buy the quality shit from the Spanish motherfuckers who dealt it. I never saw what he bought that day because he made me wait outside, but my guess is that it was heroin. And he was using me as a cover, so the family and the other dealers and everyone in the 'hood never really knew what he was up to or where he got his shit. They just saw us going for a ride.

It was summer, but by the time we got back to Staten Island, I was cold as hell, and afterward we went up to Unique's apartment. All I'd really known about Unique until that day was that he was getting money, but I soon realized just how fly the nigga was when I saw that he had two girlfriends, both living with him at the same time. He had one that was working for him, helping him hustle and move the drugs, and another, a real pretty chick, that he kept around to run the household. Unique had it all figured out. One day when I was up there, he sent me out to the store for whatever, and don't you know when I came back this nigga was buck naked fucking with both of them? That's how Unique got down. He was in love with both of them because each one had different qualities that enabled him to be who he was. Unique was a lover boy, the type of guy that listened to all the hip-hop love song records. He was both a lover boy and a soldier, and he chose his two women to reflect both sides of his character. I do think he was more in love with the hustler than the lover because that girl represented his bright future and really cared about him. She wanted him to make millions and was going to do what she could to get him there, and she was smart enough not to worry about his lustful ways with other girls. I was just fifteen, but watching their relationship taught me a lot about the value of a woman's inner beauty. I saw how she looked out for Unique and realized that without a strong backbone like that at home, a man will never succeed. Because of them, when I was ready for a relationship, I knew that I should look for a partner who really cared for me and not worry so much about superficial things. Of course, looks are important because you have to be attracted, but I didn't make them the priority. I looked first and foremost for someone who could comfort me and educate me and school me. There were so many women out there who were pretty and into themselves, but empowered women of quality were much harder to find.

The more I hung around Unique, the more comfortable he got with me, and soon I was allowed around when he and the girls bagged up the drugs. Then he was sniffing drugs in front of me, off the top of this mountain he kept on a table, but he never, ever let me get involved any further. He was looking after me even as he exposed me to the life, letting me be around it but never in it. Of course, being that close to someone I looked up to, who was doing everything I wanted to do, just made me want it more. To other people Unique might seem like he was a bad influence, but he had a heart of gold. As I grew up, I tried to live the same way. He was selling drugs—and drugs are illegal and addictive—but within his enterprise he looked out for his people and he looked out for his family. He helped the people close to him, took care of them, and he sorted out the fake ones quick and kept them far away. Just by watching Unique live, I got hands-on knowledge that I've taken with me into adulthood. It has kept me on the right path, even when the lure of the hustle had me drifting toward the wrong one.

Unique was my hero, but even heroes have bad days. Like the day Unique got so high that he fell asleep in his big pile of dope. He just nodded out. One girlfriend was so high that she didn't notice and wandered off to the bedroom, and the other had gotten so mad over something that she'd gotten dressed and left. So there I was with this nigga, all doped up, lying facedown on Drug Mountain. I sat him back in his chair, brushed him off, and made sure he was breathing. I didn't know what the fuck else to do, so I laid him down on the couch and took a seat next to him until I could tell he was just sleeping it off.

Back then, getting high on your own supply was a badge of honor for hustlers, even though that didn't work out too well for Tony Montana. That idea came from *Scarface*, and before that movies like *Super-*

fly, which is where Unique was taking his lifestyle cues from. He knew how to hustle, he did it well, and he always had money. He sniffed coke, dope, and smoked weed. He had a shag haircut that was part fade, part afro—like a mullet for black hair. Dude used to run around like he was Tony Montana too, with a soldier by his side most days, always with guns on them. Unique was well liked, but he had no problem busting his gun out, so nobody in the 'hood ever fucked with him.

Being the poor kid I was, he'd always ask me if I had money and then pull out a stack and lay forty or sixty on me, all in twenties. He was trying to do right, but the side effect was that he showed me the spoils of drug life, and I wanted all of them. My generation of dudes, all of us for the most part fatherless, paid attention to older guys in the neighborhood like Unique and the Jamaicans. They were independent hustlers, all of them with money and looking fly as hell. That is what we wanted for ourselves: respect, freedom to do what we wanted, and the money that could make that happen. We wanted motorcycles, cars, and everything those guys had. I remember for a while Unique had a BMW 325, which was the coolest ride I'd ever seen. All I wanted was to drive it, just for a minute, but I never could because it was a stick. He promised to teach me, but there's no days off in the hustle, so he never got around to it.

I've got to hand it to Unique. Of all the dudes of his generation who got into the game, so many ended up strung out or in jail for life, but he was one of the few who made it. Like I said, he was well respected, but it also didn't hurt that he had a big-ass gun. He was a skinny nigga but dude carried a .357 Magnum, just this huge piece that he showed me one day when we were riding his motorcycle up to the Bronx. "Anyone ever mess with you, you tell me about it and I'll take care of that shit," Unique said. I fell in love with that big-ass gun, though he wouldn't let me hold it, no matter how many times I asked.

Not long after that, this older guy who was one of a bunch of drunks that hung around outside the building every day started messing with me. I wasn't looking for trouble, but these were the kind of guys who liked to roughhouse all of us younger dudes. They'd be drunk, and you'd walk by and they'd kick you in the ass or chase you into the elevator and put you in a headlock until you were about ready to pass out. They thought it was funny, but when there was a pack of them beating on you, it wasn't at all. This one guy was in a mood and was really trying to bring it to me to the point that I got scared and went and found Unique, who immediately went inside his closet, got his gun locked and loaded, and said, "They downstairs now? Let's see what the fuck this is."

We went down and the guy I was beefing with wasn't there, but he must have heard about Unique coming out because he left me alone after that. All I could think about was how cool Unique was and how nice that gun was. Since he wouldn't let me hold it, what I'd need to do is get myself one just like it. Unique wouldn't have even needed his gun to settle the situation, because he had that type of stature. Everybody in the community knew him as Uncle Unique, not Cousin Unique—because he was already a man by the age of seventeen.

How many other seventeen-year-olds have you met whose mothers let them get away with calling them by their first names? That's how this dude rolled; he called his mom Joyce like it was natural. I never understood it back then, but now I think it's because she never approved of what he was doing with his life, so he didn't recognize her maternal connection. After all, Joyce had her hands full with Brenda and Dorinda. All three of her kids were pretty bad, so I bet she got sick of trying to keep up with him. However Unique was living, he was the guy people went to when they needed something, whether it was money, drugs, or a favor, and he liked that. He liked feeling in control of people with everybody kissing his ass or relying on him in some way.

Cousin Unique let me witness his lifestyle, but he never let me sell drugs for him. He felt I wasn't built for it, and though he never said it to me, I think he saw me doing something else with my life. He also knew that his aunt, my mother, would fuck him up if she ever found out that he had let me hustle. My mom used to take care of Unique when he was a kid, and she and her sisters fought more than a few battles for him as he grew into a young adult. In his mind he owed her, so he was never going to let me into that life.

I wanted to sell drugs because I wanted to stop asking him for money. I wanted to earn it for him for real, but it wasn't going to happen. I accepted that, until Unique brought one of my homeboys into his operation. I became so jealous of the situation, especially when my boy started coming around sporting two-finger gold rings and all the jewelry the rest of us wanted. The tension between us built up until we had a fight and a falling-out that ended our friendship. I don't remember how it started, but we both put our hands up and threw fists. My boy landed one right in my mouth and then I started acting crazy. I grabbed a bottle or something and connected with his face. Then he caught me with a jab and we were both bleeding. Shit was real.

We never spoke again, and I haven't seen him since. I realized that day that I never wanted to be jealous of another man's situation. It was time for me to figure out my own. I couldn't expect my cousin or anybody else to hand me my future. It was up to me to get out there and find it.

I started branching out, hanging out with dudes from up the block. I was getting involved with groups from around the 'hood, not just the people who lived in my building. Once I started making my own moves and making new friends, it felt like I'd stepped into a new world. Physically I wasn't far from home, but in every other way, I had taken a giant step toward claiming my destiny. I was under my mom's roof, but she had no control of me, and she had no idea what I was getting into. I had a crew of guys that I knew from school who were like brothers to me, which included the friends I mentioned earlier, plus a few new guys, and a few that eventually became Wu-Tang with me. All of us started being out there, doing our thing in the world together.

Our biggest musical influence by this time was Run-D.M.C. We wanted to emulate them in every way, just like we tried to copy all the older dudes in the 'hood who looked good and acted cool. But we didn't just look to the hustlers, because there were plenty of everyday guys who worked in transit or as messengers who were as taken with hip-hop as we were. They were the ones who taught us the most about the culture that was starting to thrive. They told us about this club in the city, Broadway International, that they went to on the weekends to dance to hip-hop. We'd hang around any dude who had a good radio, because big radios were king. My man Kishaun was the only one of us with a proper blaster, a Conion, which was one of the best. We would put our Run-D.M.C. tape in his radio and just walk up and down the block. Then, later on, since my man Terelle's brother was a DJ, we'd cut school and end up at their house, listening to music and watching him spin. His favorite record at the time was Run-D.M.C.'s "Sucker M.C.'s," which is still, to me, one of the dopest records in hip-hop history. We would listen to that shit all day long, every single day. It was the best: they diss a sucker M.C. while rhyming to show how superior they are in every way. That song kills it.

Fashion was changing quickly then. People were still wearing Lees, but they had also started copping Bill Blass pants and Devil Jeans, which were these French-cut denims that had patches of cartoon devils on the pockets. Sergio Valente was happening, terry-cloth Kangol hats were it, and so were bomber jackets with Chinese letters on the side. People started writing cool shit on the legs of their jeans, usually in the same style they'd paint their graffiti tags. The way you looked became more important than ever to guys my age. If you didn't have the correct clothes, you weren't shit. Best piece of advice my mom ever gave me was that a man who stayed sharp looked respectable. If I only had three pairs of pants, that was fine, she said, so long as I paired them with a clean white pressed T-shirt, clean shoes, and a haircut. If you presented yourself well, people would want to give you their time and energy. One of the reasons my friends and I spent so much time walking up and down the block was that we watched every move the older dudes made. We were figuring out how to duplicate their style to the best of our abilities. There were a lot of guys to respect. Some dudes were good at basketball, some had a solid job which enabled them to buy the fly shit, and some were pretty-boy niggas who always had a cute girl with them.

Gold nameplates were the shit, even just one letter. My homie's older brother Bobby just had a big "B" in the middle of a square on a thick rope chain that we called a cable. He would wear it over a burgundy nylon shirt from this brand that came with matching nylon drawers, a pair of Lees, black-and-white Adidas, and a Kangol hat. Bobby always looked nice.

The gold teeth era came in when Slick Rick made his debut with Doug E. Fresh in 1985. He had an English accent and that one gold tooth at the time, and he was wearing suits or sheepskins, with all those rings and the eye patch and fur hats. He had style like we'd never seen. He was the one who elevated hip-hop from just jeans and Adidas. We saw him in concert one summer, and all of a sudden we started wearing dress slacks and Bally sneakers. When Doug E. Fresh and Slick Rick dropped "The Show," all of us wanted to look like them and to go out and do the latest dances.

In our 'hood we were obsessed with gold teeth the minute we saw them in the mouths of all the Jamaicans. I'm not just talking about the drug dealers we already looked up to; Jamaican grandmothers and grandfathers had them and they looked fly as shit too. Our older family members had gold fillings in their back teeth, but we had never seen gold right there in front when somebody smiled. Having gold in your mouth was the ultimate luxury to us. and it carried a rebel quality that we wanted for ourselves. There was a dude in Park Hill named Tino, a super-cool dude with an Ethiopian vibe, who made gold teeth. He made a full set of frames for a smooth guy with amazing style and waves in his hair that flowed to the side, named Pure, and soon everyone was asking Tino for gold teeth. By the way, peeping Pure is where I got the idea to have waves to the side in my hair. I copped his style every way I could afford to.

When we heard about Tino, my friends started telling me to get gold teeth, because my teeth were always messed up. He charged ninety dollars per tooth, and I wasn't making any real money yet so it took me some time to stack the cash for one. I made up for it later: if you look at me in the video for "C.R.E.A.M." from '93, my whole mouth is flooded with gold, even though my teeth were still jacked up. It was more important to me to have my teeth shining than looking good—the priorities were gold first, dental correction second. Having gold in my mouth made me feel powerful, and I couldn't get enough of that feeling. In the meantime, before I got that first tooth from Tino, I did what all my friends did. When we'd get a few bottles of Champale, which is a malt liquor beverage that sparkles like champagne and was packaged to look like it (the motto in their ads, which always featured black people, was "Live a little on very little"), we'd take the gold foil off the top and wrap it around one of our front teeth. Some dudes put in one, some dudes put in three, and we'd get high and drunk with our grills full of gold foil. The trick was to not swallow that shit once you got buzzed. Unfortunately they've changed the bottle, but it's still made today, so if you find Champale, try it. I recommend the pink variety.

My friends and I were the only ones our age who used to take the ferry to the train to hit downtown Brooklyn or 42nd Street in Manhattan. We'd go to the movies in Times Square, which was four dollars at the time, take in some karate flicks or whatever else was playing up on the Deuce, then we'd spend whatever money we had left on clothes to show off back in the neighborhood. Before I started selling drugs, I worked in my community's Summer Youth program each year to get some money, but it was never much. Summer Youth put teenagers to work in their own housing project. I was a janitor, cleaning hallways and stairwells, and I picked up odd jobs anyplace I could.

Of course, that wasn't going to cut it when you're talking about buying slacks, dress shoes, and jewelry, so my friends and I began to do petty robberies. We were never stickup kids; I wasn't putting guns in niggas' mouths and threatening their lives. We'd snatch a bag or a wallet, but we'd break into houses and cars mostly, grabbing what we could, hoping to leave with something we would sell for half its value just to have some pocket money. We broke into a lot of cars to steal their stereos. Two of my friends figured out that if they threw a ball bearing the size of your thumbnail through the window, it would shatter the whole thing as if it were a brick. One little metal ball the size of a pebble would get it done.

We were trying to elevate our style, so I remember around this time my friends and I started drinking wine. Our preference was Carlo Rossi, which was ten dollars for a four-liter jug. When we weren't sipping on that, we'd get some Riunite. Those sweet wines were our beverages of choice when we were sniffing coke and smoking coke cigs. The cool thing about my crew was that we shared everything we got; we were a family that way. A few of us looked old enough, with facial hair and everything, so we never had a problem getting booze. And if we ever did, one of us in the store was usually stealing some just in case.

Cocaine is a highly addictive drug and everyone we looked up to did it, so we did it too. As it is with addiction in general, soon people looked for ways to get more out of it. That's how sniffing evolved to putting it in cigarettes and joints, which became freebasing, which is a much more potent way of getting high. The guys that we were looking up to were into all of that. Of course, this eventually led to the crack epidemic.

High school was an interesting time for me, because I was going to school but not trying to achieve at all. For me and my friends, school was just part of a routine to satisfy our moms and families. My typical day during those years went like this: In the morning I'd pull up to the bus stop, which was the spot. When the bus came, some kids would get on and others wouldn't. They'd chill and figure out what they were going to do for the day. Depending on my mood, you might find me in either camp.

When I did hop on that 117 bus and head off to school, me and my dudes could be found all the way in the back. We'd have a radio with us, playing music, and we'd definitely be smoking weed despite the early hour. When we lit up on the bus, we'd hear about it from the driver, but what was he gonna do? I think he realized that he'd just picked us up out of the fucking ghetto and we didn't know any better.

Our bus also picked up kids from the Stapleton projects, which to us Park Hill kids was the competition. I'm not really sure why, but those two projects were always at odds. The way each project lived was just different, and people from one never trusted people from the other. There were always stickups, shootings, and fights going on between crews from Park Hill and Stapleton, as if it were some kind of legendary feud from way back when. It didn't mean you couldn't have friends there, it just meant that each side stuck to their own and didn't trust anyone they didn't know from the other. That's just how it is in poor communities, there's always rivalries that you're born into that may cost you your life if you're in the wrong place at the wrong time.

On the school bus, after a few stops, we'd be let off at New Dorp High School, which was on the other side of Staten Island. It was just twenty minutes away on Hylan Boulevard, but it might as well have been another country to us. It was situated among a few all-white neighborhoods in the South and Midland Beach areas. Us project kids were the minority among a working-class, racist, white student body during a time when black teenagers were coming together through the identity of hip-hop. It was tense to say the least. These white kids were no suckers, and they behaved like the school was in their hometown and we were invading it. In a sense they were right, because we were being bused in from across town, but there was nothing we could do about that. It was a terrible situation because the white kids were tough: there were a lot of leather jackets with Metallica or Kiss logos on the back, a lot of gold choker chains. They'd hang out in packs outside the pizzeria across the street from school smoking cigarettes, and they loved to yell at us when we got on or off the bus every day, calling us niggers, threatening us or making fun of us individually in whatever way came to mind. The experience of going there—and how I was made to feel while just trying to mind my own business—was so unpleasant that I wasn't open to learning. I could barely concentrate, let alone take in knowledge. I was only there to prove a point to my mom and to make it through another day, nothing else. The racism and bias extended to the teachers as well. Not all of them, but several let me know that they were barely tolerating my presence and had no intention of trying to teach me. After I asked a question in class, I even had one ask me why she should waste her time trying to teach me when I'd never amount to anything. This wasn't a school where a poor black kid was going to be elevated in any way.

I remember one time around Easter when I was a sophomore. Me and my little Fat Albert crew were feeling ourselves, so we decided to wear matching outfits to school. We'd gotten some money and all bought leather jackets, because back in the day we didn't have a problem dressing like each other. So we decided to go to school all leathered out, with our radio and everything. We got on our matching navy-blue bombers, our navy-blue leather pants, and a few of us had the Bally sneakers that the Get Fresh Crew wore on the cover of their first record. I added some aviator sunglasses, and we were blasting M.C. Shan's "The Bridge" at the bus stop. When the bus came, we hopped on and got high as hell on a few joints at the back.

When we got to school I was so fucking high. My second or third class was gym and I was so stoned that I missed half of it. When I got to the locker room, there were people in it from the class before getting changed. This one white kid walked by, and I decided to bump him because I didn't give a fuck.

"Get the fuck out of my way," he said.

"Get the fuck out of your way?" I asked.

"Yeah, get the fuck out of my way."

This dude was big, he played football—but I was so high and so fed up with the bullshit from the teachers and the harassment from the students that nothing mattered. "Fuck you, you fuckin' prick," I said.

He turned around. "What? What the fuck did you say?"

And then he came at me, and when he did, I automatically punched him in the mouth as hard as I could. We started fighting, and before I knew it, the whole locker room was shouting and getting involved. Then it seemed like the whole school suddenly came downstairs in front of the gym as multiple fights broke out. The tension between the black and white students that everyone felt every single day finally exploded.

No one was even taken to the principal's office, because by the time it was over, none of the faculty knew how it had started. The security guards at the school were so outnumbered that all they could do was herd this crowd of fighting students out of the building and into the parking lot, because it had grown into a riot. At least two hundred people were involved, most fighting and the rest cheering us on. What can I say? I acted stupid that day, but I just couldn't take any more. In the end it didn't change anything and nobody really won because it was too messy of a fight. But it did bring a lot of tension to the surface that everyone was conscious of going forward. Both sides tread a bit more lightly after that.

For all of these reasons I fucking hated everything about high school except lunch. The lunchroom was like a fashion show for the kids from the projects. We would be in there flashing our clothes, bragging to each other about what we had on. There was one teacher who really hated it, and hated me for that matter, but I was too busy checking out the hottest shit to care about him. We were ridiculous. When people started wearing Tommy Hilfiger, I got a pair of Tommy cargos and left the tag on, letting it hang down my leg so everyone could see. If a dude came through in a Polo shirt or jacket, someone would be like, "Oh yeah? I got Polo socks," or they'd pull their jeans down to show their Polo drawers. When we weren't leathered up, that's what we were wearing.

Style has always been very important to me, and even at fifteen I did everything I could to stay ahead of the game. I was into Bugle Boy jeans before they were a thing, and of course Lee jeans, which were the standard if you were young and black and into hip-hop. Me and my friends used to go around ripping the patches off of other kids' jeans if they weren't Lee. I used to carry an extra Lee patch in my wallet, run up to them and say that I was the Lee inspector and that I needed to see their jeans. If they weren't wearing Lee, their patch was coming with me. Some people got mad, but usually they laughed because I was always funny about it, and sometimes I'd have extra Lee patches I'd give them. If you had Lees you were good, and if you had Lee pinstripe jeans, which came in black or burgundy, you were really good. We were also into the surf brand Ocean Pacific because they had the cool T-shirts back then. And since I couldn't afford Ballys at the time, my favorite sneakers were my yellow Converse high-tops.

Hip-hop artists started performing at certain clubs in the city in the eighties, but not too many people from the Staten Island projects were taking the ferry—and then the train—to go see them. Some of the older dudes went, and lucky for me, my friends were willing to make the trek too. When we went to see that Doug E. Fresh and

Slick Rick show, it was incredible to witness how big of a movement hip-hop was becoming outside of our community. It was already everything to us. But when we went to a show and saw people from all over the city dressing and acting the same as we did, it was powerful. We got to see that it was everything to them too. The lunchroom was one thing, but one night at a club and you'd be up on all the latest styles. Hip-hop was growing and changing so fast. That's where I first saw Bugle Boys, and the blue-and-white Spot-Bilt high-tops, and Clarks on this slick-looking Jamaican dude. Everyone had gold chains, cables—more gold than I'd ever seen.

The club we went to the most was called Union Square, which was on West 14th Street in Manhattan. It was in a big warehouse-type room with a little stage at one end. There were speakers everywhere and no chairs or tables, just a bar on one side. Along with Latin Quarter in Midtown, Union Square was just about the first real all-hip-hop nightclub. And it was real as hell. The crowd was half hustlers and half hip-hop artists, with break-dancers and project kids from every borough. You felt the energy the moment you got on line; the place was electric and exciting and dangerous. You would see multiple fights a night, you would see robberies, and you might get hurt if you weren't careful. But no matter what, you'd see people and hear music that would blow your mind. Everyone wore gold chains, but whatever you wore you had to be ready to fight for because dudes snatched chains and designer glasses, and girls snatched earrings right off of each other in the middle of the dance floor. I remember whenever Salt-N-Pepa's "I'll Take Your Man" or Big Daddy Kane's "Ain't No Half-Steppin'" came on, the chain snatching was off and poppin'. People took Cazal glasses right off people's faces, and I heard about some guy getting his shoes snatched off his feet. In the winter it was common to see a girl outside, all upset because another girl had stolen the fur coat off her back. I'm telling you, these clubs were vicious. At Union Square, there was a chillout room behind the dance floor that was anything goes as well. You'd head in there and see people rolling up blunts, sniffing cocaine, puffing on woola joints (which is crack rolled up in a blunt with weed). That was fueling the scene, and it was on the edge. Anyone from back then will remember woolas or coke cigarettes, both of which smell very delicious. When I got high off of one of those, I felt fresh, I felt invincible, I felt on top of the world, the same way I did when I put on a new pair of sneakers.

My friends and I got caught up in the drug aspect of the culture, but it never became a lifestyle to us. There were two sides to crack in that era: the fly, flashy, 'hood-rich-and-famous pose of smoking crack, which was the next level of doing coke and being fabulous; and there was the horrible side that destroyed lives and ruined families. Getting high was a phase to me and my friends. As we saw people we knew get tangled up in the dark side of it, we moved away. But for a while we thought it was the coolest shit and we liked to be high because it motivated us. When I was sniffing coke at fifteen years old, I didn't look at it like it was bad for me. I saw it as being down with my crew, who were all about getting fresh with money, clothes, and hoes. We were going out, renting cars, and going to the clubs. We'd light up, huddled up in the staircase, rhyming, wearing Polo gooses, V-Bombers, Avia sneakers on our feet. What we got addicted to was the glamour, style, and money that we saw all around us in hip-hop culture. That was the real drug. As hip-hop changed, me and my crew changed too, always evolving with the style. We picked up break dancing and graffiti, and soon we started freestyling and writing rhymes. We moved on from Run-D.M.C. to the gangster style of Big Daddy Kane, the well-dressed moves of Slick Rick, the dance-hall swagger of the Jamaican artists like Shabba Ranks and Yellowman. Later we were taken in fully by the wise street thug knowledge of Rakim and crews like EPMD. It was hip-hop in every form that we could never get enough of. We were addicts for that shit.

In the early days, in the clubs like Union Square, everyone was dressed up, dancing, living life to the fullest. It was the hip-hop Studio 54. Pretty girls were everywhere, wearing Gucci boots and jewelry. You'd go there to learn the latest dances and see the latest styles. The guys who were thieves and crooks used to wear velour suits and dope sneakers and have Caesar haircuts with waves and half-moon parts. They'd have flattop fades, gold teeth, or just a Yankee hat pulled down real low. Those were the guys we admired, and eventually I was one of them. The music was always dope, but it was filler compared to the excitement. The scene was growing before our eyes from week to week.

A lot of people don't know that young Raekwon was a big dancer. I knew how to break-dance and was always up on the latest moves. When Heavy D or KRS-One came on, I was the first one out there doing the Walk or the James Brown or whatever my current favorite move happened to be. That was all good, but when a hard track like "Eric B Is President" by Eric B & Rakim came on, the energy of the club changed immediately. You'd see the robbing types stop dancing and start wandering around looking for chains to snatch. Usually what a crew would do was spot a dude who looked like he couldn't defend himself and dance near him like everything was cool. Then the youngest or smallest member of them would sneak up, snatch the chain, and run. It would be easier for the little guy, often a young boy they'd snuck into the club, to get away in the crowd. When the dude who'd gotten robbed tried to grab him, he'd find himself blocked by the bigger, older guys in the crew. My friends and I watched these packs of kids from Brooklyn, usually from the Fort Greene or Brownsville projects, and we were blown away. Brooklyn was running shit back then, and those niggas loved to get at anybody they felt was fresh. They were not playin'.

My friends and I were all about the energy, the scene, and the culture. We did all we could to get out there and show our style. One way to do that was always having the right hairstyle, which changed quickly so you had to keep up. I always tried to set myself apart from my crew, so I was the only one who rocked the Gumby cut, which went up high and to the side. I had a straightening comb to lift my hair straight up, high as it could go. That was my thing, and it looked dope on me. I even put a little piece of blond in it for a while to take it to the next level. Since my crew couldn't afford to get cuts every week, we learned to do it ourselves. My friend Sheldon from the neighborhood was the first: he got a pair of clippers and taught me how to do it. I fell in love with it, and for a while I was cutting hair in the staircase, trimming guys I knew from all over Park Hill, making some quick change. I couldn't afford a good pair of clippers, so I got some cheap shits and did my best. Those things were loud as hell, and they'd get hot—so hot that my hand would start burning. I'd go as long as I could, then take a break to let them cool off. To sharpen them up, I'd dip them in my mom's cooking oil that she fried chicken with. When they got warm, the whole room smelled like chicken. I did a good job, but clippers cut when they're too hot or too sharp, so a cut might look perfect at the time, but two days later I'd see the guy and he'd have a mark on his neck from my subpar equipment. No one ever got mad, usually we'd laugh about it. Dudes used to come to my mom's house to let me cut their hair in my room, and when she would check up to see what we were doing, she was always happy to find me giving haircuts. At least that was something constructive that wouldn't land me in jail.

My friends and I followed the trail of hip-hop all over the city. We'd go all the way up to Harlem, to the Rooftop, which was another club that was always poppin'. We'd have to roll deep too, because we weren't from there. But we'd go and we'd get out on the floor and do our thing. Hip-hop was evolving around us and it was our life. Those days were the very beginning of modern black culture as we know it today. These clubs, this music, and everyone who was drawn together by it were a part of history and creating a black identity that is now known around the world.

Those times were historic and valuable, and we felt it back then as it was happening. My friends and I got to see our favorite artists perform in intimate settings that were mind-blowing to us. When I saw Rakim in a club back then, the curtains opened and there he was sitting on a throne, all dapper in his Gucci suit. I saw Just-Ice in his big Kangol hat, Heavy D out there dancing, Queen Latifah, and Salt-N-Pepa. I got to see all of these groups at a very young age, and it made me love hip-hop more than anything else.

Now, like I told you, I had odd jobs here and there, from Summer Youth to selling newspapers to even bagging groceries at the local A&P. That kept me in weed, wine, and whatever, but those wages weren't enough to fund my taste for clothes and shoes. So me and my homeboys got to robbing chains in the clubs, or robbing dudes whenever we saw a chance, stealing car stereos, and hustling in small ways where we could. We'd get an 8 ball of coke or an ounce of weed and smash it up into smaller Baggies. We didn't stay out on the block because the Jamaicans would have killed us if we tried to hustle in front of a building where they had a drug spot. We made do with little sales here and there to get our clothes allowance.

We stayed fresh however we could. I remember one day U-God and I were in Brooklyn, because we used to do little robberies with some homeboys who lived there. One of them was named Kato, and he had originally lived in Staten Island. By the time we were in high school, he had moved to the Farragut projects with his family. We were all going to Union Square that night, and U-God and I had recently bought some Gucci sneakers we were excited to wear. I had a fresh fade, my Bugle Boys on, and a green-and-white striped button-up shirt that matched my shoes. The shirt wasn't a Gucci, but I'd snatched a Gucci tag off a shirt in the store and sewn it into the back of mine. So if some girl was dancing with me and saw it, she'd think I was all in Gucci. That's why I've always loved Biggie's first verse on "Sky's the Limit": "While niggas flirt, I'm sewing tigers on my shirts, and alligators / You want to see the inside? I'll see you later." I remember those days.

Anyway, U-God and I were looking good, walking to the train in Brooklyn, when this van pulled up with an old man driving. It stopped, the back door opened, and eight kids jumped out. We could see that all that was back there was a mattress. There were eight of them and three of us and it didn't look good. Luckily the old man recognized Kato because he was from Farragut. He called Kato over as U-God and I realized that these were stickup kids and this was some bad shit.

"Yo," Kato said when he came back over. "They was getting ready to throw you in the van, rob you, and do some other shit to you, but I talked them out of it. I'm tellin' you, they know me and they still asked me, 'Yo, could we rob you all?'"

It's a good thing nothing went down, because U-God used to carry a butcher's knife on him at all times, strapped to his body, hidden in his drawers. But that wouldn't have done much to scare off eight crazy niggas. These psychos probably would have used it to carve us up. These motherfuckers with their old man driver had made a job of cruising around, throwing dudes into the back of their van, taking their shit, and doing whatever the fuck else to them. In that era, Brooklyn hood niggas were notorious for behavior like this, just robbing people anywhere they found them, not caring who saw it. That shit was fucked up, but in a way it was a compliment. Clearly me and U-God looked like money that day.

CHAPTER 4

YOUNG THUGS

When you grow up in the 'hood, your crew dictates your life experience. They are your extended family, the people you learn and grow with. You become a unit, known to everyone else on the street by your connection to the others, and your collective swagger determines the level of respect you get. This begins young, as soon as you start school. My crew was a diverse bunch of dudes, some no longer in my life, some still friends, while a few became the men I've made musical history with.

I met U-God in the Summer Youth program, and right away he became part of my little Fat Albert gang of friends. Our mothers went to the same school in Brooklyn growing up, so they encouraged our friendship. He wasn't from my neighborhood proper, and he didn't go to my high school. He went to McKee High School close by in New Brighton. He didn't live in the projects, either. He and his family lived in a house, and he had this little room in the attic where we'd smoke weed and watch karate movies.

At a young age, U-God was a hustler. He worked at the Statue of Liberty, in the souvenir store, where Method Man, aka Clifford Smith, Jr., who I knew from the neighborhood, worked too. From what I understand, and I'm not naming names, but some of the kids who worked there regularly stole from the safe and register. I don't know if it's true, all I do know is that one day U-God showed up with some real money, and the next day he went into downtown Brooklyn and bought himself two thick gold cable chains. U-God always had fly gear, and there was no way he was affording Bally sneakers and expensive glasses on the minimum wage at the Statue of Liberty gift shop.

I admired U-God because he always looked fresh and he loved to go out. We became dancing partners at Union Square and we started meeting girls and shit. He was the first of us to get a gun; I remember him bringing me up to his room to show me his brand-new nickel-plated .32. Man, did he love that thing. We were up at my boy Blue Man's house one night, waiting for him to do something before we went somewhere, and U-God got his gun out to show it to me and next thing I knew, the motherfucker was pointing it at me.

"Yo, don't point no fucking gun at me, man," I said.

We were kids and he was just having fun. We didn't treat guns like toys—they were for our protection—but still, they got us excited.

"You think I'm going to shoot you?" he asked. "You know I'd never shoot you. There ain't even one in the chamber."

He pointed the gun at the window next to him, pulled the trigger, and BAM! The gun went off and the window shattered because there sure as hell was one in the chamber. He could have killed me that day. Kids play with guns all the time, and too many times that's exactly how they die. Don't ever let someone point a gun at you in jest, whether they think it's loaded or not.

Our friendship was all about staying fly, going shopping, and getting off of Staten Island as often as we could. We used to go to Brooklyn to get clothes and check out the fresh shit in all the department stores downtown. My friends and I were professional thieves by then, stealing car stereos and getting a hundred dollars a pop for them. That was good money because I could get a nice shirt for forty dollars. One time after I'd done a robbery, U-God and I went to Albee Square Mall. When we got off the subway we saw a crowd of about thirty niggas across the street from us, looking like they was trying to fight each other. It didn't look right, so we kept it moving. Our guess was that those kids went to Westinghouse, which was a technical high school with a bad reputation. Kids fought in the halls and robbed each other and there was a lot of gang activity. Even for Brooklyn, kids from Westinghouse were rough.

We walked a few blocks up, then stopped to look in the window of a sneaker store and noticed that the same gang was now behind us. Something was up, but we were outnumbered so we tried to pay them no mind. U-God had a shopping bag from A&S because he'd bought a shirt, and all of a sudden one of them tried to snatch it. When U-God didn't let it go, it was on.

"The fuck you niggas tryin' to do?" he said.

"Oh you trying to be tough? You acting like you fucking tough?" one of them said.

We were about to be lunch for these motherfuckas so I stuck my hand in my pocket and acted like I had a gun.

"Yo, back the fuck up!"

One kid didn't believe me and started walking at me. "What you got? What you got?"

"Yo, yo, keep coming, motherfucker," I said. "Hell yeah! I'm gonna blast you!"

It was a close call: the guy thought I was bluffing, but his friend didn't, and that guy put an end to it. They turned around and let us go. From that day forward U-God never left the house without his gun. Going shopping was dangerous back then because there were always niggas waiting to jump you when you came out of the mall, or on the train, or waiting for the ferry back to Staten Island.

It was worth the risk to us because all we cared about was gear and music. I still remember the day I got my first pair of Nike Air Force 1s, plain black. I was sixteen years old. That's a classic, all-American shoe. When Reebok came out with the Blacktops, though, they took over our neighborhood. Back in the day when a hot shoe came out, everybody got them, because it was a status symbol. There was a whole summer that you'd see those heavy-looking black-on-black Reebok high-tops with the graffiti-style logo on every pair of feet on the block.

My crew and I loved traveling, taking the trains just for the sake of going anywhere. We'd cut class, hop on the A train, and ride—even though the A train was the scariest line to be on at the time. We'd watch motherfuckers get wild, but we were never worried about it because we had that gun with us. It was liberating and it gave us confidence. We never waved it around, either. We knew that if one of us pulled it out, we were shooting someone. That rule was in our hearts.

The craziest shit happened at the back of the A train, which is where we'd hang out. We rode it from Staten Island all the way to Queens and back. We'd watch kids get on and off, and sometimes we'd catch a kid slippin' and he'd lose his coat or his chain or whatever he'd just bought from a department store that day.

When we were back home in the projects, hanging in a stairwell, U-God was our beatboxer. He imitated all the Doug E. Fresh sounds, making those clicking noises with his mouth, and I was the MC. I had plenty of time on my hands by this point, because after I got suspended for that huge fight at school, I stopped going. I never told my mom about the suspension, so for a long while she thought I was at school every day. When I wasn't riding the train or going to see movies in Times Square, I'd be at one of my boys' houses or hanging in other buildings around the 'hood where her friends wouldn't see me. I spent a lot of time at my friend Jarnell's because not only was he a cool cat and a great dancer, he had his room hooked up with black lights. We'd go over there, smoke blunts, drink Private Stock and Old English malt liquor, and watch kung fu flicks all day. After that we'd go out into the neighborhood and see what we could get into. Usually we'd end up piling into this abandoned car that was behind our building. We'd get in there, roll up the windows tight, light a blunt or two, and smoke until it got real foggy. Once the doors were closed, nobody was allowed to open a window or door. We wanted all the smoke locked inside to get us even more fucked up. That was a fad in our neighborhood: if you ever couldn't find one of your homeboys, you'd go check inside the car out back and usually he'd be there.

The truth is, I was a burnout back then, and so were my friends. Nobody was trying to get a job, and everybody was trying to hustle whatever they could. I was living with Moms and starting to get into the crack economy that had quickly swept over the projects. Everyone we knew was starting to sell drugs here and there, mostly in and around the high schools, away from the Jamaican drug spots. I wouldn't say that me and my friends were real drug dealers yet because none of us were making big money. We'd get a little 8 ball or whatever, break it down, wrap it up, and at most make four or five hundred dollars off of it.

Some dudes knew how to flip it better than others, and over time I became one of those dudes. But back then I was partnering with guys around the neighborhood who weren't business-minded. We used to get high off our own supply, which is one of the cardinal rules you don't break if you want to be a successful drug dealer. I was a teenage high school dropout with no job who spent all day listening to music, getting high, watching movies, and hearing about who'd gotten robbed or shot or stabbed. I knew every single hip-hop song that came out, start to finish—from the work of DJ Jazzy Jeff and the Fresh Prince to the Ultramagnetic MC's to Public Enemy. I had no other focus than loving hip-hop music and trying to get by.

I would fuck around with a couple of girls, but I was no super lover man. None of my boys had girlfriends; that just wasn't our thing yet. Some of them had females they would fuck with, but they were more like friends. And as the drugs started to take over, all kinds of girls around the neighborhood got turned out. I remember this one pretty ass chick who fucked damn near the whole 'hood after getting high for two weeks. You'd see her coming down the block and anybody could go grab her. None of us were about relationships. We were about fucking, getting out of there, and talking about it later with the boys.

There was one girl who was different, though, one young lady whom I loved, and she lived right in my building. She was African, just this sweet little girl who never hung out in the streets. I used to see her coming and going from school and in the lobby, and I had a crush on her for a long time before we started talking. Her influence pulled me away from my friends a bit, which considering how I was living wasn't a bad thing. My African princess was cool: she didn't know much about the street world and didn't want to. That appealed to me because I didn't want a girl who ran around like we did, knowing everybody's business, including mine. Her name is Candy, and after a long, shy courtship, we ended up dating and stayed together for ten years.

I liked that she didn't know my business, but the person I really worried about knowing my business back then was Moms. She had her hands full with my siblings, but she wasn't too busy to see that her son Corey was a burnout. She had less patience with me with each passing day, and as she started to ask me the hard questions, we began to fight. She actually started to scare me, because as I've said, Moms was a fighter. I knew that if she really caught me doing something wrong, she would bust my ass up good. One time she came down the block looking for me, convinced I was out there selling drugs. She found me, and thank God I didn't have any on me. I lied my ass off about it, even though it was obvious that I was dealing because every dude I hung with hustled drugs. There was a network in the project, and word had gotten back to her about what I was up to. We both knew it was just a matter of time until she caught me red-handed and we had a showdown.

It happened late one night when I came home and didn't have the key to get in. When a kid is already doing the wrong thing, there is nothing worse he can do than show up and have to knock on his mom's door in the middle of the night.

"Where the fuck you been?" she yelled, letting me inside. "I am too damn tired to whop your ass tonight, but you better believe you're getting it tomorrow. Go to bed!"

When I went to the bathroom to take a piss, I heard my mom's boyfriend joking about me. Then he told her to kick me out. "That kid ain't doing nothing with his life but making problems," he said. "I've had enough of this. It's either me or him."

He went on and on about how I wasn't in school, how I didn't care about her or the family, and how I was selling drugs. I was offended and so angry that I banged on their locked bedroom door.

"What the fuck is you sayin', motherfucker?" I yelled. "You fucking shut your mouth."

My mom came out. "What are you out here cursing for?"

"You going to let that motherfucker talk about me like that? You ain't going to defend your child?"

"You better know who the fuck you're talking to like that," she said. "You better calm down right now."

"Nah, fuck that motherfucker. He doesn't care about me, or your kids, he just lives here. Who is he anyway? Fuck him!"

Her boyfriend was an African guy who put food on the table and was good to my mom, but he didn't so much as talk to me or my siblings. He wanted nothing to do with us and just ignored our existence. But Moms loved him, so she chose him over me.

"Get the fuck out of my house," she said. "You got to go! Get the fuck out."

I went to the kitchen, got a trash bag, loaded up my clothes and sneakers, and left. That night, it was raining and very late and I had nowhere to go. Walking down the street with my trash bag, I started crying thinking about how my mother had chosen her man over her own child.

I wandered around for a few hours, then I went to my aunt Joyce's house. She was mad when I woke her up, but she could see that something was wrong. I told her what had happened and she agreed to let me stay. She was even mad at my mom for kicking me out that way: she said no mother should put her kid out on the street in the middle of the night. She said I could stay with her as long as I needed to, but I had to be inside every night by 9:30 p.m., no exceptions.

"If you ain't inside this house by nine-thirty, don't fucking come," she said. "Don't knock, because that door ain't gonna open."

I lived with Aunt Joyce for a month or so, and I didn't once miss that curfew, because I'd never disrespect her kindness. But it was clear to both of us that I couldn't go on like that. I had to figure out my own path to independence real quick.

I was eighteen years old, not on speaking terms with my mother, and I couldn't live with my aunt's rules for much longer. I found alternative accommodations with a woman I'm going to call Marie, who was a career crack user. There's a difference between a crackhead and a crack user. A crackhead doesn't respect themselves, they'll do anything for a rock, for that quick high and that momentary escape. They'll lie, steal, cheat, and give themselves away however they have to. A crack user is someone with a problem who still manages to keep their life on track. Don't get me wrong, when they're high, crack addicts are fiends too. But users who manage to function have not yet lost their self-respect and direction in life, and that makes all the difference.

For a crack user, Marie was mad cool. She had an apartment in building 225 just down the way from where my family lived. I knew her because I'd sold to her a few times. She'd always ask me if I was holding. If I didn't have any, I'd steer her toward one of my friends and make sure she was taken care of. She was a nice lady, a good person. She just loved to get high.

One night when I was out with my friends and it didn't look like I'd be in by 9:30 p.m., it crossed my mind to knock on Marie's door. I asked her if she had an extra bed, and she said she did in her second room, but that was where she and her friends smoked. At the time I had about seventy dollars' worth of crack on me, so I asked her if they needed anything and if I could stay at the house that night.

It was better than nothing, but it was close to nothing too. Her apartment was basically empty. In the room where I slept there was a table with a tiny TV on it and a dirty mattress that smelled like burnt plastic from all the crack smoke it had absorbed. Marie had a man who lived there with her that I'll call Isaac. He was a cool dude who got high with her and also drank a lot every day.

I graduated from my aunt's house to a part-time crack house with this couple who were, all things considered, very nice to me. They would get food, and all I had to do was give them about thirty dollars' worth of crack and maybe another thirty dollars every few days for my room and board. First thing I did was get a new mattress from a secondhand store in the neighborhood. Once I had that, I was happy to have my own space for a minute while I figured out what the hell to do next.

I lived with Marie and Isaac for six months and spent that time getting my weight up with drugs: buying more, selling more, focusing every day on making money my purpose. While I lived there, I got my first gun. I put a big lock on my bedroom door, because nice as they were, when they were high they were fiends, and fiends be sneaky. To prove my point, even though I gave them bags to cover my rent and sold them what they wanted on top of that, one day I came home and found the lock busted and the door knocked off the hinges. The two of them had taken three hundred dollars' worth of crack, plus the first gold ring I'd ever bought myself, and my gun. I was furious. I looked everywhere I could think of, every single spot they might go to get high, every single bar they went to, but I couldn't find them. I sat waiting in the house and they didn't come home for days.

Marie showed up first, and by then I could not contain myself. "You robbed me!" I yelled, right up in her face. "What the fuck happened to my shit? You smoked it, didn't you? You fucking did all this!"

She started crying and saying she didn't do it and that she would never steal from me.

"You lying bitch!" I said. "I want my fucking money and where's my fucking gun at?"

I grabbed her by the hair and was getting ready to punch her in the face as hard as I could, but I just couldn't do it. Mad as I was, I didn't want to hit the lady who gave me a place to stay when I had none. She was a crack user, and in my heart I knew to expect something like this from her in the first place. Still, when it happened, it wasn't any easier to take. I'm glad that my intelligence won the day because I was one minute away from treating her real dirty. If I had, I would still regret it to this day. Nothing would have come of it because back then, no one blinked an eye when a dealer or anyone else beat the shit out of a fiend. But she wasn't just another fiend to me. It might sound crazy, but she was a sophisticated crack user. She was an older lady who talked with me about life and music and listened to me go on about hip-hop and how I was starting to rap. She'd become like a mother to me when I needed one.

This situation couldn't go on after that, though, so I cleared out and went to the only other place I could think of. My mother had a friend who was also a crack user named Terry. She lived two floors up in the same building, and I knew that my cousin Unique hung out there and sold drugs out of her house. Unique had known Terry for a long time, and they'd come to a very safe and profitable arrangement. Unique would cook up and bag up his shit at Terry's place, and casually sell to the more upscale crack clientele that Terry brought in. This went on for years. It kept Unique's operation off the street and kept Terry's user friends safe and supplied. Terry's place was never a crack house; it was always a very nice apartment where crack was sold. Usually she would invite friends over who liked to get high and arrange to have one dealer—Unique or me—there to supply what they needed. She'd tell us: "Eight o'clock, people will be there, just come by and bring the good shit." She was an undercover addict that you'd never see on the street in a daze at six in the morning.

Terry took me in out of respect for my mother and also because I'd keep her in crack. Me and Unique started hanging out in a whole new way. My cousin was cool with the situation because he hadn't gotten me into it. I'd gotten into it all on my own, so there was no way his mom or my mom could be mad at him. I was really happy to be hanging as equals, doing business beside the guy I'd seen as a father figure for so long. He still looked out for me too, the way he always had.

One night when I was downstairs in front of the building, I got into a tussle with a guy named Jerry G. He and his boy Mel were the type of old-school niggas who liked to punch you in your chest, teasing you until you put your hands up. Dudes like that were part of the landscape: they had nothing to do but sit out there drinking, talking shit and picking on younger guys and anyone else smaller than them. They'd do it until you told them to stop fucking with you, and then they'd run off laughing, just drunk-ass niggas. Maybe it's me, but I always seemed to get picked on by guys like that, ever since I can remember. I don't know why, maybe they thought I looked funny, or maybe they thought I'd take it since I was pretty quiet or whatever. One night those motherfuckers were out in front of Terry's apartment building, and I guess I was in a mood. They got at me too much and they pissed me off, and I told Unique about it. I knew he would tell them to chill out since they went to school with Unique and were the same age. I thought he could just end that shit right then and there. Jerry and Mel—they're both dead now, rest in peace—were drunks and assholes, but they weren't suckers. They started arguing with Unique and one thing led to another. Unique slapped Jerry G right across his face with his gun. Jerry started bleeding, and those guys ran off to get a pistol and Jerry's cousin Umar, a guy Unique used to be cool with. These guys were bullies who had access to guns. They knew that Unique fucked with guns, so when they took off, we knew they were definitely coming back packing.

Umar came out and got into it with Unique, who came at it cool, with respect, explaining why Jerry G deserved the slap he got. It didn't go well, and it looked like Umar was going to try to do something. That's how it was in the 'hood: you could be with a dude you knew all your life and next thing you knew you were beefing with him, pulling out guns. When dudes got in their feelings and started acting funky, friendship went out the window. Umar was a little bit older than Unique, and as he started sizing him up, getting in his face, Unique pulled out his gun.

"Yo, don't come at me like that, man. Back up off me."

"What you sayin' U? What you sayin? You takin' it somewhere else? Oh now what, nigga?"

"Man, if you swing on me I'm telling you it ain't going your way, so back up off me right now. This ain't going to go where you want it to go."

Umar put his hand on Unique's face and that was it. Unique hit him with two quick blasts, one in his arm, one in his leg, dropping him to the ground right there. Jerry G and Mel ran off as soon as they saw the gun, leaving Umar on the ground screaming and holding his arm, yelling, "Oh shit you shot me! You fucking shot me!"

That was the first time I saw somebody get shot, but it wouldn't be the last. U took off running, and I ran right back up to Terry's house, nervous as hell. U showed up a few minutes later to grab some stuff he had stashed there, and then he headed to his mom's house and I went with him. We said hello to Aunt Joyce like nothing was wrong, and I sat down to watch TV with her like it was a regular visit. Unique ducked back out to catch his breath and come up with a plan. There was a good chance those guys would retaliate and a real good chance the cops would come looking for him.

I was sitting there on the couch with Aunt Joyce after Unique left, when somebody started banging real hard on the door. It was not friendly. My aunt looked over at the door with no intention of getting up to open it.

"Who's there?" she asked through the door.

It was Umar, the dude that Unique had just shot.

"Joyce, where Unique at? He shot me, you know. I ain't going for this shit, tell him to come out. I got no argument with you, now."

"He ain't here!" she yelled. "You stop banging on my door right now, he ain't here!"

That motherfucker wasn't having it; Umar kept banging harder and harder, so bad that Aunt Joyce and I hid in the bathroom and locked the door. He was still bleeding and hadn't even called for an ambulance yet, but he'd gone and gotten a shotgun. He seemed about ready to kick the door until he'd broken it down. My aunt wasn't having that from a guy she'd known since he was a kid who used to come by to play with her son after school.

"Umar, what the fuck do you think you're doing to my goddamned house?" she yelled. "You stop this shit right now!"

She opened the front door and started cursing his ass out like he was still in middle school, telling him to put the fucking gun down and go the fuck home. Umar made his case, showing her where Unique had shot him. It was a no-win situation because Unique wasn't there and Joyce was not having Umar's anger. Dude was so frustrated that after Joyce closed the door, he let off a round in the hallway, straight into the ceiling. It left one hell of a hole and it's a miracle it didn't hit somebody walking down the hall upstairs.

A few hours later one of Unique's soldiers came by to tell me to stay put. A few hours after that Unique came through. To say the least, Joyce was not happy with him. He asked me if the cops or anyone else had come by looking for him. He had been to jail once and he was still on probation, so he knew what kind of shit he was in. He didn't want to go back. He knew that the man he'd shot was a stand-up dude, but who could tell if he wouldn't snitch? Who could tell what bystanders wouldn't snitch?

U was ready to bounce. This shit had happened in broad daylight, and even if the parties involved kept it to themselves, people were gonna talk. This shit was all my fault. I wasn't big time enough to handle it. I was still a junior hustler, and I'd called on my cousin to back me up when maybe the situation didn't call for it.

Unique brought me downstairs to see the 1982 Oldsmobile 98 that he'd packed up.

"I got to get out of town for a little bit," he said. "I'm not trying to go to jail, you know what I mean? I'm going to North Carolina for a month until this shit cools off . . . you wanna come?"

CHAPTER 5

STREET LIFE

Unique and I jumped into the 98 and we were gone, off to North Carolina. I was eighteen with nowhere else to be—I didn't have a pot to piss in. Unique had packed the essentials: his crack stash, a stack of cash, a few guns, and nothing else. We headed to a town near Raleigh called Wilson where Unique knew two brothers we could connect with. They were from the neighborhood and they were like us, niggas getting money, just older. They'd gone to Carolina to find a new life, kind of like retiring, even though they were still hustling. Those guys were thinking ahead, like proper OGs. They were looking to get out of town and go to a place where they could settle down, make money, and have their own thing without worrying about young guns coming for them. They were smart, thinking outside of the box and outside of the 'hood. Unique never told them why we'd come down, he just played it like he'd taken little cousin on a vacation to see the world outside New York.

It was the first time I'd been on the road, and I loved it. I left with nothing but the clothes on my back, but Unique took care of me. We stopped off and had us a steak dinner, and he gave me some money to go shopping for clothes once we got there. Then we drove straight through to NC. His boys were happy to have us because, like I said, Unique showed up with drugs, guns, and everything you'd need to do a little business. These were dudes Unique had never really run with business-wise, but they'd always been cool with each other. It was open arms, but at the same time, Unique was known for having weight, so they figured there was something in it for them. And Unique knew that if he connected with them, he'd be able to make money while he laid low. Looking back, I think he knew he was going to end up back inside. He just wanted to put it off for a while. I'm thankful he chose to spend that last vacation with me.

For those two months Unique and I rotated hotels. We never let anyone know where the stash of drugs, cash, and guns was located. U had a few girlfriends in town. He liked one in particular quite a bit, but he didn't want to stay with her. She was a church chick. We took life day by day, chilling wherever we wanted, staying in one hotel then changing it up so no one knew where we were. It was safer that way.

For the most part this was exciting and fun. We sold drugs, we hung out, we made money, we got girls. And Unique's friends, the two brothers who were our anchors there, they were mad cool. I bring this up because when we got back home, it really fucked me up when I heard what happened to them. Real talk, these motherfuckers were crazy. They got money, they loved to gamble; they lived on the edge. Apparently one night these two brothers started playing with a revolver and they threw down a bunch of cash on a game of Russian roulette. They put one bullet in the cylinder, they spun it, put it on the table, and they stared each other down. And they went through it, putting the gun to their heads back and forth and pulling the trigger. And that night one of them blew his brains out in front of his brother.

WE went home after two months, and I went back to living with Marie and Isaac, temporarily, making sure they never got the chance to rob me again, as I began hustling once more. By then Umar had gotten into more trouble and was in jail for armed robbery or some other shit, so Unique didn't have to worry about dealing with him. Unique did have a warrant out on him, though, so eventually he was hauled in and locked up. He had violated parole, and it was his second major offense, so the judge handed him a few years of hard time.

Unique was sent to Sing Sing, the infamous maximum-security prison upstate in Ossining, New York. It's where murderers like mob hit man Frank Abbandando and David Berkowitz (Son of Sam) had done time. It was no joke, and it changed Unique almost immediately. I went to see him shortly after he was incarcerated, and he was a different guy. He had a thick mustache (he'd always been clean-shaven) and was fully institutionalized: everything neat, creases in his pants, hair cut short, in shape, all of that. He knew I was selling crack, so he told me to set myself up at Terry's house. If I was going to do it, he wanted me to be as safe as possible. It was the blessing I was looking for. Terry was like a sister to Unique. It couldn't have been a safer environment for such dangerous business.

At that time, I felt successful if I ended up with four hundred dollars at the end of a night. It was enough to keep me in fresh haircuts, sneakers, and maybe a new goose when winter came. But once I started hanging out with Terry, that number went way up. Terry helped grow my enterprise with her built-in clientele, which got me hungry to build even further. I reconnected with a homie I'll call Jamie. I'd known him for years and he was making real money, mostly in a building down the block. We started hanging out as friends first, going out to Brooklyn to get some food and weed. Soon I was riding with him when he went uptown to score. We got cool with each other, but I never approached him on any kind of business shit, out of respect for our friendship. I just went along and watched him do his errands and take care of his business. Aside from Unique when I was younger, I never wanted to work for anybody but myself. I wasn't going to ask Jamie about it because I was just happy to have a homie who respected me and liked hanging out with me. That being said, it came to a point where he did start handing me packs, supplying me as a friend so I could go sell at my spot. When he saw that I was moving it quickly, he got curious. I brought him over to Terry's to see what I had going on. After that, everything went to the next level because Jamie was in the game for real. On a scale of 1–10, if what I was doing in sales was a 3, Jamie was a 12. And when a 12 meets a 3, he don't respect him or trust him right away. But once he did trust me, it was on. In no time, he turned Terry's house into a gold mine.

Jamie was my man and I learned so much from him. He was the kind of guy who knew how to handle his money. This was good for me to see because I didn't know how to save or plan or anything like that. I'd been living day to day, hand to mouth, for my entire life. The thought of keeping cash for a rainy day was alien to me. Jamie taught me otherwise. He had cars, he had fly shit, but he wasn't spending his money every chance he got. Hustlers who catch real money quietly are superstars. They are the ones who really know how to get it.

Terry's apartment became like a crack country club. I'd never call it a crack house or anything negative like that, because it was a nice place. Her friends were all everyday people with jobs who just liked to smoke crack on the down low. This wasn't uncommon at the time: in the way that people sniffed coke on the weekends in the seventies, people smoked crack in the eighties. When Terry wasn't high, she was like a mom to us, cooking meals and teaching us things because she was constantly reading books and magazines. She would sing, she would dance, she would talk about life. She was thoughtful and philosophical: a real Maya Angelou type, but on crack. She'd make chicken, rice and peas, potato salad—dishes that made you feel at home. Plus she was a great baker and always had a homemade pie or cake on the counter. She was a well-respected lady in the community. She kept a clean house, with candles all around her living room and art on the walls. Her house didn't smell like crack and neither did she. Nothing about her suggested that she had an addiction, but she did.

Terry showed the same degree of sophistication when it came to business. She allowed a select number of her friends to hang with her and smoke when she was smoking. Even though her house was like our storefront for moving product, she had standards. The clients were never strangers off the street. They were friends of hers or friends of friends, and everyone had to be vouched for. I know that Terry felt comfortable with us as her suppliers because we were young boys. She felt safer than she would have if dealing with a supplier who was a grown man. It enabled us to have a kind of auntie or mother-figure relationship with her, and both sides were happy with that.

Once we got rolling, we got so busy that we had to hire someone to work with me up in Terry's house. It didn't hurt that Jamie and I went the extra mile and our shit was better than most. There were two products the Spanish guys sold up in the Bronx: one was crack that they'd already cooked and the other was cocaine. If you bought the crack, nine times out of ten it was synthetic crap. Jamie knew to buy the cocaine, then come back to the 'hood and cook it. That's what I had been doing and that's what Unique used to do. And we had Terry to test the product, because there's no better judge of quality than a sophisticated crack user.

On a typical night of business, we'd all have a meal together. Then me and my partner—sometimes it was Jamie, sometimes our worker at the time—would go in the other room and smoke weed, watch TV, and chill. Terry's friends came over to buy bags or sit with her and get high. She had a core group of five or six friends who used to come every week, relying on her to supply the good shit. Most of the time, that crew alone was all we needed. If they really got after it, they'd be good for eighteen hundred to two thousand dollars. Usually we'd break up the night by going out for sandwiches. I'd always get pastrami with yellow cheese and mustard, black pepper, and jalapeños, heated up, along with a juice or grape soda. Eventually my partner and I would fall asleep on the couch until Terry came in to wake us up and buy more for everybody. This would go on all night. It would be five o'clock in the morning and she'd nudge us and say she needed seven, eight more bags. That might sound like a crazy situation, but we loved it. From our perspective, it was one-stop shopping. When it comes to hustling, the less you have to move around with substances on you, the safer you are.

We were moving a minimum of seven hundred dollars of crack a night. Our quality was good, so word got around that we worked out of this low-key clubhouse and if Terry liked you, you could come through. When shit really started popping off, we'd have so many people in there smoking that my partner and I would put on gas masks we'd bought. With seven or eight people getting at it in the other room, the air was not right. Fridays were our busiest time, since most of our clients were working folks and most of them got their paychecks on Fridays. They'd show up after a long week, and some wouldn't leave until either their money or our drugs ran out, whichever came first. Sometimes they'd be there all weekend.

My man and I kept the Baggies in our drawers, knowing full well that we were surrounded by fiends. We had a deal with Terry that she was the only one allowed to come into the room to buy because we wanted to stay as anonymous as possible. For every ten she sold, she'd get a bonus dime bag for herself. Still, there were times when I woke up to find her face close to mine, as if she was leaning in for a kiss. She was checking my breathing, seeing if I was knocked out deep enough for her to slip a hand down my pants to grab a bag. Fiends are very scary when they're high, and at those times she looked more like a witch than the nice lady who had served me dinner earlier in the night. Terry never ran around like a weirdo during the day, but she was a different person on the pipe. When the door to her smoking room would open, sometimes I'd catch a glimpse of her fucking some dude or another. I knew it was going down when she'd come out of there in her robe to ask for more bags.

I'm lucky that she looked at me more like a nephew than a drug dealer, because I was young. A fiend with no heart could have taken advantage of me in any number of ways. I knew she had this split personality because of the drugs, so I did my best to keep the balance between giving her what she wanted and getting what I needed. That being said, she did some sneaky shit and was always hustling me for more crack. A few times when she was coming down, she told my partner and me we had to leave if we weren't going to give her anything free. But for the most part it worked out.

We did so much business that our supplier was selling us quarter kilos of coke for twenty-five hundred dollars. This was a really good deal in the mid-eighties. Things were good, but word had gotten around that we were up there doing our thing. There was a Jamaican guy in the building, down on the second floor. He had a Puerto Rican working the street for him, and the two of them started getting competitive. They'd see our regulars coming and would try to steal them away, offering them shit before they even got to the lobby. Jamie didn't like that one bit. He decided he should smack the shit out of the Puerto Rican kid since he was a dude he knew from school.

We'd heard all this from a fiend, by the way. You can never trust a fiend, but Jamie still wasn't having it. Maybe a week later, Jamie and I were exiting the building when we saw the Puerto Rican kid come out the back door. Jamie had his gun of course, and he was ready to do something. Thing is, the Puerto Rican kid had his baby in his arms and was walking toward his car where his baby mama was waiting.

I tried to hold Jamie back, telling him we'd get at the guy later, but my man got into it anyway.

"Yo, I heard what you've been doing. If I catch you getting in our shit, if I catch you trying to stop what we doing, you're going to see me again."

The kid kinda blew it off and said something real dismissive like, "Yeah sounds good," and got in the car.

Jamie didn't like that, so as they drove off, he shot up the car real good with the nigga's baby and baby mama inside.

"What the fuck you doing, bro?" I yelled, grabbing his arm to get him to stop. "You could kill the baby, man!"

He said something about showing them we wasn't playing, and I couldn't believe what kind of shit we were in now. This was going to cause a war. The worst part about it was that Jamie didn't live in the projects like I did; he just came there to sell drugs. Since I lived there, this was going to come right down on me. I had a gun and wasn't scared to use it, but I'd made it this far without having to kill anybody. I wasn't looking to start over something I didn't even do. In the end, the kid and his partner let it go, and stopped going after our clientele. I guess they figured there was enough business for all of us and that getting into a turf war would ruin all that. This was the first time I realized how lucky I'd been. But no one stays lucky forever.

THERE was something else in my life that had me thinking of ways out of the drug game and that was Candy, my African princess. By this time we had a really nice relationship going. It had started as a schoolboy crush, just seeing her out in front of the building, saying hello, the way these things go. I'd walk her to the store when I saw her and do anything to make her laugh, and we became friends until one thing led to the next. We got close, but her parents didn't like me. They were very strict Africans, the type that didn't consider African Americans to be like them or related to them in any way. They knew I was a street thug, so I'm sure they were worried for their daughter. They'd snatch her out of the hallway and slam the door in my face when they saw us talking, and they more or less forbade her from seeing me. Of course, we saw each other anyway, it just took a bit of running around.

My life had settled into some kind of normalcy, but not the kind most people are used to. I was getting money, I had a system going with Jamie. Even though I wasn't on good terms with Moms, I was taking care of myself and getting by. My occupation was nothing for a grandma to be proud of, but it was an improvement over how I was living when my mom kicked me out. I'd found a way to support myself and I was totally independent. That part was great. But the dangers of hustling, even as safely as I was doing it, had me worried day in and day out.

Candy was the person who kept me in check because she was my connection to life beyond the streets. She listened to my problems, she gave me advice, she told me to be careful, and she held me back when I got too headstrong. I held on to her tightly because she was a good person and we really cared for each other. When I wasn't hustling, I'd take her on wholesome dates to the movies, dinner, or dancing. The more money I made, the more I tried to stay off the block altogether to avoid the shit that came with just hanging out.

One evening Candy and I had plans to see a movie. I was going to scoop her up around seven in my aunt Joyce's car. I spent the afternoon up at Terry's because at the last minute, she decided to have her fiend friends over, which was guaranteed money. I made fifteen hundred dollars in a few hours, but it cut into our plans and we had to skip the movie. Candy, as usual, was cool. She told me to stay there and take care of business and come get her when I was done. We could see a later movie or not see a movie; she didn't mind either way. She was understanding, the way a supportive partner should be.

When I'd sold the fiends everything I had, I got out of there, feeling good with a nice stack in my pocket. I grabbed the car and rolled up to my family's building to grab Candy. Since I was in such a good mood, I decided to stop for a minute to talk with a few of the homeboys I hadn't seen for a while who were sitting out there. These were guys I'd known for years, all chilling on the fence pole like always. As we were talking, we recognized this one dude we knew called Maurice in a gypsy cab rolling by. I was sitting beside a dude called Cent, who turned to me real quick.

"Yo, was that Maurice?"

"Yeah man, that was him," I said. "I haven't seen him in forever."

"I'm gonna shoot that nigga when he come over here," Cent said. "Watch this shit."

Everyone started laughing, thinking the dude was kidding, even as Cent pulled out his gun. He was acting mad, but in a way that seemed like an act.

"Yo, yo! You funny, Cent. Stop the bullshit," someone said. "You playin', right? What Maurice ever do to you?"

Dudes made a few jokes and the laughs continued, but Cent wasn't laughing. His eyes got hard. When the car pulled over, Maurice jumped out and started walking toward us real serious. All of us realized something was about to go down. Everybody scattered, most of them across the street. Since I was right in front of my family's building, I decided to run in there.

Through the Plexiglas of the lobby I watched Cent point his gun at Maurice and pull the trigger. Nothing happened—his gun jammed. Then it was on: Maurice pulled out his gun, a Glock with a 22-shot clip, and he started blasting. Cent ran toward me, heading for the lobby, with Maurice coming up behind him, shooting the whole way like the Terminator. He had twenty-two shots in that clip, so he was just getting started.

The lobbies in all the project buildings were nothing but Plexiglas and steel, with no place to hide. There was a row of mailboxes and a little open alcove at the base of the stairs. As soon as I saw what was happening, I hit the ground and started crawling toward the stairs. My best bet was to either run up them or hide under them. Cent came in at top speed and hit the deck, trying to unjam his gun so he could fire back. It was no use: Maurice came through the door a few seconds later and emptied his clip. The place filled with smoke as bullets ricocheted off of the steel and Plexiglas, flying over my head and pinging all around me. It happened too fast for me to stand up and try to run, so I kept crawling until I was under the stairs.

I stopped moving when I heard the bullets stop coming, then the door slammed and I knew Maurice was gone. That's when I felt a hot searing pain in both legs. I knew I'd been shot. As I thought about shooting back, I realized my gun had slid out of my pants. I looked and saw it lying on the floor in the middle of the lobby among all of Maurice's empty casings. I didn't see Cent. He had run off already.

I pulled myself up and hobbled up the stairs to my mother's door on the second floor. Before I knocked, I pulled my pants down to check my legs and saw two bullet holes in each one. I was in shock, but they weren't bleeding too badly. They were small .22-caliber bullet holes.

"Damn," I thought to myself, "that nigga shot me, just fucking around going after someone else. Out of all the shit I've done, this is how I get shot?"

Then I knocked. My little sister answered and said she'd heard the gunshots. It was a strange moment, but since the bullets had passed through my legs and hadn't hit any bones, it almost felt like I'd just been punched really hard. My mom took one look at me, shook her head, and called for an ambulance. I managed to get back downstairs on my own to collect my gun. I gave it to my little brother and told him to hide it in his room for me. Then I went outside to wait for my ride to the hospital. I found out later that somehow Cent hadn't even been hit. He was right there in the middle of the floor but he managed to escape without a scratch. It took more than half an hour for the ambulance to come, and the whole time I was sitting there, I was too pissed off about the whole thing to feel any kind of pain. That would come later.

At the hospital, the cops questioned me and didn't believe me when I told them I didn't know who shot me. I wasn't gonna tell them shit. Even if they'd roughed me up, nothing the cops could have done would have made me feel worse than when the doctor stuck a catheter up my dick. That tube felt like it was four feet long going in and even worse when they pulled it out a few days later. The bullets didn't kill me, but I thought that tube might. Trust me, getting shot is one thing, a catheter is something else. It was one of the most torturous things I've experienced in my entire life.

Two bullets had gone through my right thigh, missing my bone and major arteries, which is a miracle. On my left side I wasn't so lucky. One bullet passed through, but the other hit me below the knee, just under the cap, shaving off a piece of bone as thick as my thumb. Of the four that passed through my body, that one did the most damage. To get it clean, the doctors had to cut out so much bone and cartilage that my knee and my mobility have never been the same. Combined with the muscle damage from the other bullets, I was in for a long, slow recovery. I spent two weeks in the hospital and over a year healing.

The first morning I woke up in the hospital I knew I had to make a decision: would I go after Maurice or let this go? He hadn't meant to, but he inflicted permanent damage to my body. Was it worth going to war? Was it worth killing a nigga and possibly doing time for it? That night Maurice called me in my hospital room.

"Yo man, I'm sorry, man," he said. "I didn't know that was you in there. You seen he was going to shoot me. I know you seen that—he was trying to kill me. I wasn't going to let him shoot at me. So I did what I had to do. But I'm real sorry you were there. I wish that didn't happen."

I didn't want to hear any of it because I was still so mad about it, but at the same time he was being a real-ass nigga and I had to respect that.

"Yo, man," I said. "It's all good. Don't worry about it."

The cops had Maurice's name and knew what happened, but I still wouldn't help them build a case against him. They visited me a few times, asking questions. I found new ways not to answer until they finally gave up. When I got home, I didn't say shit to people in the neighborhood either. I walked with crutches and had bandages over my legs. The doctor told me that if one of the bullets had entered my body a few centimeters closer to the bone, I'd have been paralyzed. The craziest thing about all of this is that Maurice and I are now family because one of my cousins and his sister had a child together.

I spent the next year at my mom's house recuperating. This spelled the end of my relationship with Candy for a while. As cool as she was with my occupation, once I'd gotten shot, all she could talk about was how none of it would have happened if I'd just picked her up on time instead of choosing to make a few thousand dollars. I didn't think that was fair, but what the fuck could I do about it when I couldn't even walk right?

I slid into a depression, which was made worse by the constant pain of my wounds. They were tricky ones to heal, especially the one that had destroyed most of my kneecap. Every time I walked, or flexed my leg, the wound reopened. I was constantly changing bandages, and it seemed like it would never close up and grow new skin. It also took me a while to deal with the constant soreness in the other leg where the bullet had passed through the muscle. I wasn't even twenty years old but the aches and pains had me feeling like an old-timer.

After a month or so I was able to go downstairs and sit outside to get some air. I'd chill on the fence that ran along the front of the building and hang out with whichever homeboys were around. When I felt up to it, I'd do some dips to keep my upper body in shape, but since I couldn't move around much, my world became mostly internal. I began to write rhymes more seriously. For the first time, I put them down in a notebook that I kept on me. That notebook became my confidant as I recorded everything that I saw around me. I also found myself digging into Moms's record collection, getting back into the classics. I started examining the music I'd heard all my life with a deeper respect.

At this time I also discovered the Five Percent Nation of Islam. Sitting outside my building, I engaged with brothers in my project who had devoted themselves to the Nation. A lot of them had learned about it in prison and had survived there because of it. From where I was sitting, surrounded by drama and drugs and poverty, and having been accidentally shot by one of my homeboys, the teachings made a lot of sense.

The lessons are a guide to becoming a self-realized African-American man, and they began to make me think about what I was going to make of the rest of my life. I didn't want to spend my life hustling, and the only other thing I cared about was rhyming. I started using my notebook as a blackboard for myself. I made lists of goals, created a map to my future success and security. I knew I'd go back to hustling because I didn't know how else to make real money, but I was going to take that money and find something else. I'd follow any lead I came across that might take me into something different. I'd never thought that way before. Recovering at home, I engaged with my family again after a long period apart, and I realized the stability family could bring to my life. I started looking out for my little brother, who was ten years younger than me. I made sure he kept his head together as he grew up.

The rhymes I was putting to paper back then weren't complete songs or anything like that. I don't think I ever used one of them on a record, but in a way they were more important than my rhymes that the world knows. Those little lines, those verses for the fuck of it, taught me to think in poetry. That notebook was my gym, it got my thoughts in shape. It was where I sharpened and refined my skills beyond freestyling off the top of my head.

This became my preoccupation, and it was how I kept my frustration at bay as time went on. Until then, my identity had been hustling, getting money, being fly, and looking high. Stuck at home and barely moving around, I felt like I'd lost my purpose. I've always loved nice things—the best that I could afford—and I wasn't gonna depend on nobody to take care of me. I was waiting to feel better so I could get back to that life.

Once I was well enough, able to move around without crutches and without too much pain, I had to get back to hustling. I felt like I'd lost so much time that I took to it more seriously than ever, because I was motivated to find the means to some kind of security. I had Terry's spot of course, but I wanted more. So just like Jamie had done, I set up shop in additional houses. I also scrambled in and around my family's building, picking up extra sales from anyone in need. I hired a few guys outside of my arrangement with Jamie. We would get up before dawn because in those early morning hours, out on the street, there was always a rush as the sun rose. It was eerie shit watching the crackheads who'd been up all night come out to the street in search of more. If you were out there holding you could make a lot of money real fast.

Despite how determined I was, it was tough getting back to work with my kneecap all fucked up. When business was good, I'd be at it for hours and I wouldn't have time to get home and change the bandages. Just going about my day, my pants would rub against my injury and eventually wear the bandage off. Some days I'd be out there with blood soaked through my pants and all down my leg. I'd have to get the iodine out when I got home and clean that shit up, hoping I wouldn't get an infection.

Increased business meant increased risk. As carefully as I was choosing my houses and my business partners apart from Jamie, I had a few close calls. One night, coming out of this lady's house after selling off all my shit, I was counting my money as I opened the stairwell door. A pair of cops were coming up the stairs, and when they saw me, one said to the other: "Bingo, we got him."

When they searched me, they didn't find nothing but my money on me. The worst thing about it was that while they had me up against the wall and were patting me down, they busted my injury wide open and my knee started bleeding all over the place, coming out of my pants and onto my sneakers. I was in pain and pissed off.

"Yo man, what the fuck?" I said. "You got nothing on me, I ain't got nothing!"

"Where did all this money come from?" one cop asked.

"Yeah, that's my money."

"What are you doing up this early in the morning?"

"I'm just coming from the club."

He knew that was bullshit. I was wearing a simple jumpsuit, not dressed to impress. This cop knew me too, and I knew him. He was aware of what I was doing in the neighborhood, he just hadn't found a way to bust me for it. These same two guys had locked up my homeboy's entire family not long before this, and I'd seen it happen. I was in the hallway with a few other dudes, and we saw them coming in time to get out of there, or else they probably would have taken us in too. Cops like these guys were on a mission. They wore plain clothes, they'd park their undercover cruiser far away, then walk down and sneak into a building hoping to rush up and catch you in the mix.

"I should take your money," one officer said.

"Yo, give me back my money. That's my money."

He looked at me for a long minute, then looked at the stack of cash in his hand like the law didn't fucking matter. Then he threw it all over the floor. Playing cat and mouse with cops like them was a part of the hustle. You had to be on your guard at all times to survive. That was a wakeup call for me to take my business inside again and not be so greedy. As fast as I was trying to bank money in order to get out of the game, I didn't need to be making early morning sales and I shouldn't have been on the street like everybody else. Then and there I decided to tone it down. I left the early morning stuff to my lieutenants, and one guy in particular that I trusted. We got our system flowing real tight and started making a lot of money. It was a good thing too, because the War on Drugs was on. The cops started going crazy, snatching up anyone and everyone in sight when they decided to rush a project.

My crew and I stayed alive because we were clever hustlers. We did most of our business at night, not out on the street during the day for the whole neighborhood to see. We were respectful too: when we saw kids coming back from school, or mothers coming down the street with groceries, we'd shut it down, clear the way, and let them get upstairs safely. I might have been dealing drugs, but I was raised with manners and taught to have respect for family values. I looked at what I was doing as a business. It wasn't some kind of game or contest to see who was the biggest, baddest man. The guys out there being blatant fell hardest. They ended up either busted or dead, oftentimes because someone they'd disrespected snitched on them.

For the next two years I ran a successful operation—part of it with my own crew and part with my partners Jamie and, of course, Terry. We didn't get busted, we didn't get killed, and we made money. We had consistent product and for the most part we sold it discreetly. My enterprise became even more established, and soon we knew the block and the block knew us. We knew how to get by and stay above the law.

But there's a saying: if you don't eat with the wolves, the wolves will eat you. That holds true in the 'hood. Too many homeboys saw what we were doing and wanted in. On top of that, there were dudes who wanted to take over my spots, and it got to a point where I had to decide if I was going to do something about it or let it go. I never went the violent route. Instead, I'd find a new house and do everything I could to keep my spots on the low. I wasn't trying to take over the world, I just wanted to make money and chill. I knew no other way to survive. I had other ambitions, but I needed to eat, and hustling was a full-time job. I had my notebook, I had my dreams, and along the way I'd gotten signs that perhaps I had another calling. But I didn't see a path to realizing those intentions yet. Deep down I knew I had something, and the more I developed my rhyme skills, the more other people saw it in me too. I just needed a push, a partner, a collaborator. My desire was there, but it lacked an outlet. I needed a mission and a vision to believe in. I was a soldier, loyal and ready to fight a war. What I needed was a general.

CHAPTER 6

I WATCH MY BACK LIKE I'M LOCKED DOWN

I was twenty-one years old and I'd made a life for myself, dangerous as it was. With every passing year I became more aware that it wouldn't last forever. I'd been shot and nearly paralyzed. Somehow I'd managed to evade the cops, but I started to feel like a reckoning was coming my way. It didn't help that in 1988, the NYPD created TNT, the Tactical Narcotics Team. It was a hundred-member task force designed to target drug operations throughout the city. Their focus was street hustlers, then they'd use the information they got from those arrests to build cases against higher-level guys who they'd hand off to the federal antidrug units. In Queens, the TNT arrested twenty-something street dealers on their very first day of operation. Then they branched out to Harlem and every other borough, including Staten Island. This increased my drive to find some other way to live, because it was just a matter of time before I'd be caught up in their net—directly or because someone snitched. After living my own way since the age of sixteen, I sure as hell wasn't getting a day job. How could I think of working for UPS or the Transit Authority? Putting in all those hours a week to take home half of what I'd make in one good night of hustling, tax-free?

I started to look for any opportunity that crossed my path. I was always hoping to find an avenue into music, which was the only other thing I knew how to do. For years I had loved putting words together, so long as it was outside of school and on my own terms. It was my hobby when I had any kind of idle time. I'd arrange rhymes in my head by subject, always on the fly, inspired by whatever was in front of me as I vibed out, watching the world go by. I had an arsenal of lines at the ready that I'd entertain myself with. If someone started a cypher wherever I might be, they could count on me to jump in and drop some bombs. While I was bedridden, recovering from my gunshot wounds, I organized these rhymes into my notebook. The act of writing them breathed new life into my hobby and allowed me to regard it with a more serious eye. I also spent that downtime analyzing the words of my idols Slick Rick and Rakim, and I tried to build rhymes in their honor. I was devoting myself to rap more than ever, but I kept it to myself and never told my homeboys just how deep I was into my pen game.

The first person I did tell about it was someone I hadn't seen in a while: Robert Diggs, aka the RZA. Growing up, he had been involved in hustling and robbery here and there, but he had never been an all-out street dude. When I saw him again, he was visiting one of his cousins who lived in Park Hill, and he told me how he was spending all of his time on music, chess, karate flicks, and the lessons of the Five Percent Nation of Islam. He had a four-track studio tape recorder, some turntables, a sampler, and a sequencer. He was making beats in his little home studio. I was interested in that creativity right away and started chilling with him. I liked going to his spot because he was a calm and collected fella, and I knew that if I gave him my time I'd always end up learning something. It was good to have a safe haven like that during the day when there was so much heat on the street. I found RZA's passion inspiring because he had the energy of a man with a vision. Everyone else I knew didn't look beyond the way they were living. RZA's mission was to be a rapper, and he told me straight up that he knew in his heart that it was his calling. He said it might take some time, but he knew he could get there: like playing chess, he had to think, plan, and make the right moves.

I'd known RZA since we were kids. His cousins in Park Hill went to my school, and he lived with them at various times growing up. When we reconnected and started to hang out, it gave me some hope that my dream of getting into music might come true. Not only was he a Five Percenter, he was also a DJ and an MC and was teaching himself to be a producer. If anyone was going to help me achieve my dream of being an MC, it was him. But that was still a ways off. When we reconnected, RZA learned that I had rhymes, but he wasn't concerned with me. He was too busy getting himself a record deal and pursuing his goal of being a solo artist.

RZA's place was a couple blocks away from the Stapleton projects. It was this safe, open-door spot where brothers could chill and listen to him do his thing when the block got hot. His crib was a small studio apartment, and it was twisted—just full of sound gear and books and VCR tapes. To the untrained eye it looked like a messed up secondhand store, but RZA had a system and knew where everything was. It was clear from the doorway that this place served one purpose: music. It was full of records, turntables, and recording equipment. There were no other household items aside from a little TV, a bed off to the side, and a clock radio. His records were everywhere: all over the floor, stacked against the wall—just crates and crates of disco plates wherever you looked. The heart of the operation was a table that held his four-track studio tape recorder, sequencer, and sampler.

His sound board was enough to make samples and beats, record vo-cals, and make demo tapes. RZA was a different kind of dude: he didn't make small talk; he was focused and serious and liked to lecture on whatever subject he was into discussing at the moment. His inter-ests consumed him, and his passion for them made it seem like they were the most important pursuits in the world. He wasn't for every-body, but I was comfortable in his environment and curious about everything he was doing. He quickly became like a brother to me.

He would open up *Supreme 120 Lessons: For the Nation of Gods & Earths*, one of the handbooks of the Five Percent Nation of Islam. He'd choose a lesson for anyone who might be there that day to dis-cuss. It was a scene, with all kinds of dudes who were living all kinds of lives coming together. We'd talk about who we were and what we believed in. I always stuck around longer than most. After a while, when I wasn't hustling, anyone looking for me knew I could be found at RZA's. Everything going on there was opening my eyes, my mind, and soon enough my entire life, to something greater.

When we was chillin' just us, RZA would be over in the corner making a beat while I was reading the *Supreme 120 Lessons*. All of his creativity was the backdrop to my growing knowledge of self. I used this new perspective to redefine my view of life from top to bot-tom. The lessons are a series of questions and answers that explain the Five Percent Nation's view on the origin of the African-American man. They give us a lens through which to view the past, present, and future—and they gave me hope that I could lift myself out of the situ-ation I had been born into. The lessons taught me to see myself as the god I am and not to be held back by any external constructs.

I had first gotten into the teachings of the Five Percent Nation when I was a bit younger. The religion was founded in Harlem in 1964 by Allah the Father, who had formerly been known as Clarence 13X and originally Clarence Edward Smith. He was a student and follower of Malcom X and a member of the Nation of Islam. As he began to disagree with their view on the origin of man, he split off and founded his own group. The fundamental belief of the Five Percent Nation is that 10 percent of the people in the world know the truth of existence, but those few and the people who work for them choose to keep the rest of the world in ignorance in order to control them. They have succeeded in keeping 85 percent of the world in that state, but there is a remaining 5 percent of people who know the truth and are determined to enlighten the other 85. The Nation has a system of Supreme Mathematics and a Supreme Alphabet, which were created by Allah the Father and are the keys to understanding humankind's relationship to the universe. The Five Percent Nation also teaches that black people are the original people of earth. Black men, who are called Gods, and black women, who are called Earths, are the fathers and mothers of all civilization. There is no idea of a higher God in the Five Percent Nation; every black man is God. It is empowering for people who have been repressed by society to be taught that they themselves are God.

The Five Percent Nation started to take hold in my neighborhood around 1985. It really took off in 1986, when Eric B and Rakim came out (everyone already knew that Rakim was a Five Percenter). Suddenly everyone I knew wanted to be one, or at least have a name that made them sound like they were. Overnight the dudes I was hanging with changed their names to Supreme DeShaun and Love God and God Universal. I thought to myself, "Damn, I need a nice name too. Something dope as shit."

There was an older god from a different neighborhood who used to hang out in Park Hill. He was a notorious criminal that all the girls liked because he was a good-lookin' bad-boy crook. His name was Shallah. I always looked to the older brothers for guidance since I didn't have a father figure in my life. I'd always hang around and listen to what they had to say, and Shallah used to kick the knowledge of the Nation to me.

I valued the fact that he always tried to build me up. And he never tried to take advantage of my high regard for him by involving me in one of his stickups or other crimes. He did make one demand though: he told me that I had to come up with a name to prove to him that I was taking the teachings seriously.

"Yo, tomorrow when I see you, you'd better have a fucking name," he said.

All night I tried to come up with something, and I couldn't think of shit. When I saw Shallah the next day, he asked to hear my name. All I could think to say was: "My name is Young God Allah."

"Your name is Young God Allah?"

"Yeah," I said. "Just call me Young God."

That's what I went with. When we weren't robbing car stereos, my friends and I began to hang out near the circles of older guys. They'd talk through the teachings and we'd listen in. To all of us on the brink of dropping out of school, what we heard was the next level of maturity. All those brothers would gather at night on the basketball court behind the building. They'd circle up in a cypher and discuss self-knowledge. Once I'd taken my name, Shallah brought me into it. They would quiz me too, asking me to recite the day's mathematics. To answer that question, you'd look at the date. You'd have to know the attributes that corresponded to each number, plus the attributes for the number that was the sum of the two numbers. For example, if today was the 25th, today's mathematics would be wisdom, which is 2, power, which is 5, and refinement of all born into God, which is 7. You had to memorize all of this, because you couldn't come into a cypher with paper or a book. On top of the corresponding attribute, there was a lesson that went with it that you were expected to recite as well. When I first started joining the brothers, so many times they would tell me I was close. Then they'd correct me until I learned it all the way through.

It was the most fruitful homework I'd ever been given. It made me understand who I was as a young black man. Eventually I got sharp, and they pushed me further.

"All right, now give us your understanding of what wisdom means to you."

"You mean I can't quote it no more?" I asked.

"Nah, we don't want you to quote it no more. We want to know what it means to you."

I took a deep breath and dove in. "Wisdom is the wise words that come from your mouth. You can't have wisdom without having the knowledge. You won't be able to have wisdom or create a better understanding without the knowledge."

"You're getting there."

Then in order to build me up, they'd break down what I'd said and where it went wrong. It was tough, but it was worth it. For me and so many kids from broken homes, the Five Percent Nation provided guidance and an abundance of father figures. Those cyphers were serious: they were large circles that nobody could penetrate unless they were invited to be in the group. People walking by went around us.

All of that took place before I started hanging with RZA, so I had a good degree of self-knowledge. It had started with just trying to follow the crowd, but I had found myself in the teachings. After a while, I also decided to change my name again. I had run into brothers with names like Supreme, Bar-Sun, Bar-Shar, and some older dudes with dope names like God Kim, Raevon, Teewah, and U Dahl. I realized that Young God made me sound like I'd be young forever, but when you're young you don't want to be considered a kid. So it was time for a change. I looked up lists of names and didn't see anything that felt right. I liked the brother Raevon's name and I liked my man DeShaun's name—they both sounded authentic to me—so I wanted something with that ring to it. I came up with Raekwon, but I didn't want to take that as my first name.

When I was up in my mom's house studying my lessons, I used to doodle on a piece of paper all the time. I usually drew the number 7, which represents the Nation, and the crescent, which is part of its symbol. Above that I would write "Allah." One day, I was drawing and my little brothers were playing with the TV up way too loud. I shouted "Shhh!" at them, trying to hear myself think. As I was looking at the paper, staring at the word Allah, and hearing myself say "Shhh!" it all came together. My name would be Shallah Raekwon. Turned out most people in the neighborhood didn't know how to say Shallah, so to them it was Shay-la, rather than saying it the way you'd say Allah, just with an S sound at the beginning. Then it got shortened to "Shy," as another nickname, which had nothing to do with my name at all. It was cool if they didn't know how to pronounce my name as long as they called me by the proper one, but that wasn't happening.

At RZA's, I'd sit and study the lessons or write rhymes. When he took a break, we would talk about what I'd been reading. Discussing it with someone my age was enlightening because it felt like two equals learning together, and I felt wiser every day we hung out. Learning from RZA, I also felt that I could be an artist myself. I became his student in a way, absorbing what he was doing as a young producer, chopping up music history with him as well. I had been such a music junkie all my life that I realized that I knew what good music was. As I listened to RZA make beats, over time I felt confident enough to start giving him my opinions on them. Then I felt confident enough to start sharing the rhymes in my book. He was into it, encouraging me to continue to grow.

When I went back to the 'hood, I told Jamie I was going to be spending more time pursuing music. He understood; he had always thought I had the skills to be a rapper. At the same time, there was business to be done: spots to hit and drops to make. He wasn't going to be supporting me financially, but he was willing to let me back in on a buy when I needed to make money. I had one foot planted in each world.

I respected how hard RZA was going after his vision, and I wanted him to win. Deep in my soul I felt that he was something special. A lot of guys talk and don't do shit, but not him. He was walking his talk. He knew where he wanted to go and he wasn't sure how he would get there—but he never doubted the value of his talent.

RZA was like me in that he liked to get off Staten Island and move around New York to let all of that influence into his life. We started traveling together into Brooklyn and Manhattan, up to the Bronx, and all over. He already had connections in music, so we went to producers' houses including Easy Mo Bee. At the time he was making beats for RZA and his cousin Gary Grice, aka the GZA. RZA was already so slick that he had copped a pile of prepaid car service vouchers from one of the record labels he was talking to. He would use these to get us all over town. I was used to public transportation, so that shit was amazing to me. He would make a call, the car would show up, they would take us where we wanted to go, and he would sign this piece of paper and that was it.

Falling in with RZA and GZA and the crew of dudes always coming through there happened naturally. It began to feel like I was on a team. Out of all the guys hanging out, I was the only one who showed up every day. I was ready to go wherever RZA might be going to make connections or buy gear or records. He saw I was serious. As I began to get a taste for what types of beats worked with the way I liked to rap, I found myself developing an idea of my style. I began to think beyond clever rhymes and started to form stories in my mind based on everything I had seen hustling and living in the projects. Up at RZA's, I'd hear a beat that matched the movies in my head and I'd tell him to let me drop something on it. Soon he was putting beats aside for me.

"You like that one?" he'd say, giving me a sly look. "It's yours."

This was a whole new world. Once I had a beat, it was like starting an engine inside me. I pulled together pieces of rhymes I'd been carrying around for years. All the snapshots in my mind, all the moments I'd lived, all the characters I'd met blended together and made their way into lyrics. In the past I'd only ever freestyled over a break from a popular song or to a homeboy beatboxing. Now I was designing my verses around beats made specially for me. When we hung out, we'd battle rap without calling it that. Instead of snapping on each other, we'd just try to outdo each other. I'd bring out something dope from my book which would inspire RZA to bring out something from his book. It was a mental exercise that sharpened our pens. He would always listen to me carefully then be like, "That shit is dope . . . but check this shit out." We went at it like that for hours.

I know why he liked having me around so much: it was like hanging out with his biggest fan who also happened to have some skills. Back then there was no bigger fan of RZA than me, and that's a fact. I used to take the tapes of his demos that he'd give me and play them for everybody back in the 'hood like it was my job. I'd get in Jamie's car and we'd roll all over blasting that shit.

One day when RZA and I were hanging out he turned to me and said, "Okay, we gonna do a song together today."

"You serious? You wanna do a song? How we gonna do a song?"

"Yo, listen, we gonna do a song, what are you talkin' 'bout? Let's do this."

"Hell yeah, let's do it." I had no idea what was gonna happen next.

That first song we did was called "Food," a straight-up rap concept song using food as a metaphor. It was inspired by a rhyme that Cappadonna (aka Darryl Hill) had dropped in a freestyle years before. Cap had been a figure in our neighborhood circles for years and was real tight with U-God. He was a couple years older than me and so famous for his freestyles and storytelling rhymes that we called him our 'hood's Slick Rick.

I'd been a fan of Cappa ever since I first heard him and this one line had resonated with me: "I take control of the mic when I bleed it, listen to the sound that's played and I feed it, chunks of the lyrical art that I provided, dissolves in your mouth, you can't hide it." I recited it to RZA and suggested that we do something called "Food" that used food as a theme in the clever way Cappa had done in that rhyme—clearly I was always meant to be called the Chef. RZA loved my idea of building on that food-related theme, and since he'd seen that I was a quick writer, he set me loose while he got a beat together.

I wrote about sixteen bars, though at the time I didn't even know what bars were. I just started making rhymes and kept going until my thoughts on it were exhausted. RZA helped me shape what I'd put to paper. He introduced me to the importance of starting and ending a rhyme and editing them into verses that build to a peak. He sent me home that day with a tape of what we did, and I was on top of the world. I hopped into Majestic's car and we rode around blasting that shit all fucking night.

I was at RZA's every day, and I saw all manner of dudes from the neighborhood come through to see if they could get on. RZA started making demos with dudes we both knew like Method Man (born Clifford Smith), U-God (born Lamont Hawkins), and Inspectah Deck (born Jason Richard Hunter). He tried people out and enlisted the best talent the projects had to offer. I watched RZA and GZA's every move, picking up what knowledge I could about the record business. I observed how they maneuvered with producers and the record label executives that were starting to get curious about them. Every day filled me with energy because I could see their work paying off right in front of my eyes. Watching them pursue their label deals, I learned what labels expected of an artist. I saw how they needed a single to push, how contracts were structured, and later, how they tried to shape your image.

On a more personal front, since GZA was really involved in the Nation, every day he came around, he'd push me further into the mathematics. He'd choose the most advanced lessons for us to study together. We would build our knowledge and then the two of them would put me on the spot to see if I was really about the Nation or just posing. They were insistent about applying the lessons not only to our lives but to our music and lyrics. I didn't see GZA as much as I would have liked to, though. He lived in Brooklyn and only came to hang with RZA every once in a while, but when we were all together, he treated me like a little brother. He had lyrics, he had rhymes, and he worked the knowledge into his verses as well. Without even trying, GZA taught me a lot.

I felt sharper rhyming with RZA and GZA than I ever had on my own. With a better sense of how to craft a verse, I continued to study my heroes, but with a different set of eyes. Rakim, Slick Rick, KRS-One, Big Daddy Kane, Heavy D, Run-D.M.C., and Kool G Rap—those were the legends I looked to for inspiration. All of them managed to be wise and true to the street, but still fun. That was the type of artist I wanted to be. I would work on shit all night so that I'd have something fresh to bring to RZA's the next day. I wrote about imaginary drug dealers, street hustling, and stickups, lacing it all with bits of knowledge and Five Percent lessons when I could. Even though I was doing everything to exit that street life, I was RZA's drug-dealing rapper friend. That existence and swagger was what I knew best, and it was a lane he wanted filled in the musical family he was beginning to form. But all of that got put on hold when RZA got a record deal from Tommy Boy Records in 1989.

When that happened, RZA really became talked about. When someone in the 'hood gets a record deal, they are regarded as a celebrity and a hero, and it's like that person's success belongs to everyone. None of us knew where to go to try and get a record deal. There weren't professional studios around where you could make real records, and nobody was thinking about making songs. Everybody was just rapping for fun and some were making little tapes so they could show off on the block. RZA's moves were on another level, and people noticed. I made sure to stick close to him and GZA because I could tell they were going somewhere. And when those guys told me I could rhyme, it meant so much more to me than when dudes from around the way were impressed.

Hanging with RZA and getting more serious about music felt like reconnecting with something. Growing up I'd always had a crew. Our members, our goals, and motivations changed and evolved as we got older, but that camaraderie was always present in my life— and it was always based in hip-hop. The music changed and our style did too, but at every phase, all of us would get together and rap. It was freestyling in the staircases of the project buildings, or out front on the street, or behind the buildings while we got high. Everyone in the neighborhood did it. At any time, even if you were just passing by, you could expect that someone hanging out in a cypher might throw you the rhyme. It didn't matter if it was corny or everyone laughed, you just had to come up with something then pass it on. That was all I'd known. But now I was writing rhymes and dropping bars with purpose, which was a whole new world.

I brought all of RZA's music back to the 'hood and told everyone how dope he was. After he caught that deal, niggas wanted to make tapes and play their shit on the block too. Soon the whole thing became about who from the neighborhood was getting bumped the most in the cars coming down the block. It happened quick, but I have to say, we were the guys that set it off, and I was there first. It didn't take long for Cappadonna to have a tape that I think he did with the Blif Brothers.

RZA's artist name on Tommy Boy was Prince Rakeem, and his single and EP were called "Ooh I Love You Rakeem." Once that happened, his revolving door studio days got put on pause. While he focused on making it, I didn't see him for about a year. Unfortunately, the song didn't perform well commercially and he got dropped. It didn't surprise me because the music had nothing to do with who RZA was as an artist. The Rakeem record was a soft, lover-boy track, and RZA was not known for making music like that. He was a dude who spit knowledge, wisdom, and understanding in his rhymes. The record was what the label thought would sell because that kind of hip-hop had gone mainstream.

By contrast, when I heard the GZA's album, *Words from the Genius* (he was called the Genius by the label), I was blown away. That motherfucker rapped his ass off. But he too was misrepresented by his label, Cold Chillin', in much the same way. The wordplay on his record is still some of the dopest I've heard, but the label pushed him to be more of a flashy Big Daddy Kane character that the girls would love. That ladies' man vibe was not really him or what he was saying in his music. Unsurprisingly, his project didn't connect commercially either. We did have a good time the day they shot the video for the Genius's "Come Do Me," though. He and RZA are cousins and they have a big family, so I'd already met a lot of their relatives. This included Russell Jones, aka Ol' Dirty Bastard, who back then was known as the Rap Professor Asan Unique.

I was catching up with Dirty when the director asked us to be in the shot they were doing, which was a party scene. I was not ready for that at all, because I was scared to see myself on TV. They wanted me in the video on the dance floor dancing with some girls. I was feeling shy about it, so I declined. Which was fine, because Dirty, who was drunk on forties and full of energy, got right in there. I got to be in the last scene they shot. It featured GZA walking down the street with a girl, passing by a building being painted. RZA and I played the painters. That was the type of corny shit I felt more comfortable with, because I was not ready for prime time. Still, I couldn't wait to get home and tell my mother I had been in a video that was going to be on TV. It was an indication that I was getting somewhere with music, and the crew I was hanging with was the real deal. After that experience, all I wanted to do was rhyme every day, perfecting what I'd begun to think of as my craft. My mom didn't see it quite the same way.

"That's dope," she said about the video. "That's real nice. But you still need to get a fucking job."

Moms had a lot to worry about, because when I wasn't with RZA, I was still living the hustle life. As the eighties wore on and the money kept flowing, the stakes got bigger. There was so much money around that dudes started getting cars and more guns and living out loud more than ever. Once Rakim was photographed with a Benz, everybody wanted one. We didn't have luxury dealers around Staten Island, so what dudes like my boy Jamie did was build one from junkyard parts instead. Dudes would find a Mercedes frame and then piece the rest together at a body shop. When Jamie's car was done, he was so proud. We went rolling in that thing like the T-Birds did in "Greased Lightning." He probably got the frame for five grand, put some rims on it, dropped a proper engine and a big sound system in, and he was set. We'd roll around listening to straight drug-dealer rap, just two hustlers living the life.

I didn't have a car, so when I wasn't with Jamie, I'd get rental cars: Corsicas, Maximas, Grand Ams, Rivieras, Cadillacs, and Chevy Malibus. You'd be lucky if you got a Jeep or a Thunderbird, which was the fastest fucking rental car I'd ever seen in my life. A bunch of us would pool our money, get a car for a few days, and go driving. Back then it was something like sixty dollars a day, so we'd get them for four days and each cover one. Now mind you, I didn't know how to drive, but I sure as hell was getting my money's worth out of this rental. My boys could all drive, and they drove fast. This one time I threw a temper tantrum in the back seat demanding to drive until they finally let me. We were in the back of our building when I took the wheel and realized I had no idea what I was doing. I laid onto the gas with the car still in park and the engine roared.

"Aw man you don't know how to drive," said one of my boys. "Get out of the car, man."

"No man, I can do this! This car different is all."

They started to teach me, letting me drive circles around the parking lot, eventually the street, and then the neighborhood. These guys were all older than me and they had more experience in the world, plus they didn't have an apartment of siblings to look after on a regular basis. So many nights I missed out on going out to clubs with them because when I lived at my Moms's one of my jobs was staying home and taking care of the little ones when she wanted to go out. My boys would come to my window in their silk shirts and dress pants, with fresh haircuts, black shades, and shit, telling me to come down and join them. The one time I didn't have to babysit, they had two rental cars and were ready to drive uptown to some clubs. I put in my money for this red Thunderbird, and they were so happy I was there that they let me drive, which I had learned to do by then even though I didn't have a license. Our cars were full, and with my boy driving the other one, we started racing side by side on the BQE doing seventy, eighty, ninety miles an hour. I was looking at nothing but my boy's car, trying to beat him, when the guy in the passenger seat started yelling.

"Yo! Look out up ahead!"

The traffic in our lane up ahead was at a complete stop, but I didn't see that until it was too late. Luckily the guy in the other car did and was able to hit the brakes quick enough so that we could cut in front of him, barely in time to avoid ramming the cars stopped in front of us. It was fucking scary, and I could've killed everyone with me. My boys made me get out and into the back seat right there, and that was the last time I ever drove with them. I learned my lesson: to this day, I've never driven that fast again.

It was a different story for my boys, though. They were such skilled drivers that we would get from Staten Island to Brooklyn, across the Verrazzano Bridge, in nine minutes flat. That's a ride that takes twenty-five minutes without much traffic. My friends would compete to see who could get the best time. I think my man Killer, who we called K, held the record. He and I used to go to Brooklyn and spend all our money on clothes and weed and food, only to realize that we had no money to pay the toll back home, which at the time was around six dollars. K would get ready, bobbing and weaving through traffic as we approached the toll booths, deliberately speeding up. He'd be up to about eighty miles an hour when we'd race through them, both of us with our hoodies up covering our faces. We'd get hyped listening to EPMD and fly through there on some *Dukes of Hazzard* shit, feeling like the sheriff was in hot pursuit. We would keep going, fast as we could through the streets, then park the car in the back of the building. Then we'd run all the way up to our roof, looking down the street to see if any cops had followed us. When we were clear, we'd give each other a pound and laugh our asses off.

It was always better to have rental cars because you didn't know what could happen. One night I had my uncle's Buick and was out with K after hustling. We'd sold through what we had, and it was about two-thirty in the morning. We wanted to chill out with some weed, so we went out to a weed spot we knew in Bushwick. We were making our way back slowly, having nowhere else to be. At a stoplight we saw this kid crossing the street, eyeing us kinda funny. We were near a project, so we figured he was going over there and didn't pay him no mind. He had a bag in his hand and a ring on, and he kept looking at us. I kept looking back at him, because back then if you looked away, you were a sucker. My man rolled down the window and said, "What the fuck you lookin' at?"

"You think you're something sweet over there?" he said.

What we didn't see was his man coming at an angle from behind him with a gun. That guy let off twenty shots into my uncle's fucking Buick. We stepped on it and got out of there, and we're lucky we didn't get hit. But explaining those bullet holes in the side of the car wasn't cool.

I'd rent a car just to go out to Brooklyn to buy weed and eat. We loved this place called Cheffy's on Nostrand Avenue, close to Crown Heights. It had the best Jamaican food, but it was notorious as well. It was in a bad neighborhood and there were shoot-outs and all kinds of shit happening on that block. There were no Jamaican restaurants in our area on Staten Island, but we'd see the dealers come back with these plates and we'd ask them where to go. I'd always get stewed beef and rice or curried chicken or jerk chicken and it was heaven. But going to get that food was dangerous. You had to bring your gun to get your plate at Cheffy's.

One time I went out to Brooklyn with Jamie. We left our guns behind, because we were just going to get a little bit of weed and a meal. He didn't like to take the Benz out there because it attracted attention, so we hired this African cabdriver we knew. He'd take us and wait while we ate and did our business. We got some food, then went over to the storefront where we copped weed. It was one of those spots with Plexiglas and a dude back there behind it. It looked like a convenience store, but no one was buying the dusty products on the shelf. Now, Jamie had this diamond ring that he always wore and a chain on, but he wasn't really shining more than that. He only bought about forty dollars of black weed, a strain of what was called chocolate on the street at the time. We smoked a lot of black weed back then, and chocolate was big with us. It was moist but broke up nice and it tasted like chocolate. We got the weed, and when we came out of the store some dudes jumped out of a car with guns pointed at us.

"Yo, freeze, we sticking y'all niggas up. Don't fucking move."

Jamie was still drinking his Snapple from lunch and threw it at them without hesitation. As we started running, we heard those guys letting bullets fly behind us. We ran from Nostrand Avenue and Eastern Parkway all the way to the Brooklyn House of Detention, which was about three miles away on Atlantic Avenue. The guys had gotten between us and where we'd left the cab, so we had no choice but to run the opposite direction. Then we had to get all the way to the Staten Island Ferry to get home. Jamie's favorite diamond ring had flown off when he threw the bottle, so we took a loss that day. But considering that we didn't get shot in the back, we were willing to take it. We swore never to go to Brooklyn again without guns on us. That was a close one. I still don't know if it was because they recognized Jamie, since he also hustled out in Brooklyn, or if we were just in the wrong place at the wrong time. That's just how it was day to day. You never knew if going to get some lunch might cost you your life. I didn't know any other way of living, but I damn sure wanted to. I loved being out there, walking tall, living for hip-hop, staying high and fly, but in my mind I heard a clock ticking and I felt like my time was almost up. I knew if I didn't find a way out of the 'hood, no doubt those streets were going to make me another faceless statistic.

CHAPTER 7

SIX MAN SYMPHONY

When the Prince Rakeem project didn't pop, RZA was dropped from Tommy Boy and ended up back where he started. His dreams weren't dashed, though. This setback lit an even bigger fire inside him. He wanted to take over the industry, so he returned to making music on his own terms, not caring about what any label wanted from him. He crafted symphonies from samples on that little studio setup with a newfound energy, and once again started inviting guys from all over the projects to come around and drop verses. He wasn't creating complete songs, just capturing ideas and freestyles set to the beats he made day in and day out. RZA was searching for talent, looking to draft players for his team. All those different voices gave him a lot of inspiration, and since he was the type that could comfortably move between different groups, he got to fuck with guys who didn't necessarily fuck with each other.

RZA is a smart guy. He was putting his ear to the street, getting in touch with what kind of hip-hop New York was vibing on. He had so many beats in his library and was constantly working on new ones, so having an open-door policy with rappers from everywhere was like running his own test kitchen. He already knew that he wanted to start a crew with various voices and styles, because the best hip-hop we were hearing was coming from collectives like the Hit Squad, which had been formed by Erick Sermon and Parrish Smith from EPMD, and included rappers like Das EFX, Redman, and K-Solo. There was Boot Camp Clik, who came from Brownsville and Bed-Stuy, and on the West Coast groups like N.W.A and Tha Dogg Pound were going in that direction too.

In every collective, each member must play a role that makes the entire group stronger. RZA knew this and designed his roster accordingly. I was the first call he made, because he knew that if I was feeling the beat, I was able to come up with lines quickly to suit any song, right on the spot. He also knew I was a loyal soldier and had been supportive of his journey from the start.

"Yo, man, Shal, I think we can do this shit," he said. "We need to do a session. I need you to get in touch with Method and Universal God. We need to get serious with this shit."

"Yo, word. Let me holla at them."

Up until then, doing sessions at RZA's was important to me, but optional. I liked being there, but if I had to do something else, it was no big deal. I could tell from his tone on the phone that day that things were going to be different. I felt it, and I was going to honor it. I knew RZA had the talent to make it; in my opinion the record company had just sent him in the wrong direction. When he called, saying he wanted to make all of us professional rappers, I took him mad serious.

RZA wanted everyone who was going to enter this next phase with him onboard and committed, which meant coming through to contribute verses, and working on them until they were perfect. This wasn't hanging out no more; everyone involved had to take it serious and show up to do the work of making a demo featuring all of us. Dirty and GZA were RZA's family, so they were already down. I called Meth, and he was down, but we had a couple of problems with the rest of the team RZA had in mind. U-God was in jail for selling drugs, and Cappadonna was too. Luckily, Inspectah Deck had just gotten home from jail, so we had him.

It was cool to be coming together with these guys on a mission like this, because most of us had known each other forever. Like I said, RZA and his brother and cousins were some of the first friends I made back in second grade when I moved out to Staten Island. He was always a cool dude, always a guy who shared what he had, like gum and candy—and there's nothing more important than sugar when you're a kid.

Cappa and U-God were my friends from Little League baseball that I used to pool my money with so we could buy as many cookies as possible. They were just twenty-five cents, so with a few dollars we could pile up fifty of them plus some Drake's cakes and sit in the hallway of one of our buildings, sipping on milk and eating it all. (Cappa and U liked the chocolate chip joints, but my favorite was the coconut Drake's cookies. When those were out at the store, I would get myself some Fig Newtons. I could eat a hundred of those shits.) That was our move after school, until we got a little older and started sneaking up to the rooftops instead.

Up on the roof, we felt empowered, towering over everybody, and that's where we started writing graffiti and talking about hip-hop as we traded the cookies and milk for weed and wine. RZA was never a part of that, but back then he got me a job selling the *Staten Island Advance* to people in cars waiting to go over the Verrazzano Bridge. That's where I first hung out for real with Dirty. RZA and his whole family were always snatching every chance they could to make money, and they were never afraid to put in the work. Selling newspapers, with the odd tip of a dollar here and there, could make you seventy dollars a day, but it was up and down, and at the most I made forty-five. I didn't care that I wasn't the best salesman, because for me it was about hanging out with RZA and them. We also hung out in school, mostly at gym playing kickball, and our mothers were friends, so we always heard about what each other was up to.

I met Meth a little later, in sixth grade. He had recently moved from Long Island and lived in building number 55, which eventually became one of the most notorious drug buildings in all of the Park Hill projects. We met through a guy named Saji who was a DJ that we were both cool with. Saji had two turntables set up in his room, and he would put his speaker in the window when he was cutting records. He played all kinds of fly shit that me and Meth and a bunch of other dudes would go there to listen to. Meth and I also ended up in the same sixth-grade English class. At the time I'd started writing rhymes, and he'd watch me, knowing that I sure as hell wasn't paying attention to the teacher.

"Yo, what you writing?" he asked me one day.

"Yo, I'm writing my rhymes, man."

Next thing I knew Meth was sitting next to me in English, and we started getting in trouble because we weren't doing schoolwork, but we were back there working. Meth told me he wanted to learn, and I told him the shit was easy, you just had to say whatever came to mind and make it fly. We started building each other up, showing each other our shit, and I remember he had a rhyme called "On a Mission" inspired by the Salt-N-Pepa song of the same name. It was all about being on a mission to catch this girl with a fat waist, looking at her hair and shit. We would talk about all our favorite rappers at the time, from Whodini to Dana Dane and, of course, Slick Rick. From the start Meth was a fast writer like me, maybe even faster, so in sixth grade we started going back and forth, trying to impress each other, both of us getting better with every round.

And there was Cap, the best rhymer of all the guys our age in the 'hood. When we were young, he and I used to get candy, then jump in one of the stray shopping carts that were always around the parking lot and race our friends. Or we'd play in the big dumpster behind the buildings where they threw out mattresses, jumping up and down on them like a trampoline. We'd play tag, and we'd play booty up, which was a game where you threw a dodgeball against a wall and someone had to catch it off a bounce. If you missed three times you had to run up there, put your arms on the wall, and stick your booty out while your friends threw it at your ass as hard as they could. No matter what we were doing, we'd stop to look when a nice car rolled by, and Cap was always the first one to spot it and make the joke we all made when we saw a car we wanted: "That's my car."

Eventually a few of our mothers chipped in and got us bikes, which meant that we were mobile, rolling all the way from Park Hill to New Dorp on BMX bikes (Mongooses were the best). That ride would take about fifteen, twenty minutes, which feels like forever when you're a kid. All of us would compete to see who could hold a wheelie longer than a five-count. Cap and his dudes were really fast on the bikes, I'm telling you. I was good at wheelies, but I'd watch them and think, "How the fuck they throw it up like that going so fast?"

We were kids, but even then all those dudes had good hearts, all of us down to share, and I'm saying this as someone who often had the least to contribute. When we got older, we all went to different high schools, so we didn't see each other as much. But even so, I remember RZA loaning me clothes and trading me sneakers. And me, Cap, and U-God getting together to tailor our jeans when the style changed and bell-bottoms were no longer the shit. None of us could afford new ones, so we did what we had to do. U-God was a great tailor, by the way. He could sew a seven-inch sway into a tight profile like it was nothing.

Those guys are also how I learned to snap, because we all snapped on each other like motherfuckers for years. Now, Cap, he ended up in a special ed class, and it wasn't because he wasn't smart—it was because he never went to school and had a family that didn't care much about him one way or another. He hadn't completed enough credits, so he ended up on the short bus with kids much younger than him, which became a never-ending source of snaps. Me, I've always had fucked-up teeth, so that was where they started when they went in on me. U-God had big long ears, which all of us would smash on. Everyone had their flaws, and not one was missed by friends and neighbors when it came to the snaps.

Even though I didn't hang with all of them every day when we were younger, when I thought about these guys, I remembered nothing but good times and realized that we'd had as much fun as we possibly could whenever we did get together. We had gotten older and hadn't seen each other as much, but hip-hop had touched us in the same way and united us through our shared gift of rhyme. Coming together to make music, even if it went no further, was the new chapter, and it was every bit as fun as sharing candy and snapping on each other used to be.

We started working together and individually at RZA's on a lot of things, some that evolved into songs and some that never saw the light of day. RZA was working to find the flow of the group and every member within it. He had a vision of us as a unit that maintained distinct, individually recognizable voices. Since there were so many of us, it took him time to get the best out of each man, and to find a way to organically combine that into a whole. It was important to him to get all of us on our first track, which he did, on a song called "Six Man Symphony." We were so proud to take a tape of it back to our neighborhoods to play on the block. Leading up to that moment, RZA had been both ringleader and cheerleader, playing each of us the other guys' songs to get us inspired. I had my "Food" joint, Meth had done a song called "Panty Raider," and so on. He got us appreciating one another, and we got familiar with each other's style. It inspired us to sharpen our rhymes, and in my case at least, it pushed me to think of rhymes that would play off the other guys' nicely. When he got us standing next to each other, the chemistry was there. Everyone's flow seemed to get better, and it brought the best out in each of us. We became rap homeboys overnight and started hanging out together because we loved what we'd done on that record. We bragged about it, and when somebody would throw it on their boombox, whichever of us were around would get together and rap it live on the street. Passing cars would stop and crowds would gather to watch us do our thing and we began to get a lot of attention.

Like I told you, RZA was on a mission to succeed in the industry in any way, so we weren't his only outlet. He was also fucking with a bunch of dudes from Stapleton projects. There was a DJ named RNS out there that RZA had known for years from DJ'ing parties, and that guy was producing too. It was through him that RZA met Ghostface Killah (born Dennis Coles) and a few others. So RZA started to develop a Stapleton crew as well, which began to inspire rap battles between the two groups, because our areas are legendary rivals to begin with. It also started a debate about whose mixtapes were the hottest: RNS's or RZA's. For real, RZA took some notes on what RNS was doing, and in his way, paid homage, but RZA always had his own thing going on. They were pulling from each other, to tell you the truth, so it was a competition from the start.

It became more complicated when RZA decided that the missing piece of his puzzle was Ghostface, who was definitely the best rapper Stapleton had to offer. He was the only one from Stapleton that RZA wanted to bring over to our group. Ghost and I had gone to junior high together, but even dudes who were friends as kids became enemies by the time they got to high school. That's how deep the Park Hill–Stapleton rivalry went. I knew him as part of a notorious stickup crew that everybody watched out for. When Park Hill dudes saw them coming, they got their guns ready. Ghost was a little different because he had a history of visiting Park Hill to mess with one of our guys' sisters. So when he came around, it could go either way: he'd either be up there to see his girl and hang out or be on some stickup shit.

Guys from Stapleton were very different from us. They smoked weed dipped in a mixture of angel dust (PCP) and embalming fluid that they called "wet," while dudes in Park Hill sniffed coke and smoked blunts, sometimes with crack rocks in them. Those are two highs that don't really mesh together, which increased the friction when the two sides met. I've smoked wet a few times: the leaves smell like mint, which is deceiving because they smell harmless. You roll them up with dry weed and smoke them, and it makes you feel like you've drunk five gallons of Bacardi and got spun around over someone's head five times before getting dropped back on your feet. You'd get that feeling off of two or three hits from a tiny pin joint.

On wet you walk down the block like a zombie: eyes open wide, body moving slow, mind moving way too fast. People on dust look like they've seen ghosts, and if they're real high they need someone to hold their hand just to get them down the street. The last time I tried it, my boys and I had bought it way up in Harlem and we rode the subway all the way home, high as hell, and it was the longest ride of my life. People came on the train and jumped right off when they got a look at us. The niggas I was with started doing crazy shit, pulling their dicks out and pissing and shit, because dust puts you in a devious state of mind. Five dudes got high off of one of those tiny joints, so if you didn't have a lot of money, it did the trick. But that shit wasn't for me. There were many times at RZA's when Stapleton dudes would come around high and do crazy shit—like pull out a razor blade for no reason—and RZA would have to talk them down. Ghost wasn't like that, but he got down with dudes who were. He had never disrespected me, and he'd never tried to rob any of the crack houses where I made my living. He did have beef with plenty of the street guys in Park Hill, though. He stuck plenty of them up and even cut the face of a guy I knew. The guy wasn't a number one homie, but I took it personal because I was cool with him.

When we started hanging out at RZA's, the first thing Ghost and I did was reminisce about going to Junior High School #49 together. We had a teacher named Mr. Bruns that our entire class snapped on all day long for looking like Fred Flintstone. He was a chubby fella who wore his pants way up over his stomach and had a funny walk. He was a good guy and he did his best to teach us, but there was no way he was getting his point across with a room full of students snapping on him like it was our job. He had no choice but to snap back if he was ever going to get through a lesson, so that's what he did. And he was good at it too! He used to say things like: "Yo, I had a shirt like that once. And then my mother got a job." I can't tell you one thing I learned from a book in that class, but I sure as hell learned a lot of new snaps. We came up with all kinds of new shit to call Mr. Bruns, my favorite being "fruit bowl–looking motherfucker." Any other teacher would have quit, but this guy got it, and by letting us snap on him and snapping back on us, he got us excited to be in his class more than any of the other teachers. The other side of that coin was Ms. Panza, a strict Italian lady who made it clear who she cared to teach and who she didn't. She was the type to tell you that if you didn't want to learn, you should leave her class because you weren't going to be shit and you weren't worth her time.

It was good that Ghost and I had those memories in common, because I'm telling you, Park Hill and Stapleton were sworn enemies. At nine and ten years old, we witnessed gang wars between the Paris Crew out of Stapleton and the Avenue Crew out of Park Hill. These were battles that would happen in the street, with everyone really going at it. One time I even saw some dude's mother get knocked out. That might sound crazy, but the beef went so deep that when one side would see the other side's gang coming up the block, everyone out there would jump in, mothers included. Motherfuckers got cut, motherfuckers got hit in the head with bats; it was real nasty shit, and it went on for years. Even after that period of street violence cooled down, the rivalry did not.

Stapleton dudes were always ready to rob you, while Park Hill dudes just wanted to make money. Generally we were better hustlers than dudes from Stapleton, which is why they liked to come to our 'hood and start shit. Park Hill dudes were the ones hanging out in different boroughs, looking fly. We had more money since our project was slinging upward of a hundred thousand dollars a week in drugs. We had the best weed spots, access to more drugs, and rental cars. We were the guys going to clubs, stealing people's girls, and dudes were jealous of us. Plus, like I said, Stapleton dudes were all smoking wet, which makes people crazy. I remember one time when I was still going to high school, this guy from Stapleton named Ron, who was older and real dusted, tried to steal my shearling coat as I was waiting for the bus. His eyes were bloodshot and insane, and there was no way my jacket was going to fit him, but he started pulling it off me. I was wrestling with him when this girl Ellen Brown, whose brothers were in the Paris Crew, came up and smacked him real hard in the head and told him to leave me alone. Me and her were cool forever after that—she was a badass fighter—but I never heard the end of it in my neighborhood because a girl had saved me from losing my coat. That being said, I swore to myself then and there that no one was ever gonna come at me and almost take something of mine ever again.

The point of sharing this 'hood history is to say that RZA fucking with Ghost and then taking Ghost away from RNS was a big deal. Like I told you, RZA was a nomad, so he liked to come and go between Park Hill, Stapleton, and everywhere else on Staten Island, and he did so with no problems. He lived closer to Stapleton, which is where he hung out a lot during his time trying to make it as a solo artist. That's how he got tight with Ghost. Stapleton had a different vibe. It wasn't a Willy Wonka Chocolate Factory where every drug was for sale like Park Hill. There were dudes hustling in Stapleton, but overall there were more people just hanging out, not doing much. RZA and Ghost used to cool out there together every day, and smoke dust or whatever, because RZA did that shit for a while. That is where the Wu-Tang slang began. Like I told you, karate movies were big with dudes in our generation. When we were kids you could catch them as the late movie or on weekend afternoons on one of the local networks like WPIX or WWOR so we grew up on them. RZA loved them and introduced everybody to the Hong Kong Shaolin and Wu-Tang movies, which is where they snatched the term from.

The Wu-Tang style in those movies uses swords, while the Shaolin style is traditional kung fu. The Wu-Tang masters are incredible but reckless; they lack discipline so they get kicked out of Shaolin. RZA identified with that mystique and began to say that he and the dudes he hung with were Wu-Tang because they were the rebels in the community. Ghost and everyone in Stapleton loved it too, so Wu-Tang became a catch-all phrase for them. They'd refer to themselves as Wu-Tang, their weed was Wu-Tang, smoking wet and drinking forties was Wu-Tang, a plate of dope Kung Pao chicken was Wu-Tang. Basically everything cool or good was Wu-Tang. RZA turned all these dudes into kung fu ninjas in their own minds: they started wearing scarves and dressing like him, with everybody wearing military cargo pants and dark colors and looking mysterious. You'd never see RZA in jeans and Air Force 1s; it was always military surplus and Timberland boots, even in summer. Down in Stapleton, dressing like that became the thing to do.

After "Six Man Symphony," we all saw that we had chemistry, so RZA thought hard about the roster when he asked Ghost to join the group. RZA already knew he was going to name the group Wu-Tang Clan, because that was his thing. Wu-Tang, as a trend and idea, had become a Stapleton identity, so they weren't happy about the fact that a group with that name included only one guy from their 'hood.

Ghost wasn't comfortable with it either, and I could understand that. Beyond taking Wu-Tang on as their community persona, plenty of them had been involved in making music with RZA, so when he turned around and only chose Ghost, they felt disrespected. After all, it wasn't like RZA was forming a duo; he was making a rap posse. What RNS and those guys did in response was form their own group called GP Wu-Tang, which stood for Gladiator Posse Wu-Tang. So for a minute it looked like the whole thing was going to play out like just like the kung fu movies, with two rival schools cut from the same cloth battling for dominance. This put Ghost in a bad position, because in that scenario he was seen as a traitor by the dudes in his neighborhood, but he realized that what we were doing was bigger and better for him. He made the move because Ghost never had a problem saying, "Fuck those niggas, I'm gonna do what I want." After we really started making dope music, it was all good, but I know for a fact that RNS called RZA up and called him out, aggressively telling him he had no right to have a group called Wu-Tang with five Park Hill niggas in it. RZA had to deal with that backlash and wasn't really welcome in Stapleton the same way again—until people started loving what our group began to do. Then we were welcomed everywhere.

There was an even trickier situation that had to be handled before Ghost could be officially integrated into the group. Right after he told RZA he was down to join, Ghost got into it with my friend and hustling partner, Jamie. They didn't like each other from the start, and one day they decided to do something about it. Luckily I wasn't around when it happened—they got on to some street war shit— but I heard about it later. Ghost was dusted or whatever, hanging with RZA's brother Divine, who'd had a falling-out with Jamie over a drug deal they'd done in the past before Divine had gotten hauled off to jail. When Divine ran into Jamie that day, they started scuffling. Jamie didn't live in the Hill; he was up there to visit his mother and was about to walk into her house. Ghost, in his mind state, just said fuck it and started busting shots at Jamie, all of which went straight into Jamie's mother's house. I don't know if Ghost was really trying to kill him, but he blasted at him, not knowing or thinking about the fact that Jamie was standing on his mother's doorstep.

Jamie was mad as a motherfucker, so after they cleared out, he got his guns, hopped in the Benz, rode down to Stapleton, and shot up the whole front of Ghost's mama's house. He blasted out every single window, put holes in the door, really fucked the place up. Thank God no one was hurt at either house, but there was no way that Divine and Ghost could be in the same room as Jamie after that. This was a problem because Jamie was not only my close friend, he was also a huge supporter of ours, artistically and financially. He paid for equipment and studio time and was also tight with RZA. All of this happened before our group even got our second demo off the ground.

Stapleton dudes continued to be pissed that Ghost was in the group, but this moment was when I first noticed RZA's talent at making peace and bringing people together. He orchestrated a sit-down, between Ghost, Jamie, and Divine, because he knew we weren't going to be safe—or productive—until this beef was squashed. It's hard to let bygones be bygones when a motherfucker shot up your mama's house. It took both boys becoming men to put that shit behind them. Somehow RZA put the fire out and cooled everybody down. And if he hadn't, there would be no Wu-Tang Clan as the world knows it today. RZA further sealed the peace by making Divine and Jamie invested partners in the group, and if you look at our first record, Ghost is the only member other than RZA listed as an executive producer, which linked him into the corporate structure of the Wu in addition to being a rapper. This wasn't a big deal at the time, but it became significant later when this venture became a real corporate entity. The rest of us didn't care about all of that back then. In fact, I don't think we even knew about it. We just wanted the beef squashed so we could make some records. Like I said, RZA handled that, and it was the strength of his intent to get us out of the fucking ghetto that led everybody to shed their animosity and start something new.

Once we were able to sit in a room together and make music, RZA needed money to get us to the next level. He needed to upgrade his recording equipment, and he needed resources to press records and eventually make a video. Divine and Jamie helped out there, allowing RZA to get to work. Back then, RZA drove a burgundy Chevy van to meetings, or to pick us up to do recording sessions. He started meeting with everyone he knew in the industry who he thought could help him make his vision real. He was on a mission not just to get out of the ghetto, but also to prove that he had talent the industry didn't understand (remember, he had been dropped). His library of verses and beats kept growing, all bits and pieces in development that were all on the table when we came to hang with him. Dirty was always going through the old stuff, and together they started pulling out half-made records from months earlier that had potential. He'd introduce them to us as songs that might become album cuts, or others that might feature one or two of us, or songs he wanted to see the whole group on. Those dudes who were over at RZA's more often ended up on more tracks. Before we even had a deal, when we had completed just one demo, RZA was already plotting out the entire album.

When we weren't doing the music thing together, we were all about whatever we were doing to get by, which for me was hustling. We knew we had chemistry but weren't quite all for one and one for all at that point. We were taking the music thing with a grain of salt because every one of us was still living in Scramblesville. We hung out more, but we didn't start hanging all the time because we weren't doing that before. We mostly just got together when we did music. Making our first complete song didn't do anything to bring us together either, because it was made in pieces. It sounds like everyone is in the same room, on the same vibe, on the same day, but that's not how it was. I'm talking about our first demo as a group, "Protect

Ya Neck." It was made of verses RZA had collected from each of us, sometimes on different beats, and stitched together. He had the song in his head, knowing he'd bring Dirty in to set it off, then collect bits of what we'd all done over the past few months. And something like two days before RZA finished the record, U-God got home from jail, and dropped four lines that were used as a bridge. The B-side of that single was a song called "After the Laughter Comes Tears," which was just RZA and Ghostface.

When we heard the record, we thought it was dope, but nobody really went back to the 'hood and talked about it the way those of us who were on the first one had done. We weren't really huddled up thinking, "This shit is about to go off," because we knew it was a long shot. Everyone just laid back to see if what RZA and his family were promising us would become a reality.

The main issue was money. RZA was always getting people involved who had a bit of money because he needed it to get the music—and his whole concept for a group—into some kind of shape to bring to a label. He had a cousin named Mook who gave him some cash and used to go to meetings with him, and he had his brother Divine and a couple of others who acted like a little staff that got the basics done. We needed money for records to bring to radio stations, and we needed money to make a video, because unlike now, videos were a necessary promotional tool at the time. The rest of us gave RZA the odd buck here and there when we hung out with him, but the only thing us other guys were giving up was our time and a ton of verses for his growing library of tracks. In terms of content, RZA had more than enough. It was like a Scrabble game for him: some records needed a new verse to tie it all together, some needed hooks, but for the most part, after months of recording us, each one was almost complete. Most of what became our first album was in some state of existence before we even did "Protect Ya Neck."

What I'm saying is, that song wasn't born from a spontaneous moment of inspiration. Instead, RZA was really just focused on completing one entire track with each man on it, which he could use to express what the group was all about. He could have made it happen with any number of songs he was working on, but it just happened to be that one he chose. It represented all of our voices, which was his goal—but to the rest of us, it was like, "yeah cool, that's dope." We'd all laid down so much stuff, not thinking about any of it as part of a whole. We were just hoping it would lead to something.

"Protect Ya Neck" did allow each man to shine, and it showcased each of our individual styles. This was important because RZA was already promising dudes they'd get their own solo albums once we got signed. Ol' Dirty knew he was getting one because he was a coproducer and RZA's cousin, and he was there the whole way watching RZA. I know RZA promised Meth that he'd do an album for him, because Meth participated in making records at RZA's house more often than anyone.

As for me, I was like a member of the board, sitting back and watching it all unfold. As I took note of how things were coming together, I started to weigh in on which tracks I thought had potential. "Method Man" was one of those: I felt strongly that it should be on the album, when we got to that point because it had that great hook, "M-E-T-H-O-D Man," that Meth just killed.

After "Protect Ya Neck," RZA tried to find a small independent label or management company to sign us, but nothing worked out. We got close with these two brothers who managed a few small groups. They liked what they heard and wanted to fuck with us, but they wanted a lot more control than anyone involved was going to give up. Divine and Jamie, for the money they had put in, wanted to have a voice in decision-making, and I wanted to give my opinion too. All of us felt like these guys were going to take too much away from us. You can't hustle eight hustlers, so we let that opportunity go and decided to do it all ourselves.

I don't remember where the money came from, but we somehow got three hundred copies of "Protect Ya Neck" pressed in December 1992, and set about taking them personally to college radio stations. We drove up to Connecticut, out to Jersey, all over, but nothing really happened. Then we went to see Stretch and Bobbito, who were doing a weekly underground hip-hop show out of a basement at Columbia University every Thursday night from 1 to 5 a.m. on 89.9 WKCR-FM. They loved the record and told RZA they were going to play it on the next show. We stayed up all night listening, but it didn't happen that first week. I can't remember if it happened the second week, but each Thursday we'd be up at RZA's by midnight to listen to the show on his little clock radio. The night it happened, RZA was there making beats and me, Dirty, Ghost, and Meth were gathered around with the radio on, not paying it much mind, when there it was, "Protect Ya Neck." And I started screaming. "Yo, yo! It's on, it's on!" I turned that radio up all the way, didn't care how crispy it sounded. When they said, "That was Wu-Tang Clan," I jumped nearly five feet in the air. Then they started talking, and I don't remember if it was Stretch or Bobbito, but one of them said, "The Wu-Tang Clan, damn. We don't even know these guys' names or who these guys are, but this record is the shit!" Those guys got behind it and started playing it nearly every show for the next few weeks. And that started it all, because those guys broke artists. Labels looked at who they played, and other college stations did too. All those campuses where we'd dropped off vinyl started digging it out and playing it on the air. I was so hungry to get out of street life that this meant the world to me. It felt like a victory, and I celebrated every time I heard my voice on the radio even though I knew in my heart that this wasn't the destination. It was just the beginning. We still had a mountain to climb.

CHAPTER 8

CLAN IN DA FRONT

As ready as I was to leave the streets and pursue music, I still had to eat, so I kept hustling the way I always had. I tried to do it as little as possible because the streets were hotter than they'd ever been, and it seemed like every week someone I knew was going to jail. But hustling is a lifestyle, not a job, and it was the only one I'd known. When you hustle, even when you're doing well, every day you wake up scrambling, trying to make a living without getting picked up or stuck up, staying out of the way of your more powerful competitors so you don't get killed. I had been living that cycle for years, but now, with the possibility of a music career in my future, I was inspired to write hardcore drug-dealer storytelling rhymes more than ever. Lines like "I know this kid by the name of Gigante, a Teflon don with a Diamante" started to flow out of me every time I opened my notebook. And for once I felt like my skills were approaching the level of the heroes that inspired me, like Kool G Rap and Big Daddy Kane.

That being said, it was hard for me to believe that anything we were doing would ever amount to much fame. Shit just didn't happen that way for kids from the Staten Island projects. When you grow up a young black man in a poor urban community, you become accustomed to what is in front of you and numb to circumstances that ain't right. If you keep your wits about you and find a potential way out, you grab it and hold on with all you've got. As a fan, hip-hop was my escape from reality. The music became my identity, and rapping was a hobby until it became so much more. Rap became a calling, a skill to sharpen; a tool I could use to change my reality. I was no optimist; any hustler who is won't be alive or free for long, and I'd grown up looking over my shoulder and expecting the worst. But I was a dreamer and I had seen fame close-up a few times. Looking back on it now, I had a few encounters that came at exactly the right time, when I might have been losing hope. These moments made me feel that maybe I was special, and that maybe I had a shot at making it.

The first people I ever knew from Staten Island who caught a record deal were a group of guys who called themselves the Force M.C.'s, and they were some of the nicest rappers I'd heard. They'd come out and rock the block parties in the summer, as well as perform on the Staten Island Ferry and in Times Square. They could pop and lock, they could rap, they could sing, and they could dance. They'd do cool shit like make freestyles out of the *Gilligan's Island* and *Brady Bunch* theme songs. Those guys could really sing and harmonize, so in the late eighties, they changed their name to the Force M.D.'s, which stood for "musical diversity," and became more of a fly R&B group and early pioneers of new jack swing. They caught a deal with Tommy Boy Records and released this dope summertime anthem called "Let Me Love You." They were an inspiration to me, but they also made me realize that for an artist from Staten Island, it took a lot of work to even get noticed. The industry didn't come to us, ever.

There was one time when I felt like the music industry came to find me, and it was early on in my rap career, if I could even call it that. We used to hang with Inspectah Deck's brother, who always talked about his friend from Long Island, Erick Sermon. Now EPMD was one of our favorite rap groups, so we used to call him out, saying he was lying just to gas us up. He'd always say, "You'll see, one day he gonna come out here and kick it with us." And one day he did. We couldn't believe it, but Erick came to Park Hill and was chilling in front of the building with Deck's brother. I was with one of my homies, who told me to go down there and rap for Erick Sermon.

"Nah, fuck that, I ain't rhyming for him," I said.

"C'mon man, you got this," my boy said. "Drop some bars on him."

It took a little more convincing until I finally figured I had nothing to lose. So we went to hang with Erick Sermon, and Deck's brother was the one that set it off.

"Y'all niggas out here do what you do, one of y'all kick it for him. Sha, show him your rhymes."

At the time I had a rhyme I was working with that went something like this:

> I approve factors, write me back
> Niggas in my posse roll in black
> Slept so long, god damn I got slept upon
> Put on your vest because these lyrics are Teflon

Erick Sermon liked what he heard, and said, "Yo, my nigga, you got some rhymes." And then he wrote his number down on a brown paper bag, ripped it off, gave it to me, and told me to call him. I was only about sixteen or seventeen at the time.

I took that paper and put it upstairs in my top drawer in my room at my mother's house, and every few days I took it out and looked at it. It took me months to get up the courage to call. First time I called, nobody answered, which I took to be a sign that it wasn't meant to be. A couple months later I pulled it out the same thing happened. So in my mind I gave up on it, but I didn't throw that paper away. I held on to it like it was a lucky rabbit's foot or something. Eventually I called again and spoke to a female who told me that Erick was on tour. But just making that connection made me feel like I had a chance. I started envisioning myself as a professional rapper, then I started dreaming about money—wearing gold chains and carrying my pen and pad. This is when I discovered the power of the mind and projecting the reality you want for yourself. That small step inspired my pen game and gave me purpose beyond just surviving.

Around then Big Daddy Kane released the video for "Ain't No Half-Steppin'," and there was a kid dancing in it who had what we called a Gumby haircut, which is what I had at the time. It was the style that sloped up high to one side. I told everyone in my 'hood that it was me—that I'd heard they were making the video and showed up and started dancing and they put me in the scene. I even recorded it when it aired on the Box and would stop the tape to point to the kid that wasn't me. "Look, that's me! Can't you see me?" I ran with it and everybody believed it. I was projecting the reality I wanted in real time.

I did see Erick Sermon again in the 'hood around 1990, just after EPMD dropped *Strictly Business*. I'd stopped calling him, but I still had that paper. Then one day I heard this booming system coming down the block, and it turned out to be Erick in a black Benz 300E. He pulled over when he saw me.

"Yo, I know it's been a minute, man, sorry I didn't get back at you. I've been moving around and I've been on the road."

I was standing there by myself, shocked that this was happening. "Yo, here's a new number, I want you to come out to Jersey and I want to get you in the studio. So hold this number right here and use it."

"All right, bet, I will call you later today."

I couldn't believe this shit, and later in the day I was telling every friend I saw about it. I never did get into the studio with Erick, but the fact that this happened at all was another moment that gave me hope and inspiration and made me feel like I was getting closer, much like the time I interacted with my hero Rakim out at a club in Manhattan. I was just leaning on a wall when I saw him, dressed in black and wearing his big gold necklace with a Mercedes symbol, two other big ropes, and a hat. Next thing I knew he was looking at me, and as he walked by, he said, "What's up?"

"Peace, God," I said, letting him know that I too was in the Five Percent Nation.

That was enough for me, but later he came over again and gave my shoulder a pound. "I see you, God," he said.

That interaction might not seem like much, but it was life-changing for me. It was like he transferred power to me that made me understand that I too could be a rapper. It might sound crazy, but it's true. It was the sign I needed to give it all I had, to focus on my rhymes and pursue music any chance I got.

I was glad for these signs, because on the other side of things I kept seeing karma take down my friends in the hustle game. I felt like it was slowly closing in on me. Both of the guys who had been involved in the incident that got me shot had come on hard times. Cent was shot and killed a few years later, which surprised nobody because he was a real aggressive guy, but LL, who actually shot me, and who I became real good friends with after he started seeing one of my friends' sisters, wound up getting shot in the eye. He was never the same again—he would fall asleep suddenly because he had all kinds of nerve damage.

I'd run with the whole drug dealer profile of being some super-violent tough guy—a Tony Montana type—so I kept myself out of harm's way for the most part. All I ever wanted people to know about me was that I was someone you didn't want to disrespect. I'd run into a couple scenarios with people trying to move in on my clientele and territory, but nothing ever so bad that somebody wanted to wipe me out or vice versa. I stayed somewhere in the middle, away from the extremes where I needed to take someone out to get more business or was so big that I was a target for every hungry hustler around the way. On top of that, I tried to spread positivity in the 'hood to other dudes through the teachings of the Nation. Hustling doesn't come with a happy ending, so I pursued music as relentlessly as I'd once pursued hustling, which is how I ended up on RZA's roster. And now that I was, I planned to go at that as hard as I'd gone at hustling back when I had no future and nothing to lose.

WHEN things started moving, after "Protect Ya Neck" got radio play, RZA kicked into high gear, and the rest of us gathered around to see what would happen. He got up every day ready to make moves in the music business. He organized a kind of support staff to help him out. Besides his brother Divine (born Mitchell Diggs), RZA had his cousin Mook, who drove those of us who went to meetings in his fly black Merkur XR4Ti, which was a high-performance coupe hatchback made by Ford for a few years in the late eighties. Jamie was always down for the cause, helping out with spending money and coming along on missions. RZA also hired a Staten Island guy that hung with us named Michael McDonald, who was a graffiti writer known as Lask One and a promotions guy in the music industry. He was the perfect middleman because he knew people at the labels, he knew people at the big record stores like Tower, and he knew how to get the word out to club DJs and magazine editors about underground artists. What RZA started having his staff do was sell our vinyl directly to a few of the record stores, because the song was bubbling up and people had come in asking for it. At the same time, we started driving to Upstate New York, then to Connecticut and Boston, to visit more colleges, bringing records personally to the DJs and station managers and doing appearances if the show featured interviews.

One of those was with a DJ called WildMan Steve, a big supporter of ours at college radio, who broadcast out of Adelphi University. Not everyone wanted to make the trip, so it was me, Deck, Ghost, Meth, RZA, and Dirty. At the time, GZA was in his own universe out in Brooklyn, so he didn't come to every little thing RZA orchestrated, but RZA knew GZA had his back. WildMan Steve had been playing the record, and like a lot of people, he didn't realize how many different guys were actually on it. We all came through the door of the studio and he was like, "Holy shit, is all these guys on this record? How we gonna get you all in this fucking room?" That show was cool because he wanted to have us on the air, talking to callers, which we had never done before. After he played the record, people kept asking us to freestyle, so Steve cued up a beat—I think it was Naughty by Nature or something—and we got down to business. People on the phone lines couldn't believe they were hearing so many different rappers all united, falling in one after another. This was a breath of fresh air, something completely new.

At the same time, RZA was arranging meetings with every label that would have us. I went along with him many times, the most promising of which was a meeting with PolyGram. When we sat down in a conference room with executives, their first question was how many guys were in the group. The record was out, but there were no publicity pictures of us, no liner notes, nothing. We didn't have the money for anything other than pressing records.

"The group is eight members at this time," RZA said. Cap was still in jail and at that point we hadn't brought Masta Killa in yet.

"There's eight artists in this group," one executive said.

"Yeah."

"And you keep telling us that each guy has his own style, and each one should make his own album."

"Yeah," RZA said. "Each guy is dope. Each guy can carry an album. You're getting a group and eight solo artists in one."

I watched as each guy from the label began to smile uncomfortably. Clearly they were all thinking the same thing: "This motherfucker's crazy."

"Well, that's interesting, but that's a lot of artists for one hip-hop group, so I'm sorry, I don't think we can do it," one of them said. "We can't sign that many artists at once at the moment. We will think about it and give you a call if we change our mind."

The single continued to gain momentum, and soon it was not only being played at college stations but also on 98.7 Kiss FM because Kid Capri was a fan. And Stretch and Bobbito played it so much on their show, and talked about the mystery of who we were, that they started saying they were going to get us all to come in and perform. So word was getting around at every level of the hip-hop record business. Still, these label meetings weren't going well. Our next important one was with Russell Simmons at Def Jam. Russell let RZA know that he wanted all of us to come in for this meeting. He wanted to see each and every guy that was on the record, so we arranged for that because all of us had such respect for what Russell had done and was continuing to do for hip-hop culture.

Russell was real respectful and said he liked both songs on our vinyl a lot. But then he took one look around and smiled that smile of his and said, "I don't know man, there's really a lot of y'all." We had heard that, and would continue to hear that, but then Russell asked us something important.

"Why do you feel that you're so special?"

"I just feel it in my heart," RZA said. "Y'all don't know this because I have music from all these dudes already recorded, and it's all individual. I didn't bring it to y'all because I want the group to be signed as a unit before we even get to that. But I'm telling you, all these guys have it in them to be solo artists too. You've seen what the Hit Squad did."

"The Hit Squad is dope," Russell said, "but they're not a group. They just did one song together."

He wasn't wrong: the Hit Squad was a clique that came together for a record. Most of them already had solo deals before they got together.

"What you want to do, and what you're asking us to do, has never been done in the music business," Russell said. "And we're not really one hundred percent interested in that."

So Russell and Def Jam turned us down too, but we weren't giving up. Across the board, labels and executives were fucking with us, but nobody wanted to sign us. There was only one thing we could do, and we all agreed it was the only way: we were going to sell records out of the trunks of cars, on street corners, direct to stores that supplied club DJs, making some money and spreading the word any way we could. We'd stay on the grind, doing appearances and keeping up our relationships at labels, while forcing college radio to continue to play our music. We were going to get the funds to make a video, and we were going to start doing club appearances. We were going to do it all our way.

All the money we made from selling the records went toward more travel as well as getting RZA a bigger place where he could build a better studio with more equipment. From the moment he got that studio, RZA barely went outside. He stayed behind the board working on music, only leaving to take a meeting or to go to Sam Ash Music near Times Square, which was his favorite place to buy gear.

And that's how it went until RZA got a call from a guy named Steve Rifkind who ran a label called Loud. Actually, he got a lot of calls from Steve, for weeks, that went to his answering machine. He didn't call him back because he figured a small label like that wasn't going to be able to do what the big ones wouldn't. Steve wasn't the average small label owner though; he had been in the music industry since he was a kid. His father, Jules, and uncle Roy ran Spring Records, which was a top R&B label in the sixties and seventies, home to artists like Millie Jackson and the Fatback Band. Steve's dad played a big part in getting James Brown his first record deal and

Elvis Presley his first show in Vegas. Steve dropped out of high school to work for his dad, doing promotion, which became his thing. He moved on to Delicious Vinyl, doing the same thing there in the late eighties, and then started his own independent company, promoting rap groups like Boogie Down Productions and Leaders of the New School. Steve and his company did more and more business as hip-hop grew, because they launched the concept of the street team. They got music directly to industry tastemakers and plastered posters and stickers wherever rap fans got together, rather than the traditional route of taking out magazine ads. This was how all nineties hip-hop reached people, so they were ahead of the curve. His marketing business was doing real money, so he decided to start a label to promote artists he believed in instead of just doing the work to make other labels' acts a success. He got a distribution deal with BMG (Bertelsmann Music Group). He didn't have much cash from them to sign acts, but what he did have was the marketing machine to break unknown talent.

Steve made his point by continuing to call, and RZA took the time to look into him a bit. When RZA did finally call Steve back, after being rejected by every big label in town, he had a plan. He told Rifkind that every man would be signed to his label, Razor Sharp and Wu-Tang Productions, and that Loud would do one deal with that company. Mind you, most of us weren't concerned with the details, all we wanted was to get our careers on the road so we could move out of the 'hood.

Steve came out to Staten Island to meet us and I remember thinking, "Who is this white boy who looks like he sniffs coke talking about signing us?" In my mind, a record company executive should pull up in a limo, wearing a slick suit and carrying a briefcase. Steve was humble and young, but I could tell after spending time with him that he was a thinker and a planner. He also kept reminding us that his father was in the industry, he must have said it ten times at that first meet and greet. What he was trying to get across was that he might not have years of experience and connections but his father did and he'd been looking after Steve's every move.

I was at the meeting when RZA told Rifkind we were looking for half a million dollars, but that wasn't happening. Loud could only pay seventy-five thousand. RZA was smart enough to know that Steve's company, SRC (Street Records Corporation), with all of its marketing influence behind the group, could do more than the in-house teams at any of the major labels. The majors came to SRC to break new talent as it was, and they'd been doing so for years. So RZA knew we were in a good spot, but he was still going to bargain.

"Seventy-five thousand for the whole group?" RZA asked, his smile turning to a smirk. "You're going to give us seventy-five thousand for the whole group? Are you serious?"

Steve began listing the other expenses they would cover, from transportation to marketing and promotion, plus offering us all the profits from live shows.

"We'll think about it," RZA said, and we were out.

Like I told you, the rest of us were ready to take whatever; we just wanted to get a deal, get a record done, and have a career. But we trusted RZA's experience. RZA knew the value of what Rifkind could provide over and above the advance, but what he really wanted from whoever signed us had nothing to do with money. He'd seen how it went down when he was an artist on a label that lost interest the moment he didn't take off out of the gate. Our group was too special for that to happen, so RZA wasn't going to sign with anyone who didn't get it. Whoever signed us had to have passion for us. They had to fucking love us and be willing to put everything they had into making us successful. This went beyond money—he wanted to see a level of commitment equal to ours.

RZA polished up some of the best tracks we'd been working on, both individual and group tracks, and booked a day at Firehouse

Studios in the city a few weeks later. His plan was to have every guy there and for Steve to meet all of us, to hear the whole range of music we had and to vibe. By then our single was making enough noise that we had a number of journalists wanting to interview us, so RZA invited all of them to come down on the same day. He wanted Steve to see the potential he would be buying.

RZA brought the best of what we'd been working on to Firehouse that day, and we came hard. He brought the demo for "Method Man," Ol' Dirty's "Shimmy Shimmy Ya," and a record I had been working on with him for a very long time. It had started out as a rhyme I had called "Lifestyles of the Mega-Rich," which contained my best verses about the drug-dealing lifestyle. This went back to the earliest days of when I started fucking with RZA. He was working on the beat while I wrote lyrics and read the lessons. I stopped him when I heard it and told him it had to be mine.

"You want it?" he asked. "It's yours."

That song had come a long way. The demo now had Deck and Meth on it and was an anthem we called "C.R.E.A.M." That day that Steve came down, I redid my verse for him, so he saw us making music in action. But we will get to that story in a little bit.

Like I told you, we weren't playin' when we brought Rifkind around. We had songs up on the board to play him, there were journalists doing interviews in the lounge, all of us guys were there vibing, and everyone was dressed to impress. Steve was cool—he came in and laid back and watched everything going on. He was the only white guy in the room, so he wasn't fading into the wallpaper or nothing. And these studios were small, so he was right in it with us. He watched every guy's persona, and I'll never forget him turning to RZA when I was right there next to them and saying, "Yo, this guy Rae right here, he's the Energizer Bunny. Him and Dirty never stop." He was right; me and Dirt were always the ones running from room to room, getting niggas all amped up.

The plan worked, because at the end of the day, Steve told RZA he wanted to work with us more than anything.

"If you trust me," he said, "I can turn this group into something big, something like nothing else in hip-hop. It's just going to take me a little bit of time, but I can do it."

RZA, being a born hustler, got cocky and played it cool when he knew he had Steve on the hook. "Yeah man, that sounds good. Thanks for coming out. We like your energy, we like who you are as a person. It seems like you get it. We'll talk it over and get back to you."

As a group, we'd hoped for more money, but at the end of the day we looked at it like street guys, because that's what we were. This situation allowed us a lot of control, and though we weren't getting money up front, we'd finally be seen as a real group with a real record deal. We decided to give Loud the first right of refusal to any of our solo records, but if they didn't buy it, or didn't match another offer, we were free to go to any label we wanted. Everybody felt like this made the deal worthwhile. RZA made a point to Steve that all the dudes who had solo joints or were prominently featured on the record, like me and Meth and Dirty, were going to be the dudes we wanted to push for solo records first. I wasn't stressing about my solo career at that point—I knew I'd get to it someday—but it was an important condition to certain members of the group. RZA pitched the condition to Steve, he agreed, and for seventy-five thousand dollars, that was that, Loud had a group and we had a record deal. All Steve cared about now was getting a finished album so he could start pushing it.

After paying our lawyer and putting money aside for videos and other miscellaneous shit, each of us was lucky if we caught three thousand dollars off of our deal. I didn't give a shit about the money, though. I was a signed artist with a record contract. I was done nickel-and-diming. I was done hustling. I had a music career. When the police pulled me over now, which they did left and right in our neighborhood, I could tell them I had a job. I was a recording artist with a record deal, working on an album. The evolution had begun.

We knew shit would really start rolling once we started playing shows, but we had an album to make first. In preparation for that, each man took to his craft more seriously and started spending real studio time with RZA, weighing in on what records deserved to make the cut. Loud's marketing team started doing their thing, and our two existing songs were played on more stations every week. We started traveling from DC to Virginia and Maryland and all the way up to New England doing radio shows. Then we got flown out to the West Coast to do some radio on that side of the country to build hype as we worked on the album.

This was a fucking dream come true for me. And the squad was coming together like a team: no bullshit, no politics, just unity because we were hungry. We were cocky too. We'd roll up into interviews and tell everyone we were the new Hit Squad, but better. We took it even further and told everyone which guy in our group was a better version of the dudes in their group and other groups. Ghost and I were like EPMD, Method Man was our Redman, GZA was our Rakim, and RZA was our KRS-One. Those were some bold comparisons for a group with one single out, but that was our mentality because we knew the quality of the music we had coming. And mind you, we hadn't even introduced Cappadonna, who was still in jail, and U-God, who had just gotten home.

Before we went any further, we had to decide our names once and for all, because we weren't just going to be a gang of random rappers. A group methodology and philosophy was emerging. The music was unlike anything else—it was grimy, it was real, it was a symphony made in a basement to the beat of our own drum. It was ominous and paranoid, full of dreams and memories. It was mysterious and threatening, like ninjas, and our personas had to reflect that.

RZA had started this conversation with us after "Protect Ya Neck," as the whole identity of the Wu began to take shape in his mind. In hip-hop, names are important because they reflect who the artist is as well as their lifestyle and aspirations. Your hip-hop name is both who you are and who you want to be. In my case, I was still known as Shallah Raekwon because I was very much involved in the Five Percent Nation. I got to thinking about it, and the one issue with my name was that people never took the time to learn it properly. People called me Shallah, which was cool, but I didn't want that to be my rap name when it came down to business. I dropped Shallah and became just Raekwon because that was the part of my name I always liked best. It's a strong name that stands out, one you don't forget.

"Dope," RZA said when I told him, "because that's still your name and everybody knows you for it. So we gonna call you Raekwon. Raekwon the Chef."

"The Chef?" I said. "Like the Chef characters in the karate movies?" The Chef in old karate movies is always an old man who is good at cooking but has so much more going on. He's usually a drunk—so he's underestimated—and he comes with different fighting styles that take his opponents by surprise. He is a guy who beats dudes who think they know what he's all about.

"Yeah," RZA said. "The Chef is a dope character. We gonna call you the Chef because you're always cooking up something that's different. You can rhyme to anything. You don't rhyme to any one style—you can pull a new style out of any beat you feeling."

"Yeah," I said. "I like that. The Chef . . . that's dope."

So that was me. Everyone knew Method Man was going to be called that; he'd been called Method in the neighborhood for years. Ghostface was such a troublemaker at the time—you never knew if he was on the run, if he had a warrant out on him—plus there was a fighter in a movie we liked called Ghostface, so that's how he got his name. Dirty was Unique Ason before this, but he just chose Ol' Dirty Bastard and no one was gonna argue because it suited him perfect.

Inspectah Deck chose his nickname the Rebel because he'd felt like an outsider all his life. RZA and GZA shortened their names from Rakeem and the Genius because the crew decided they should have names that sounded like razors since they were the sharpest blades in the drawer. And U-God was already known as Universal God in the 'hood because he was still a Five Percenter at the time, so he just condensed it.

Now there was one more guy, who went by Jamel Irief (born Elgin Turner), who hung out with GZA all the time and was a real cool brother from Brooklyn that everybody loved. We thought he was GZA's right-hand man, but on the low, that nigga knew how to rhyme. When we'd battle rap in cyphers, GZA would ask us to throw his man in real quick, and we saw that dude got busy. He kept coming around and got on some records, so we decided he should be a member. He came up with the name Masta Killa (another kung fu reference of course) himself, and everybody fell in love with it because it matched up perfectly with the rest of ours. Shit was getting real and we were off and running. We had the team (aside from our man Cap), we had the vision, and we had the demos and a label. It was time to start taking over the world.

CHAPTER 9

MY SHIT

We spent the first half of 1993 recording at Firehouse, perfecting the music we'd been working on for a while. This album had to be the shit, or else our journey was over. RZA still had his game plan, but he had eight new problems. You see, everybody had laid back as this thing came together, waiting to see if it was going to get serious. Once it did, every single man had opinions he wanted heard when it came to the music and everything else. When you're dealing with dudes who only know the streets, egos come with that, so it wasn't easy. RZA couldn't do it without us, but at times we made it hard for him to do it at all. He dealt with guys wanting to come in and change their verses or be first or last on songs—all kinds of shit that had not mattered to them before the deal.

Tensions would escalate when dudes were at the studio and heard another guy's verse. They'd get competitive, thinking they didn't get enough time on the track. All of us at one point or another got in our feelings, which caused problems for RZA day to day. We made a song called "7th Chamber," which was a group record with everyone on it, and no one was ever satisfied with the order in which each member appeared. If you ask all of us today, some people will tell you they still aren't happy with it. The way the song was designed, I went first, and I remember dudes saying shit like, "Why he first? That verse is dope but it ain't all that." I'd laugh it off and tell motherfuckers, "Yo, I ain't made the order, I'm just rhyming." All of that shit came back on RZA, and in the case of this particular song, it almost became too damn much for him to deal with. He nearly dropped the track from the album to shut everybody up.

RZA never set a pecking order, but he knew each man's strengths and composed our songs so they played off each other. I've always been good at bringing energy, and I could rhyme to any beat, so he liked to have me kick off a song because it established a hyped mood. But that didn't mean I dropped my verse first. He'd have each of us come in for the day to lay down verses on a number of beats, then decide the order that guys would appear on each of those songs later. Each song was like a house he was building, but never from the ground up. He'd put the windows in, then the floors, then add some cement, put the roof on, fix up the outside . . . and boom, it was done. He always wanted a surplus of supplies, so he had dudes do multiple verses and then picked the one that worked best alongside the other guys' contributions to the track. Unless a song was a one- or two-artist venture, we never really knew which one of our verses was going to make it until we heard the finished product. The solo tracks by Meth and GZA and Dirty were so dope that nobody questioned them or tried to get on them. But everything else was anybody's guess, and constantly evolving until RZA said they were done. Hooks would change, snares were dropped, beats were switched, tempos were adjusted, and verses were moved around until the moment RZA considered the song complete. With all of these things up in the air, a lot of dudes started hanging at RZA's house and the studio just to see where their shit was gonna land. RZA's constant reworking of the material could be frustrating when it came to us having to adjust or create new tempos to our verses, or writing new ones altogether under pressure, but nobody was mad that it was making the music better. When he started dropping in the karate-movie samples and skits, we knew the album would be monumental.

We believed in the team—RZA, with GZA and Dirty coproducing— and we knew the songs were dope; we all just wanted to be on the album as much as possible. I was excited whenever I went to the studio. I was focused and ready to tear it up. I'd ask the other guys how I did when I got out of the vocal booth because I respected their opinion and I wanted my shit to be tight. They might say, "Nah, that shit ain't all that." It was competitive to the fullest, so if a guy didn't make the track and you did, the motherfucker might not want to talk to you for the rest of the day. It never boiled over, but there were many days where we really didn't like each other.

It was hilarious too, because we all engaged in some devious shit. I remember sitting there, listening to a song being made that I knew I wanted to get on, with my bandmates sitting there telling me, "no, no, you're not getting on this one." What could I say to that? I'd be in my feelings, but I'd let it go. But in the back of my mind, I was saying to myself, "Oh yeah? I'll get RZA alone tomorrow and get all over this fucking track." Everyone was playing one game or another. We schemed to get RZA to ourselves, which kept the cycle going. If I heard that a man changed a verse on a track I was on and I thought it was better than mine, I would turn around and get RZA to let me change my verse too. Like I said, juggling that many egos was a heavy process for RZA. We were a pack of dudes with tough guy attitudes telling him, "Nah fuck that, my shit is the shit."

"My shit" were the fucking key words of the recording of *36 Chambers*. My shit versus his shit. But that's what made us great. Everybody was intent on representing himself in the illest way, so making the record became an endless rap battle. I dealt with this by doing a lot of listening to the others and treating each verse I did as if it were my last. I didn't know how many tracks I would be on, and I never brought that up to RZA, but I guess my being one of his top-tier students, and a willing party—always around to brush off my gun and fire some shots—landed me on more songs than the others. When the final track list came together, I realized that I was one of the guys with the most verses on the album. I was proud of that, because I knew how fierce the competition had been.

A lot of the prep work was done at RZA's, always with karate flicks on, like *Five Deadly Venoms*, *The 36th Chamber of Shaolin*, and *Shaolin and Wu Tang*. The sound and visuals of these films had been in our lives for years, right alongside hip-hop, so they had a familiar, meditative quality to us. Their presence in the studio during our creative process brought a vibe as necessary as every member of the group. While he was working, RZA had an ear to those, looking for the perfect bits of dialogue to include. He was really living in a whole karate fantasy world, so much that at times I thought he believed he was Asian. Like a karate master, the dude had his uniform: scuffed-up old Timberlands with his pants tucked into them and his brown leather jacket. And he was always in noodles; besides the boxes of pizza dudes brought by for themselves, there was nothing else to eat in RZA's house but noodles.

When he was ready to take the music to Fireside, RZA focused on one song a day, bringing all the bits and pieces of the track that he'd developed in his home studio to a conclusion as best he could. That's where he got serious and cut the verses or instrumental tracks that didn't fit. He had to emerge with a final cut ready for mastering each day in order to stay on budget. In the end, everybody got on the album, everybody did their thing, and it flowed so well. Some days I'd go up to the city with him, but some days I wouldn't because he was so focused. A lot of RZA's work at Fireside revolved around keeping the grittiness of the original tracks. Mind you, a lot of that lo-fi quality was a side effect of cheap-ass gear, but his talent lay in taking those limitations and making them work. His music was dusty, dirty, and motherfucking mean—and it represented who we were to the fullest. It was the soul of the group, and he wasn't going to let it get shined up. So part of the process for him was fighting with professional engineers whose job it was to make things sounds perfect. They would hear our demos and say, "What am I supposed to do with this? Yo, this sounds like shit!"

RZA intended to chop down other producers in the game the way we rappers aimed to chop down other rappers. He intended the music to sound like it was being played on a cassette tape, with all the crackle and hiss, because tapes are what we were brought up on. He refused to lose the sound he'd worked on for five years, so as much as the engineers were able, he asked them to just mix and master the music. But sometimes mixing the tracks wasn't even possible. Some of his shit wasn't even hitting even the lowest end of the decibel meter where it needed to be for it to sound good when it was pressed onto a CD. These debates went on forever, and in the end RZA probably listened to the engineers 60 percent of the time, not caring the other 40 percent how muddy the shit would sound. The guys at the mastering studio had their work cut out for them. RZA didn't do anything by the rules. He had a DJ's instinct and a composer's ear. He'd mix samples with other shit by slowing the record down, not caring that they were at two different input levels. He'd add weird sound effects from all kinds of sources, and when you asked how he did it there was always some story: "The needle broke when I was sampling it from the record, but I loved the sound it made so I kept it in." His style was as different as all of us were, and it was a perfect match.

One thing that RZA insisted on was that when we recorded our verses, they were done live all the way through. He had to teach all of us, especially me, how to get on the mic properly so that our voices sounded their best. When I'd hear other guys' shit and it sounded different from mine, I'd get upset, but it was usually too late to change it. At the end of the day the crew usually said I sounded good, but I'm a particular guy and always want things to be flawless. Sometimes our voices sounded light because we were standing too far from the mic in the vocal booth. And I never knew you could cut a take, then go back and punch in a line or a word you messed up. RZA wasn't allowing any of that. He wanted verses start to finish, recorded as they happened in the studio, so we did takes over and over until we got them perfect. We had to be taught that if you were feeling your verse and wanted it to come out dope, you had to control yourself and not move your head. Your voice had to go into the mic consistently at the right angle to sound the best it was gonna sound. RZA got frustrated with us many times, because even when he was right and just trying to help, dudes would say, "Nah, nah, my voice sounds good like this."

RZA was the middleman on so many levels, especially when we got into deciding the order of the songs on the album and the skits. Everybody had too many damn opinions, and we argued for days about which skits were whack—to the degree that dudes almost squared off. RZA would say shit like, "I hear y'all going at it, and I'm listening to y'all, but I'm just letting you know I'll probably come up with something different, so y'all chill out. This ain't worth fighting over." He was smart enough to know that coming up with something different was the best solution when arguments began to escalate. There was a childish mentality to our disagreements that RZA had to entertain while maintaining the status quo. It's a good thing that he had a library of material going back five or more years that he could turn to when he needed a solution. There's a reason why the album is a classic: it was a long time in the making.

A lot of artists say their debut album was years in the making, but I want you to understand exactly how it was for us. So before I go any deeper into the creation of *Enter the Wu-Tang (36 Cham-*

bers), I'm going to rewind for a minute to tell you how the version of the song "C.R.E.A.M." that the world knows and loves came to be, because this story illustrates our process: how everything was patched together from different pieces over time and how competition and pressure played a role in our greatness from the get-go. As you'll see, that classic first verse was rewritten at the last minute, and it's a good thing it was, because it played a key role in getting us signed.

I'd claimed the beat for "C.R.E.A.M." back in '89 or '90, and ever since then I'd been giving RZA verses for it, each one better than the last. I was into storytelling rhymes, painting pictures of drug dealers, fictionalizing things I'd heard and incidents that happened in the streets, so I compiled many stories for that track, over that beat. The version that stuck for the first verse went like this:

I know a so-called kid called Crazy Clip Claxton
Who drove around in a ragtop, maxing.
Stacks in a hearse and rocking mad jewelry
Headed to the flicks to see *Godfather III.*
Can't front, he was on some militant
Attitude up the part he was brilliant!

That was the opening verse in my mind, the one that should end up on the album. I thought it was dope, and I remember playing a demo for Jamie one day while we were driving up to Harlem to get some weed, around the time we were getting ready to sign with Loud.

I was driving and I remember him sitting in the passenger seat, eating a sandwich, when I asked him what he thought.

"It was cool, it was cool," he said, real quick, in between bites. Now, when your homie says something you did is cool, and they say it real quick like that, you know they don't think it's cool. They are just trying not to hurt your feelings. What they are really saying is,

"It's aiight, it's nothing special." He was telling me it wasn't all that, which got me thinking about the guys in the group who had told me it was.

"So what you really sayin'?" I asked. "Keep it a hundred. If you don't like it, you don't like it."

"Yo, nigga, you know I keep it a hundred nigga. I think it's dope but I think you could do something iller," he said. "You changing names and telling stories which is cool, but what the fuck? You and me are right here. We come from a hustle, why ain't you talking about our life together and whatever the fuck we been through?"

He was right. All the other guys had told me it was dope and I'd listened to them, but they didn't know me like Jamie did. I had no idea how personal the new verse would end up being and how it would set me on the lyrical path I've followed ever since. I just knew I had to try again and set my sights on reality, not fantasy. The life I'd lived deserved it.

"What you talking about? Shit is dope," RZA said when I told him.

"Nah, I got to change it."

Now in his mind, RZA had already finished that record. He'd already put Inspectah Deck on it, even though Deck and I didn't write that song together at all. Like I said, RZA was moving through the tracks, using all the verbal ammo we had given him. I had no way of knowing, but aside from a hook, the song was already done, so when I came to him I had to beg him to let me go back in on my verse.

"All right, get it done," he said. "You've got one day, no more."

I left with a tape of the track and went home knowing this was my chance to get it right. This beat and this song meant so much to me, and I knew it would be my showcase on the album, so I could not fuck around. At the time I was staying in a small house that Jamie and I had that was a stash crib where we kept our drugs, our hammers (guns), and whatever. At the time we had a young dude staying there, a guy we'd recruited to work for us that was a real stand-up kid. He was our little soldier, a born hustler but real wild. He'd gotten into something on the street and had been shot twelve times. So he was there, healing, hidden away because the beef had not been squashed. He sat up that night watching me write "C.R.E.A.M."

This kid had a colostomy bag at the time, and if you have never smelled one, you're lucky. He would go up to his room and open it up for maybe five minutes to change it out, and in that short time, the whole place would smell like shit. This wasn't normal shit either, so the house smelled like the dirtiest, oldest bathroom in the world, which did nothing but make this kid angry and hungry for revenge but he had to heal.

There I was with him, in that dank, stinking place, in the dark, because we hadn't paid the light or gas bill. I got a bunch of candles, set them up in the kitchen, and put my notebook on top of the stove because we didn't have a kitchen table. I started thinking about my close friend Jamie, whose opinion of this song mattered more than anyone else's, and why he didn't like the verse. Not only was he my friend, he was also one of the financial bosses in the Wu-Tang organization—as important as Divine—so on that level, I wasn't going to let him down. This rhyme was for him. It had to be the shit, and I wasn't going to stop writing until it was.

I had a whole lot of dried-up dirt weed that wasn't very good, but I was selling it when I could to keep a couple of dollars in my pocket. I had about a half pound of it, so what I did was go out and buy ten dollars' worth of Hershey's chocolate and put it in the bag to make it smell like chocolate weed. We smoked a little of it here and there, but we knew it was dirt, so the main thing we kept it for was to sell it to motherfuckers who wouldn't know the difference. With my pen in one hand and a blunt of that chocolate dirt in the other, I took a few hits and let my thoughts flow.

I stood there in the candlelight thinking to myself that the first line had to be flawless. I don't know how long I was there—time kind of stopped—but when the words arrived, I knew this was it:

I grew up on the crime side, the *New York Times* side
Stayin' alive was no jive.

I sat with that awhile and began to think about my life, the thoughts and memories bubbling up within me.

Had secondhands, Mom bounced on old man
So then we moved to Shaolin land
A young youth, rockin' the gold tooth, 'Lo goose
Only way I begin the G off was drug loot.
And let's start it like this, son, rolling with this one
          and that one.

It felt good, it felt right. I chose "'Lo goose," because back in the day in the 'hood if you had a Polo goose, that meant you were a stand-up nigga. When I looked at these first few lines I understood what Jamie had meant. These were snapshots of what we'd lived and survived. Why write fiction when the truth was so much iller? The words were flowing now, coming from my heart and mind. This wasn't an assignment from RZA; this wasn't a verse to a beat. This was my diary in rhyme. I didn't stop to review it, judge it, or analyze it. I wasn't going to get in my head about it. I kept going until I had nothing left to say.

I just about ran my ass to RZA's house the next day to drop it on him. He had been up all night working; the dude had crust in his eyes, his hair was all out, he just looked crazy. No one was there but us, and I told him how much I appreciated him letting me take another shot. When I got in the vocal booth, I said, "Yo, I'm going to try something. Let me try this."

I didn't want RZA to think I would insist on the new verse because

I knew he was down with the original version. Plus he was working so hard, I never wanted to be a burden. I just wanted him to understand that I liked this new version better and hoped it would work with the song as it was. To this day, twenty-five years later, I still say, "Yo, let me try this," every time I step up to the mic in a recording studio. I think of it as a blessing and a thank-you before I go in.

RZA let me lay it down, and when he heard it he said it was dope, but we needed to do it again because it didn't sound clean enough. He was never the type to gas you up. He always played it cool, which was his way of pushing us to try harder, because we all wanted to impress him. He was very clear when something was whack, but when it was dope, he only gave so much praise. It was one of the ways he kept the peace working with so many egos.

The plan was to have me rerecord it at Firehouse the next day, which was the day Steve Rifkind was coming through. What you hear on the record is historic, because it was done that day with Steve there at the moment when we were potentially getting signed. I remember choosing my outfit carefully that morning. I wanted to wear top-of-the-line shit to impress niggas and let Steve Rifkind know I was one of those dudes. I put on a pair of black Adidas Mutombos with the colorful letters on them, some baggy jeans (baggy was the shit), and a Fila velour joint. If you saw dudes in Fila velour in '92, it meant they were hustlers and they were getting money. I bought that particular tracksuit at Sign-ins in Brownsville, which was a notorious place. Niggas would wait outside to rob dudes coming out with their shopping bags. The place was so ruthless that some of the niggas working there would tip off their friends and set up the robberies. We never went there without our pieces and we let it be known that we had them too. So that Fila suit meant a lot to me.

I was so amped that day, running around the studio like always, but a little bit extra for sure. I was ready to drop my verse, which nobody besides RZA had heard yet, and here we had a dude primed to give us a record deal. This was the moment my life could change, and I knew it. Everyone was keeping it cool around Steve, but I had too much damn energy. I remember Ghost watching me that day, smiling as if to say, "I like this nigga Rae, even though you a Park Hill dude." We were still getting to know each other, but I could tell my energy was rubbing off on him.

I did my verse with cameras on me, tape rolling, and the whole crew hearing it for the first time and reacting. Everybody loved it, but I knew it was really dope when I saw Deck leave the room to start rewriting his shit. Unfortunately the guy I wanted to hear it most, Jamie, couldn't be there that day, but when he did, he gave me a big grin and a pound and told me I'd done it.

The hook for "C.R.E.A.M." came later. RZA, Meth, and Dirty were what I called our hook boys. Meth most of all—I called him Captain Hook. He came up with that iconic chorus when he was hanging with a mutual friend who sold weed. "Cream" was a word a lot of us were saying in Park Hill, and now to this day, people say it all over the world. Nobody really knows this, but the term originated with my cousin out in Brooklyn who used to come to sell crack in the 'hood. We used to ask him what he was doing, and he used to say, "I'm trying to make some cream. I gotta get that cream." We'd laugh at him and ask what he was talking about. He had taken it from a Tom and Jerry cartoon that all of us had seen. It's the one where Tom and Jerry are making sandwiches and spreading so much mayonnaise on them that when they take a bite, it looks like cream flies out all sides of the sandwich. "Cream" was his way of saying he was trying to get his spread on and do well. In the 'hood everyone is big on slang because it's a code that isn't meant for outsiders to understand. So my cousin brought that to our neighborhood and it stuck. When Meth heard the song, he realized it was the perfect opportunity to use the term because that's what the song is about, trying to get some cream. When he added the "dollar dollar bill y'all" refrain from the Jimmy

Spicer song "Money," which is an old-school record we'd been hearing since the rec room parties in the projects, it was unstoppable. He's Captain Hook, I'm telling you.

Deck hopped on the theme and came back with a deeper and more personal verse. He had a lot to pull from because he had just gotten home from jail, so his lines were straight from the heart:

It's been twenty-two long years, I'm still strugglin'
Survival got me buggin' but I'm alive on arrival

All of us could relate to that. Deck inspired me with his verses back then. One of the illest lines I've ever heard is his opener on "Protect Ya Neck": "I smoke on the mic like Smokin' Joe Frazier." I heard that line and it made me do better. Deck was at his finest, and me, I was just full of energy, so the two of us on "C.R.E.A.M." were a force. Once they heard our verses, none of the other dudes wanted to get on it because they couldn't fuck with us. As you can see, when we were moving well creatively, our best work came together in an inspired way.

That song was the highlight of making the album for me. The track is slow, it's got a different vibe from the rest, but it made sense in the context of the album because it told a story that we had all lived through coming up, in one way or another. It is one of the realest tracks on our album. After all, as a group, we had come together to make cream. There's no way RZA could have gotten us in his studio without the promise that money would be involved. That is the type of people we are. That was a draw for me, if I'm being honest, but I also wanted to be famous. I wanted to see if I could fill the shoes of my heroes, the ones whose music kept me alive through so many hard times.

Since I'm talking about highlights, I have to take a moment to tell you about watching Dirty do "Shimmy Shimmy Ya." It's a day I'll never forget. He coproduced that record, and he just wrote his shit right then and there in the studio. The song isn't a lot of lines, but the beat is so ill that he didn't even come up with a second verse. He just said the same verse twice! I was there scratching my head, like, "Hold up, you mean to tell me that same verse is coming back again?"

It was so authentic, and so Dirty. He was such a hip-hop junkie, loving the sound of everything, always in the studio like he was the man of the house. He'd be talking mad shit, running around looking at everyone's verses, yelling, "We the motherfucking best!" He'd be drunk, breath smelling like shit, everybody looking at him laughing. Then he'd go out and get a pizza, come back, and not give nobody none of it, shouting "fuck you!" if you tried to get a piece. He was nuts and we loved him for it. All of his outrageousness gave us confidence as a group. From the start, when we hadn't even done more than "Protect Ya Neck," he would say, "Wu-Tang is gonna rock the fucking world, Chef. I promise you. That's word to my babies!" When he said shit like that his eyes would get all wide and you knew he meant it. All of that energy, all of that crazy shit, is in "Shimmy Shimmy Ya," and you can feel it. We knew Dirty was never going to be a lyrical MC—we knew he was our Biz Markie. And everyone loved the Biz, including Dirty, because Biz was crazy. Dirty was like Biz with no filter.

Meth summed it up best on a radio show—I think it was Wild-Man Steve's—when he talked about us, a conversation that became a skit on the album. He said: "U-God is a psychopathic banker, Ol' Dirty Bastard ain't no father to his style, the Chef is just going to keep giving you marvelous, delicious shit," and so on. Niggas had already called me marvelous because I was known for being able to rhyme to any beat if you put it in front of me. I was also known to be a guy who had a lot of flavor, which, coincidentally was the term fiends used if your crack was good. So I was the guy cooking up marvelous shit to get your mouth watering. Ghost was "now you see him now you don't," which is how he was moving, still half in and half out of the street. Inspectah Deck, he "sees shit," which was true. Deck laid back and took it all in, he analyzed things, but he didn't want to be up front or do a lot of talking because he was still affected by being imprisoned. He wanted to stay out of trouble in every way. And of course, "the GZA, the RZA, the sharpest ones." That really did sum us up.

These became our characters within the group as our rap styles developed. Before Meth started a rhyme, he'd suck breath in real quick. That was his trademark. It went along with his lean, blunt-smoking voice. Me, I always started by saying "yo, yo, yo," like everything I did was a freestyle.

Ghost was on that tip too, more like me, writing in the moment. The other dudes had notebooks. Some had stacks of them full of rhymes. GZA had a library of books, RZA had books, Meth had books, Deck had a book, and I had one too. Ghost didn't have a book at first, but as he saw the lyrical content the rest of us were bringing, he got himself one and focused. During the making of the album, he and I used to get together and work on shit. To see where it would go, I started writing verses in his book for him to review, and he'd do the same in mine. Then maybe a few hours or a day later we'd come together and talk about them, helping each other perfect what we were doing. This brought us closer to each other than we were with the other guys. As we did this more, we started performing each other's verses for feedback, which was the best way for us to improve. Before long we were super-cool with each other and let our guards down on who we were.

Coming to rap school with these guys was a whole new world for me at first, because they all had books and pens and pads and I had nothing. I used to write lyrics on the old pizza boxes I found lying on the floor of RZA's studio or on the junk mail stuffed under his door. I was different in every way from them, and I even wrote different. I never wrote in a straight line; I'd start in one corner of the page and build sideways and down. It made sense to me because I'm a lefty, but all of them used to snap on that. It was just comfortable for me, but what I didn't realize was that writing that way also helped me find my style of delivery. When I'd recite my words, chopped up and written in a type of pyramid, I did so with an uneven type of bounce. The words were arranged in small blasts that got longer as the verse went on and got further away from the small corner of the page where they started. That's probably why I started everything with "Yo," because that always fit perfectly in the corner.

I'd tell stories, but never with the smooth lyrical flow of a Slick Rick saying something like: "Once upon a time, not long ago, when people wore pajamas and lived life slow." Because I'd write in these pyramids on whatever I could find, the wider the piece of paper, the longer the verse. The shorter the page, the shorter the verse. Dudes used to point out that I rarely said a full sentence, and that sometimes I should. I hadn't even noticed because I was following the chop and bounce of my flow. It wasn't a problem, but it was a tendency I had to pay attention to. Remember, I was a street rapper, and I had never tried to make songs. I had just learned to construct dope rhymes, usually on the spot. Now I was training; I was studying and finding my lane. And for the first time, using full pages, bound in a notebook.

We looked out for each other when it came to our styles and delivery, making sure to keep everything fresh. We didn't want any of us to repeat what another guy did. You had to come clever, you had to come hard, you had to be flowing, and you had to be individual. Being around intricate, lyrical dudes who said a lot of shit, I aimed to do the same, but without imitating their type of flow. If you look at my verses, you'll see that I say a lot of things, paint a lot of pictures, with one thing in common: all of it is hustler shit, because that life is in my DNA. RZA knew I was dope, but he also knew I would never be one of our more complicated lyricists like GZA or Deck. I brought energy, I could get anything started, and he always told me that I had a rapper's voice.

When RZA made us, he was building his own Frankenstein monster, and he busted his ass to make sure this debut album would be the jolt of electricity that got us our solo deals. We named the album *36 Chambers* because it represents everything we are in a very exact way according to the Supreme Mathematics. It was an invitation to enter the world of the 3–6 boys, because three plus six is nine. There were eight of us at first, but Masta Killa made nine, which was always the plan because there are nine planets in the solar system. We are the nine planets in our solar system of rap.

Now think about it: six times three is eighteen, and one plus eight is nine again. We all represented seven because that is the God Number in the Supreme Mathematics. Seven represents God and nine represents born, which means "to bring into existence." So the way we saw it, we were nine members here to make our knowledge born. That's how we broke down the thirty-six chambers. We came from four different areas of New York, so 9 times 4 is 36. And the four chambers of the heart times nine men is thirty-six.

I was so amped about my new life, my new crew, and everything we were doing. I was in the best mind frame. I wasn't worried about the business or nothing. I was part of this movement that RZA had envisioned that made me feel truly understood. I was with my brothers who knew and loved me, and drove me to constantly be better at rhyming. They were the best crew in the world. And if I ever forgot that, Dirty was there, drunk off his ass on forties, to remind us every fifteen minutes. We could never shut that guy up. He might have been drunk, but he was right.

All of us were there at the final mastering session and at the listening party we had for Loud six months later when the album was done. We even got up and performed some songs for them, hard like it was a concert. Motherfuckers were sweating bullets, giving it their all, because we wanted them to feel it. We wanted them to really fucking listen to our shit.

But over the next few months leading up to release, when it came to the label needing things from us and having deadlines to meet, that was a problem. Motherfuckers were expected to listen and do what was asked, but with this crew? There was no listening. Nobody could control all of us at one time, unless there was money involved or the incentive to get on a track. If we had a photo shoot? Not everybody made it. We had to do radio? Not everybody made it. That's how it was even in the beginning when we were excited, and it got much worse later on. Nobody ever slowed down and thought about the big picture. Nobody ever really considered that for a lot of these important promotional responsibilities to be fulfilled, they needed all of us. Because let's not forget, we were a group! The mentality reminded me of a dumb hit man. A hit man might be instructed to do the hit and drop the gun, but a dumb one would do the hit and walk away with the gun. That's how this crew was, not thinking about consequences and never fully listening. It wasn't on purpose; it was just that none of them respected time or punctuality. There were of course those of us who were where we were supposed to be—for the most part I was one of them—but with a lot of the guys there was always an excuse. So it became the case that if you didn't do what you were supposed to, you got what you got.

The photo shoot for the cover of the album is the perfect example of this. The guys who were there when we were supposed to be—me, GZA, Ghost, RZA, Deck, and Method Man—are on the cover. Other dudes came later, but by the time they arrived the cover was already shot. We only had one day to get it all done. Personally, I couldn't believe this behavior. Usually I'd scratch my head for a moment about it, but I always had to let it go.

The album cover concept was us dressed as ninjas because we'd done a show like that and people loved it, and obviously our music

and album were steeped in karate imagery. And with two guys missing, it offered the perfect solution. We'd decided ahead of time that
everyone would be blacked down, wearing shit that everybody wore
on the block: black Champion hoodies, black pants, all black. Not
every dude showed up in a Champion hoodie, but whatever. The
label had given us these round Wu stickers that they wanted us to put
all over the walls of the set, so what we decided to do was put those
on the hoodies in the logo spot. We didn't have a wardrobe, but when
we did that, it looked like something—like we were in uniforms.
Then since not every man was there, we put stocking caps over our
faces and our hoods up—so in the end we had the right number of
men in the picture, just not all of them in the group. Probably the
cheapest wardrobe expense of any major hip-hop album released in
the nineties.

In the end it worked. Looking at the photo makes you feel like
you are about to be kidnapped by lyrical ninjas. And since we went
with the face stockings, we were able to have two members of our
management team stand in for the guys who didn't show up. This was
the first of many times at Wu-Tang Clan photo shoots that whoever
was there and whatever friends were around got in when other dudes
didn't show up. We would just put our "extras" toward the back so
you couldn't tell they weren't us. When we got famous, which came
real fast, so many times the photographer didn't even know who was
in the group and who wasn't. Since we always rolled with a big entourage, dudes would get in the photo because why the fuck not? Other
members got mad, but I always thought it was funny when pictures
came out in magazines and there they were, some of our boys standing there like they'd dropped bomb verses on our last record.

CHAPTER 10

WU-TANG CLAN AIN'T NOTHIN' TA F' WIT

When you're from the 'hood and you do something that registers in any kind of mainstream way, it generates energy. Some people root for you out of pride and others root against you out of jealousy, but either way, you're talked about in the community. No matter how people feel about you, they all start fucking with you, acting like they know you, telling other people they know you, coming to your shows, and feeling like they deserve a piece of you. And that's because whether you care to or not, you represent them. This happened to us immediately, the second we had a single out. We saw it firsthand when the Clan started to go out to the clubs together, and we really saw it when we started to do gigs.

We were a reason for people from Park Hill and Stapleton to come out and have fun, and I understood that. That had been me, after all, but mind you, our crew of nine already had more than enough friends and family to fill a room without even trying. Straight up, our entourage was seventy or eighty strong without even putting the word out. We were never the types to tell people we knew not to roll with all of their friends. When we started moving as a unit to clubs and wanted to make it known we were there, it was normal for us to show up with a group of three hundred coming in behind us. That freaked a lot of people out, but it also got the word around that what we were doing was a serious fucking movement. That meant something to us, because beyond our careers, we wanted to represent Staten Island, our home, the forgotten borough.

The first serious show we did was at the Fever up in the Bronx after we were signed in early '93, while we were making the album. The Fever was a legendary hip-hop venue; if you played it and rocked it, you were somebody, plain and simple. It had been a hip-hop mecca in the South Bronx since the late eighties because legends from Sugar Hill Gang to Fab 5 Freddy to Kurtis Blow all got started there. We knew to bring it hard because it was an important show, with Staten Island supporting us and people from all over being there, plus we had Steve and the entire Loud staff coming too. It was in the Bronx, the birth-place of hip-hop. You bring your A-game or you stay the fuck home.

I always thought that Wu-Tang should show up to a gig as group, but it never was that way until we had our own bus. So we all got there however we did, with whoever we brought. Fever was the spot, so that night it was crowded and hot, with no fresh air to be had. The whole place was rockin', full of people getting drunk and fucked up. Ghost came with his Stapleton crew, there was a bunch of us Park Hillians, GZA brought his Brooklyn brothers, and RZA had his squad. We had a lot of Five Percent brothers around us, acting as our security, because they were a part of us too. We didn't have a DJ then, so RZA asked GZA's dude DJ Allah Mathematics to play with us at that show, and he soon became our guy. We didn't really know Math beforehand, but he was a good brother, definitely solid. He went on to design the Wu-Tang logo and later became a producer that worked with us. That night we ran deep the way we always did, which showed everyone we were doing something significant. We had something to prove, but we weren't there to fight with anyone. We just wanted to get on and show our respect for the Bronx and Harlem and their legendary status in the culture of hip-hop.

I think we got three grand for that show, so each man walked away with three or four hundred dollars at most, but we didn't care. We were there for the action. Backstage, the vibe was the same as it was in the rest of the club—everybody smoking and drinking and hanging out. It stayed like that at our shows, even when we got to playing big venues. If you went from the front row to the back of any place we were playing, it would be hard to feel a shift, because we were always behaving just like real fans were, sharing the same energy and there for the music.

It was a hell of a night. The Fever was so jammed that some of us ended up jumping on top of the bar to perform, because the stage was too crowded with all of us on it. Dirty was crazy drunk, telling everybody in the club that we were the best, before, during, and after we got onstage. As far as I remember, the show was dope because of the energy, but we only had four mics, so we had to play tag, passing them to each other verse to verse. Of course every man started eye-balling each mic, forming his opinion of which one sounded the best and angling to get that particular one when it was his time to shine. This was a regular thing onstage in our early days. There were never enough mics, so we all decided for ourselves which was the magic mic. We became like a pack of wolves fighting over one perfect lamb, not realizing there were three other lambs that tasted pretty good right there ready to be eaten. Whatever the sound was, the crowd went crazy for us and how we got down. The Staten Island kings crushed the fucking building in the Bronx that night.

Onstage we worked out real quick that Ghost and I were the group's Energizer Bunnies. We got the crowd hyped up, establishing the vibe and dropping rhymes on the fly. And early on we came out with stockings over our heads, a signature that of course ended up on our album cover. Our intention was to be seen as mysterious 'hood ninjas, because ninjas are different from karate masters: ninjas are assassins who don't want to reveal themselves. At our early shows, we'd come out with the stockings on, then take them off when we'd do our first verse.

Except for Ghost. He kept his stocking on the whole time back then for his own reasons. He was mixed up in a lot of shit, so he didn't want nobody seeing his face where they could easily get at him, like a stage. Ghost had been a troublemaker all his life, a dude who came from robbing and stealing and cutting niggas. His stocking was staying on because chances were, there were guys in the audience who were going to recognize him for one thing or another, but didn't yet know him by the name Ghostface Killah.

My God, those early shows were so unorganized. The DJ would play the music and we'd be up there, throwing mics at each other and shit. But that energy drove the show; it was spontaneous and felt like it might all fall to pieces but somehow came out right. That's what people came for. They could see that we were there to impress them as much as we were there to compete with each other. They were getting a real live show, and they fed into it too: if one of us got on and killed it, they weren't going to cheer unless the next guy got on and came correct.

That mode never changed, even when the group got more professional. Once we were touring nationally and internationally, there was never a question of us doing a light show or anything extra that required coordination. Not only would something like that have been against the spirit of our performance, but it also would have required rehearsal. No set of managers or guardian angels in the universe was going to get the entire Wu-Tang Clan to rehearse. The extent of our cooperation was letting RZA decide the set list. We followed his lead on that, but onstage, we were set loose, all of us out to rhyme, come hard, and be better than the last man.

There was a friendliness to this competition, but if one guy's energy was off, it threw the whole show. When a member had a bad night, he heard about it from all of us afterward. It was a real love-hate bond, because you wanted to best your brothers but never rooted for them to fail. It was like a race where you wanted to come in first with your two best friends taking second and third.

At our earliest shows, I was never nervous for more than five seconds when I took the stage with the Wu-Tang Clan. That never changed, even during the worst of times. When you're a crew, the pack gives you confidence when on your own you might slip. Until he left us, all I ever had to do was look at Dirty, our ring leader, to calm my nerves. From the start, his energy was "Fuck it, we don't give a flying fuck," no matter what we were doing. Our energy was straight from the staircases of the projects to whatever stage was having us. We were unfiltered, always.

I remember one crazy show we did out in East New York after "Protect Ya Neck" and long before the album dropped. We didn't get paid; we just did it to represent. When I showed up, the club was so crowded that I didn't understand how our various entourages would get inside. It was yet another underground place with like two mics, no real stage, and no backstage. The sound system was trash, and from the start there was a weird energy in the room. We did our thing and we hung out afterward because we were never the types not to hang out with the people who came to see us. We were all at the back of the club chilling when we heard the shots go off. It wasn't one or two; it was continuous, and everyone started rushing toward us. I heard at least twenty or thirty shots fired, and none of us could escape because the entire club was stuffed up against us with our backs to the wall.

We never found out how it started or ended, but someone led us out a back door into an alley. None of us got hit or hurt, but this vibe became a regular thing at our early shows, because we brought out the type of audiences that got so hyped that anything might happen. After that night we realized we needed to keep guns on us when we did shows, especially those of us, like me, who had been shot and forever wanted to be protected.

There I was, an artist now, but still having my gun on me when I went to clubs in New York to perform. I wasn't happy about that at all, but we were playing the spots we could. As much as I felt like I'd gone legitimate, I was still dealing with the same type of shit I dealt with on the street.

When we played shows, our friends and sometimes our members got into fights with bouncers because each guy's entourage felt entitled to get inside, and that's how shit got started. Dudes would flex on security, and although those of us in the group just wanted to focus on the show, we rolled with guys who were ready to go to jail if they didn't get into the club. It was a problem, because some promoters were too scared to book us when they heard that bouncers at other spots had been stabbed working our shows. We developed a bad guy reputation that wasn't a lie. None of us were saints, and as a unit we began to intimidate other rappers in the game because no one around New York had our level of fans representing. Niggas began to know that when Wu came out, Staten Island and Brooklyn rolled up real deep.

OUR lives changed with all of this notoriety, but that was nothing compared to how shit evolved once we headed out on our first real tour. It was a beautiful thing, a happy time for all of us, because we had legitimate jobs now and were escaping the 'hood. Our first tour was about five weeks and it swelled from there, eventually taking us across the entire country. The record label took care of our travel and hotels as we went from radio appearances to interviews to shows to signings at record stores. We had a tour bus, and none of us had ever seen the inside of one of those before. We must have looked like curious aliens from another planet the first time we stepped inside.

Most tour buses are the same. There is an area with a curtain and a little front seat dividing the driver from the rest of the bus, and there's a front lounge with a TV and stereo, couches and a table, plus the kitchen and the bathroom. The next section has all the stacked bunks, each one with curtains you can draw shut, and then there's a back lounge with couches and another TV and stereo. We called the little bunks our "shells," and we called that middle section where the bunks were "the shell block." Dudes would be like "yo, gonna jump in my shell, God." Most of the members liked their shells, but I didn't fuck with mine. I couldn't sleep through the night in one of those little-ass bunks because I felt trapped, so I slept on a couch in the back lounge.

Those were the days, man. We all got to know each other, and we got tight-knit like a family. Dudes were cooking, watching karate flicks, playing oldies, smoking blunts, and telling stories like it was the greatest summer cookout we'd ever been to. Our time together wasn't even about our music until we got off the bus to do our job. Back in the neighborhood, each of us hung with our own cliques, but it was just us now.

You learn a lot about motherfuckers when you go on a road trip with them. Some guys played chess, some guys played spades—there was a lot of gambling going on—and all of us cooked the food we liked to eat. Best of all, we shared the music we loved and discovered that we all loved the same shit. This was music we'd heard as kids, all the great soul music that brought back memories. We were building bridges on that tour, all of us excited because we knew it was our big break. So much funny shit happened that I'll never forget.

I remember a real wild gig at Norfolk State University. That city was one of our biggest markets, so it was fucking packed. We had an after-party where we might have performed another song. Not sure about that, because all I can remember about that night is the hot bitches. The place was full of the most beautiful, young, smart college girls we had ever seen. A lot of us had never seen so many college chicks, so this was like dying and going to heaven. We were on our shit, and girls were on us. I'm not going to get my friends in trouble, because some dudes were in relationships at the time, but we were young and we were hunting.

Me, I was like Rick James's little cousin, a Super Freak in the making, so this was a playground. Some guys kept it square and respectable, but those of us who didn't have anyone to report to were out there flipping chicks together and doing everything you could ever want to do. To a nigga just out of the hood, just free of hustling, thinking he'd never have anything but that kind of life, this was a living dream.

I had this one chick who was on me all night. We hung after the show, on the bus having drinks, and then at the after-party. I had played hard to get with this one, talking to other girls who had come to get autographs. I let them go off with some of the other guys, because this one was so fine I had to make her mine. She and I fucked around a bit, then we went back to my hotel when it got late. I invited her up to stay, telling her we were leaving early in the morning. I said she didn't have to worry because I was a good guy, but at the same time, I wasn't there for no bullshit. She said okay to that, so I thought this was a done deal.

We were in bed, grabbing at each other, and she was saying shit like "I want you, nigga." But after I grabbed the condom and was ready to go in for the kill, she put her hands down between her legs and stopped me.

"Yo, what's that about?" I asked her. I was thinking the worst. "Don't you tell me you got a dick down there, because I'll go fucking crazy."

"Nah," she said. "That ain't it . . . I need a little something."

"What do you need? Right now? Are you smoking crack or some shit?"

It wasn't that. She wanted money to fuck. She was a stripper used to getting paid for her time. Problem was, I didn't have cash on me, only my ATM card. I thought about trying to find a bank, but then I came to my senses.

"You know what? You got to leave, this ain't even worth it to me. No disrespect, but if that's what you were after, you didn't have to let it get to the point that my dick is aimed at your pussy before you start playing games."

"I just want five hundred dollars."

"I ain't never paid for pussy in my life. That's not my thing. I have to tell you, if you were honest with me about this earlier, you'd probably have that five hundred dollars in your pocket. But now you don't."

"Well I can't do nothing then."

"Okay, well, neither can I. Good night and goodbye."

She left me so pissed off and horny that I went into the hallway to see if there were any other girls around. And when I did, I saw the girl I'd just sent away go into another guy's room, I wasn't sure if it was one of our crew or not.

"Ain't that a bitch," I said to myself.

The next morning, we were heading back to Richmond. When I got on the bus, I found that same girl sitting in the back lounge. There was another girl with her, and the two of them let it be known that they were coming with us to our next show. This was some bullshit, but I sat down nonetheless. As the bus pulled out of the parking lot, the two girls started arguing. The girl I'd been with was the calmer of the two, but at some point she said something like "You know better than to keep talking to me like that."

And that's when all of us started gassing them up.

"Ooooh! You gonna let her say that? You ain't gonna let her say that."

We weren't trying to force a fight; we were doing what people from our 'hood did when they were fucking around. We didn't know that these two knew each other, or that they had a past beef that hadn't been squashed. As these girls kept arguing, the entire Wu-Tang Clan stopped talking, which didn't happen too often. We started shooting each other looks, until it progressed to the point that some of us had to get between them to keep the peace. No matter what we said to them, these girls refused to chill, and since the bus was already moving, we couldn't toss them off. The one I had been with was now sitting on the couch, and the other girl was being held back at the doorway to the back lounge.

"Listen," that girl said to the other girl. "I'm no kid, so don't you fuck with me." To tell the truth, this was all talk, because she was not acting like a grown woman.

"Yo, I will fuck you up!" she shouted, pushing through the wall of Wu-Tang members keeping them apart.

That chick I'd been with didn't say a word, she just quietly pulled a knife from her bag. When the other chick came at her, she slashed her across the leg.

"Oh shit!" all of us shouted at the same time.

It took five of us to keep them apart, because now homegirl was acting like she was just getting started with that blade. The bus driver, who was an old Southern redneck white guy, started screaming at the top of his lungs. "You stop that bullshit right now! What the fuck is wrong with y'all?"

This was a bad cut, bleeding everywhere. The poor girl looked like she'd had a small steak cut out of her thigh.

"You motherfuckers gassed that bitch up," the girl with the knife said. "That's what she gets."

The injured girl started yelling about calling the cops and getting everyone arrested. I felt for her because she was a real pretty girl who had never been cut before, but nobody on that bus wanted to see the cops. Before the girl could make good on her promise, the bus driver yelled that the police were pulling us over. Can you believe that shit? Everyone snapped to alert and got calm real quick. We made sure no weed was out and we were good, but the cut girl was still making all kinds of noise.

"Yo, shorty . . . you got to calm down," I told her. "Please, shorty."

Wouldn't you know, the minute the cop walked up to the bus driver's window, she calmed down? She waited until the last possible minute to chill.

I don't know if he got a ticket, but we didn't get searched or nothing. When we drove away, the bus driver let us know that he'd had it with us.

"I'm driving straight to the next destination and I'm not stopping no matter what you say."

The girl with the cut was inconsolable. We got her a bandage from the first aid kit, but she needed stitches and a hospital, which wasn't going to happen until the bus got to where we were going. She was threatening revenge, saying it would be impossible for her to work—all kinds of shit. Everyone in the group took turns trying to calm her down. We didn't want her starting further shit, because it was clear that the other girl knew how to fight, and we didn't want a dead body on our bus. We talked to her, we offered her money, we tried just being a friend—but nothing worked. In the end, one Wu member, who shall remain nameless, got her to calm down and relax, convincing her that it was better to take an L that day than seek revenge. My dude was masterful.

Being from New York, we had never seen females acting quite like this because we didn't hang out with strippers. These chicks were something else, and I'm telling you, the girl with the knife had me so open the night before that I may have never paid for sex before but I'd have given her ten thousand dollars to hit it if I'd had it on me.

One of our friends traveling with us got hustled much worse that night. He slept with some girl he met, and when he woke up in the morning, the girl was gone and so was his Mercedes 190E. He might have been drunk and slippin' that night, but all of us learned that Virginia bitches were ruthless. On tour after that, we watched how every girl around us moved. We learned to hide our money when we took our clothes off and to make sure the girls we were with were giving it up for free. It's funny, because we were street smart in the city, but here we were out in the country having to learn a new set of rules when it came to women. We didn't even know those girls were strippers. All we knew was that they were really good-looking bitches.

Experiences like that bond you with your crew. We learned to love, respect, and understand each other to the fullest on our first tour. We became a family—a family that did rock star shit. That was another thing I learned: if you have the opportunity to do rock star shit, you'll do it.

If you were staying in a hotel we were at, you'd definitely see doors opening, niggas flashing they ass at anyone passing in the hall and shoving girls outside buck naked. One of us was always running down the hallway getting up to something. We did shit just to laugh about it on the bus the next morning. Our tour was the greatest vacation any of us had ever taken, because it was the only vacation most of us had ever taken. It had a nostalgic quality too, because it was nothing but oldies and classics on the stereo: Marvin Gaye, the Jacksons, the Stylistics, the Delfonics. All of us would reminisce and share stories, then we'd play a show at night and party after. The momentum kept building as we made our way across the country, all while our album got added to more stations.

We were well into tour life, on our way to Los Angeles, when U-God got a phone call that switched the mood from day to night. He came out of the back lounge crying.

"Niggas just shot my son," he said.

His little baby boy wasn't more than three or four years old. He had been with a babysitter, a girl we all knew, who apparently was fucking with more than one guy. One of the dudes got proud and jealous and shot at them, and accidentally hit and wounded U-God's son. The real issue was that it happened in Stapleton, and I could tell right away by the look on Ghost's face after he made a few calls that the guy who did it was one of his boys. Weeks of being family went out the window. That one phone call burst the bubble we had been enjoying on the road. It jerked us all back to feeling like we were in the 'hood, dealing with the shit that had dragged us down every single day since the day we were born.

U-God was livid. He wanted to fly home and kill the motherfucker. And he wanted something from Ghost that couldn't be given. Ghost embraced U-God and kept it real and told him that he felt bad, but what else could he do? Ghost could not control what had happened in Stapleton when he was away any more than any of us could control shit in Congress. We all gathered around U-God and encouraged him to stay, because we knew that if he went back, he was going to do something he couldn't come back from. He had too much to lose now.

"It wasn't on purpose, God," I told him. "Bullets don't know names. You can't do nothing in response."

He kept to himself for the next few days, not eating with us or talking much, just lying in his bunk, only coming out for the show. It was a terrible time for him, but in the end he didn't fly home. He finished the tour and never went after the guy, and today, his son is a happy, healthy man. Regardless, this event put a damper on the last leg of the tour, and it put distance between U-God and the rest of us that lasted for a while.

It was a complicated situation, so everyone gave him almost too much space. We understood his mentality: on the street, an action like that demanded a swift reaction. But now here we were, asking our brother to go against his nature. And why? Was it for his sake or the rest of ours? I think it was for both. He had to swallow a bitter pill, and we knew it wasn't easy, but we had nothing to help the medicine go down. All of us were raised as hunters, taught to believe that respect in the 'hood mattered more than life itself. When we were disrespected, we were supposed to say "fuck it" and let the bullets fly. I don't know if I could have been as strong as U was. He did the right thing, even though it wasn't what he wanted to do, and I'll respect him for that forever.

THE road was our escape, but we could never leave our pasts fully behind. Having time to ourselves to think on our lives for the first time brought things to the surface that we weren't expecting. Ghost was hit particularly hard, to the degree that one day while we were chilling on the bus, driving down the highway, he said, "Yo, something makes me want to open this window and jump."

"What?" I wasn't expecting to hear this.

"Something is going on in my mind. Something is not right in my body. I feel like jumping, you know what I mean?"

"Nah I don't know what you mean. You ain't jumping, nigga. Are you crazy?"

Ghost had two brothers at home with muscular dystrophy, plus he wasn't used to being away from his usual guys and best friends. He felt guilty about being out and having a life while his brothers were home sick. Even though he had nothing directly to do with it, I know he also felt bad about U-God's son getting shot. Sometimes he looked around at all of us having a good time and just wanted to end it because it felt so wrong.

It's hard to help your friend when their mind goes somewhere so dark. All I could ever think to tell him was that he was no good to anybody in his family if he was dead. When you've never been away from home, you discover things about yourself, and Ghost was coming face-to-face with issues and feelings that were overwhelming him.

Tour life definitely threw some of us out of rhythm at first. If we weren't staying the night somewhere after a show, the bus would leave at 2:30 a.m. Guys would still be at the after-party or in a hotel room gambling or whatever, so it always took longer to rally the troops. We'd be doing radio the next morning in a new city as soon as we arrived, but a lot of dudes hadn't even gone to bed until 4 a.m., so that counted them out. Dirty always went missing, and a few times we had to leave him behind. To his credit, he'd always find a way to get to the next destination. Sometimes he knew he was getting into it and would say to one of us, "Don't wait on me, I'll meet you in South Carolina."

Eventually everyone got unified, but these dudes were so fucking crazy with what they expected the rest of us to deal with. Take the first time we went to Canada. I'm not positive about this, but I remember us deciding at the beginning of the tour that we were not going to bring firearms on the bus. Like I said, with this group there was no listening, so dudes had guns anyway and we were going across the border. But a couple guys, who shall remain nameless, made an announcement as we were heading through Upstate New York.

"Yo, I got that thing on the bottom of the bus and shit," one of them said. "You know, that thing."

"Yeah, me too," the other one said.

"The fuck, nigga?" we all said. "You serious? What you got?"

"TEC-Nine."

"I got a pair of Glocks."

There is no legal circumstance that allows a US citizen to bring a submachine gun across the Canadian border, and these guns were unlicensed to begin with, so we had a problem. We stopped in Buffalo, rented a hotel room with a safe for three days, and put the four guns in there. We had been traveling across America with four illegal guns like it was nothing. I kept scratching my head, wondering what my brothers were thinking.

When we got to the border, we got the full Canadian Mountie treatment. This isn't unusual for musicians coming into Canada; the border patrol loves to search tour buses top to bottom. I'm just not sure they always have as much fun with it as they seemed to have with us.

They got everyone off the bus and then came out with a big box full of weed. The guns were one thing, but weed was essential.

"You know we can lock you up for this, right?"

They knew we were a musical group, and started asking us what kind of music we did. We told them we were the Wu-Tang Clan.

"Never heard of you boys," they said. They were acting kinda funny, a little loose, like they were possibly joking, but still very authoritative.

"If you're a group, why don't you sing us something? Show us what you do."

My mind went back to the movie *The Five Heartbeats*, when racist police pull over a fictional band in a small Southern town and make them sing on the side of the road. I couldn't believe it, but the same thing was happening to us.

"You want to hear us perform?"

"If you're a group, yes we do. Sing us something."

It was nighttime, so all of us were out there, some dudes in their socks, no shoes on, freezing while these guys made us freestyle. We had some routines we used to break into when we did radio, so we jumped into those while they looked on. I still couldn't tell where their heads were at, because they didn't look mad, but they didn't look like they were enjoying it either.

We did our thing hoping they'd get into it, figuring they couldn't turn around and take us in after all this. But you never know. Of course Dirty was such a character that he managed to break through, so finally it seemed the Mounties were amused. We got away with so much shit in life because Dirty was so obnoxiously funny. We were minutes away from going to jail in Canada, but you'd never know it, because there was Dirt laughing and making faces. I credit him with earning us a pass that night. The Mounties kept calling in backup guards, so it became obvious that this had shifted and now they were just having their friends come around to see the free rap show. There were about ten of them by the end of our border cypher. When we wrapped it up, they waved and let us drive off into the night. They kept the weed, though. I hope they kept it and enjoyed it—off-duty, of course.

On tour, each dude had a daytime and nighttime personality, which meant we might clash, but the next morning or a couple of days later we'd all be friends again. I definitely had arguments with a few guys, over everything from a bitch we were both trying to fuck the night before, to shooting dice, to one of us just having an attitude. Someone might not get you food or would use your phone charger; anything could set off a fight when you're living that close.

Any existing beef would be squashed over a meal. We'd be on the bus in the summer, air-conditioning busted, with dudes cooking anyways. We had a crockpot, two hot plates, and a few skillets, and that's all we needed. We'd make rice, shrimp with peppers, tofu, pinto beans, all kinds of shit. We were so good at making meals that we stunk the bus up, pissing off the driver to no end. Dudes made filet mignon and so much fish. We'd stop at supermarkets and come out with six carts and a fifteen-hundred-dollar bill. We made the bus refrigerator into more of a freezer by stacking it with ice packs so we could pile it high with meat and sausages and cold cuts and frozen shrimp. My specialty was shrimp with red peppers, which I'd hit with Season-All and a little lemon. While I finished that up in a skillet, I'd have niggas getting bread ready so we could throw it on a hero. That was my shit, the shrimp and pepper sandwich, but dudes did all kinds of things, including heating up tomato sauce inside the teapot. It was all out in the tour bus kitchen. If someone had opened the windows, all of the goodness would have flowed out like smoke from a chimney. Of course some dudes didn't eat meat or fish, so they made all kinds of vegetarian sandwiches. The GZA made the greatest vegetable sandwiches I'd ever seen, everything cut to perfection. Even with all of that food going around, I loved touring because I always dropped weight from all of the energy I burned onstage every night. I felt like an athlete during his sport's season.

I remember waking up from a nap to find GZA driving the tour bus and thinking, "My crew is amazing. These guys can do anything." It really was our chance to realize that all of us could be something other than what we were raised to believe we could be. Being on tour was like a test for each man to decide if he was going to run with the devilish mentality he'd always known or blossom into his fuller potential. We talked about everything on that bus: the meaning of life, the color of water, what we wanted from relationships, and what we believed happened when we died. Dudes pulled out documentaries and audiotapes on the Illuminati and we went all the way down that rabbit hole. Most of us had never had enough free time and space in our lives to think about anything past what we would do to survive week to week. I'm telling you, the Wu-Tang tour bus was like a traveling dorm complete with classes and study groups and lectures. It was that on the high end, plus rock star shit. By which I mean partying, gambling, and living it up. All of us were thinking that this was it; this right here was our new lifestyle, and it was gonna last, just the way it was then, forever.

CHAPTER 11

STRIVING FOR PERFECTION

When we got home from a month on tour, I had made a couple of dollars. Those dollars increased over the next year and a half as we did more shows and sold records and CDs. I felt secure and I felt mature, so I made some smart decisions like getting myself a condo, a driver's license, and a car. I'd always blown money when I had it, but now I was blowing it the right way. I had to make my first rock star purchase with all this loot, so I went and got my very first chain, which was a big-ass gold dragon on a square figaro link, plus a gold ring I loved that I put some stones in. I had grown up worshipping Rakim and the Fort Greene cats, the Supreme Magnetic crew he ran with, and since they always looked dynamite to me, there was no question I had to get real jewelry now that I was on.

Come to think of it I bought some clothes too, because I've always been big on getting fresh. A hustler don't stack his money—he shows it on himself for the world to see—so I got new sneakers, and for winter some top-of-the-line North Face gear. I wasn't the guy who bought three thousand dollars of clothes in one trip. I'd hit all the stores, looking for maybe three ill pieces, and if I found them, I'd consider it a come-up day. I slowly stacked my closet because I knew money was coming in, so shopping could be a regular thing for me now. I started making the rounds at different stores too: Saks Fifth Avenue, Lord & Taylor, Barneys. It was a different experience than what I was used to in Downtown Brooklyn and Brownsville, at places like Simon's and S&B's in Bushwick. For one thing, I didn't have to worry about getting robbed coming out of Saks, so I could leave the gun at home.

I got a crib, because before that I had been bouncing between my mom's and our stash houses or wherever else I chose to stay for a while. I decided to get a place in Northern Jersey, away from Staten Island because I felt that I wouldn't grow if I stayed local. I thought of what artists I admired had done, and usually they moved away as soon as they could. I thought of Rakim's line, "I write my rhyme while I cool in my mansion." So I called my first place my 'hood mansion, because it wasn't the biggest but it was all mine.

Getting your own place grows you up, so I found myself caring less about sneaker drops than furniture sales and thinking about couches instead of clothes. I took pride in that shit and got creative with my interior decorating, creating a sleek, colorful style that matched mine.

I got myself a blue Acura Legend down in Virginia, where I had a crew of homies I liked to go stay with, and I used to drive it up and back going to visit them all the time when I wasn't on tour. I remember rolling in that car playing nothing but Wu shit, Nas, and R&B like Mary J. Blige. You know you love a car when you wake up in New York around ten in the morning and decide to drive seven hours or so to Virginia to see your boys.

All of our lives were forever changed after *36 Chambers*. For the first time in our lives we had legal and regular money coming in. And we had done what we set out to do: we proved that Staten Island had talent, and we'd gotten ourselves out of the 'hood. Throughout 1994 and 1995, according to RZA's master plan, the solo records began to drop, starting with Method Man (*Tical*), and Dirty (*Return to the 36 Chambers: The Dirty Version*), plus RZA took time for his side project Gravediggaz (*6 Feet Deep*) with Poetic, Prince Paul, and Frukwan. That group pioneered what critics call horrorcore due to its mix of hardcore gangsta rap, heavy metal, and horror movie imagery. There's a twisted and dark sense of humor to it, which you can see from the aliases those guys adopted: the Undertaker (Prince Paul), the Gatekeeper (Frukwan), the Grym Reaper (Poetic), and the RZArector (RZA).

As far as all of these projects went, I supported the whole group and didn't think about when my time would come. If one of us won, we all won, and if each record did well, the bags being offered for every other solo record were going to keep getting heavier. It made sense for Dirty to go first; he was an undeniable character. And Meth had so much energy in what he was doing; he was very creative at the time. I was forever the loyal soldier and focused on boosting whatever album RZA was working on to make sure it was tough. Without getting in his way creatively, I tried to help him micromanage those albums and was very vocal with my opinions. I tried to help RZA see how he could best let each artist's personality shine through, whether it was with beat selection or suggesting how verses and hooks could be improved.

I was definitely critical, but it's because I've always wanted everyone to be fly. I laid back and paid attention; I was the one who would quote their own verses back to my brothers to remind them of their illest moments so that they would shoot higher. I was a mascot and a general manager at the same time. I would tell niggas when I didn't like something, and most of the time, the other brothers would agree with me. I know sometimes I made dudes feel judged and uncomfortable and it put me into situations, but I had to be honest because all I cared about was seeing every single one of us be the best we could be. I never wanted my brothers to forget that we were now regarded as one of New York's most interesting groups of all time. That was a championship trophy we had to respect and hold. You have to remember, we'd been working hard at it, but it happened nearly overnight and none one of us were even twenty-five yet.

I looked at us like a rookie team that had gone all the way, so we owed it to ourselves and our legacy to be our best. I took it real serious when RZA turned to me one day and said, "You ready? You're coming next."

To tell the truth, I wasn't sure I was ready. I was comfortable with my position, but there was no way in hell I was gonna let Wu-Tang down.

I'd always gotten along real well with Steve Rifkind and made sure he was taken care of when he was around. Whenever he came to the studio now and again, I'd chill with him and show him my appreciation, and since some of the members weren't as approachable, he and I were able to form a closer friendship than he had with a lot of the guys. I was always comfortable talking to Steve, so I became a bit of a mouthpiece for the group. I also learned a lot about marketing and promotion from him. I guess I shouldn't have been surprised, but I was honored when RZA told me that Loud was ready to give me a solo album deal for half a million dollars.

At the time I'd have been happy with thirty thousand, so this was a fucking good day. I was nervous, though, because my album was coming up behind Dirty's and Meth's, so my shit had to be hot. I enjoyed rocking and rolling with the team, but damn I wasn't sure I was ready to be out front alone. I was comfortable hyping the crowds with Ghost by my side, because I knew my brothers were at my back. A solo career put it all on the line, with no one there to carry you if it went wrong. I started thinking long and hard about what my album had to be.

Out on tour, cliques formed within our group, and those bonds remained once we got home. GZA and Masta Killa had been tight already, so that wasn't new; Method and U-God were close and they got closer; RZA, Dirty, and GZA were always a unit because they were family; and Deck kind of did his thing. The biggest change was that me and Ghost got to be good friends. We bunked up on the road when hotels didn't have enough rooms for all of us, and we started spending our time on the bus occupying the back lounge together.

I remember the day the tour bus rolled into L.A. for the first time. He and I were in the lounge, looking out the windows, starting at palm trees, loving the sunshine, and I remember counting all the Mercedes-Benzes I saw driving up Wilshire, thinking about which model I was going to buy myself one day.

"Yo, I just fucking love it," Ghost said.

"Yo, I was just thinking that," I said.

We continued to show each other our rhymes and push each other to go harder, so the one thing I knew about my solo album was that I wanted Ghost all over it. Having my brother from the Clan involved would give me the confidence and swagger I needed to pull off a classic. RZA loved the idea, knowing that through my album, Ghost would get more attention than he'd ever had. My record would be the springboard for a Ghost solo joint.

It just made sense. We were the guys on tour who went shopping together. We were the pair up at the front of the stage like Dapper Dans, rocking Clarks Wallabees, the same style hats, and the same fly gear. We were the Wu-Tang Energizer Bunnies; we had a different hype vibe than Dirty, but we brought the same level of excitement to the live show. The videos for "C.R.E.A.M." and "Can It All Be So Simple." were huge at the time, and those featured the two of us big. Those were song tracks, rather than lyrical recitals, and in concert, with those sing-along choruses, the audience felt that shit.

A lot of the imagery in the music videos that went with those songs came from my ideas and suggestions too. I was there giving a lot of input when Hype Williams and Little X were editing, which is to say that I was definitely a pain in they ass because I cared about what was going on as much as the director. To be real, I wanted to be the director. The way I saw it, they wouldn't have a job that day if it wasn't for me, so I had every right to see the angles they were shooting and to oversee everything. I let it be when it wasn't a song I was featured on, but when it was, I was all over that shit. When it came to the video for "C.R.E.A.M.," I went so far as to have all my Virginia niggas roll up with their cars, so we had Lexuses, Infinitis, and I even made RZA come correct with his Mazda MPV because I referenced it in my verse.

As you can imagine, I was coming at my solo album with even greater concern and focus. Ghost and I got to chopping it up and decided to approach it not as my record featuring Ghost but as a duo joint, like an EPMD album. RZA was down with that and we both agreed we'd let on any Wu members who wanted to get on the album. Now it was time to turn to the content. Ghost had been admiring my pen and my lyrics for some time, which were straight from the pages of my life—a life he was still living for the most part. Ghost was a bad boy from the badlands who hung out with a crazy crew, and since we'd gotten signed, he was still wiling out more than any of us. Like I told you, Stapleton niggas would rob you while Park Hill niggas were just out to make money, so it was in his blood. The way I saw it, I was Al Capone to Ghost's Frank Nitti, and that's how I characterized us as a duo. That image clicked with me, and I began to think of the album as our version of *The Godfather*.

"You know, the way you put your rhymes together, you taught me without even teaching me," Ghost said to me one day.

That was a big compliment. I had never tried to teach Ghost to rhyme because I didn't have to. He had that. I just got him thinking in a Mafia-inspired criminal cadence, which was my vision, since I thought of the Clan as our own mob, complete with a similar type of loyalty. In fact, I wanted to call the album *Wu Gambinos* to really bring it with the Mafia imagery. That was my working title, and that's what Steve Rifkind and everyone at Loud planned for the album to be called—until Steve's father, Jules, who had been a music mogul since the 1950s, got a call. As Steve related the story to me, his father got a phone call from "someone in the family" with the message that the Gambinos were not going to allow their name in my album title. So I changed my mind on that real quick, and kept it as a song title only.

When I thought deeper about the Wu, I realized we were the type of crew who fought and argued amongst ourselves, but nobody could pop our link and break our chain, which gave me the idea of the title: *Only Built 4 Cuban Linx*. In case you don't know, Cuban links are the biggest, strongest gold chains money can buy, and they don't break if a nigga tries to snatch your chain. The dudes who wore Cuban links were drug dealers and hustlers—every single one of them niggas with guns, money, and cars. Cuban links were the chains I noticed on the dudes I looked up to growing up; the guys with everything I wanted. It was the perfect title because my album was gonna be about getting money, living large, shining and flexing. My album title could not be ordinary. It had to be over the top.

Ghost, a stone-cold crook, felt it, and the moment we got our heads around the name and image, we were off to the races. The title technically came from a freestyle Ghost used to spit, which went something like "Built for Cuban links niggas who pull strings, sporting pieces of ice carved in rinks."

I told RZA the album was going to be Mafia, mob shit. It was going to be my story, real serious, and RZA was down. I started watching *Scarface*, *Across 110th Street*, and *Godfather* nonstop for inspiration.

I decided to give Ghost half of my entire album advance because I wanted him to really feel like we were a duo, and because I've always been about my team. Later on I wondered if I was crazy, because that nigga wasn't even from my neighborhood, but when it came down to being creative, Ghost was by my side so it made sense. Our creative appreciation was already so strong that I'd let him have one of the best rhymes in my notebook long before we even got started on my shit:

Yo, back on the block, rocking graveyard rocks,
One chain of pain on the block.
So I'm fed up son, trying to keep my head up, word up, Paul.

Ghost loved that rhyme so much that I let him have it, and he brought it on all kinds of freestyle shows. He loved my rhymes and he loved me—and I felt that love—so giving him a piece of my pie felt natural.

We started talking about how so many of our favorite artists, from Marvin Gaye to Stevie Wonder, Luther Vandross, and the O'Jays, had done their best work by getting away from home to a foreign location. We decided to do the same and made plans to write the record in Barbados. We told RZA to give us whatever beats he thought suited our vibe and said that we'd bring him back an album.

"Why you choosing Barbados?" he asked.

Ghost and I just wanted to be near water and trees because both of those things made us calm and happy.

"Yo, that's dope," RZA said. "Yo, I'd want to be there too. Just make sure you come back with some shit."

We scheduled eight weeks to write the entire album, and I was all over RZA for beats before we left. I wanted to paint a picture, and I wanted unusual shit. I told him the beats needed to glide and the tracks had to flow, because I wanted people to feel like they were watching *Scarface* through their headphones. I wasn't writing songs for the club—I didn't see no one dancing to my shit—but they were going to hear it fucking bumping out of every Acura, Jeep, Benz, and

Bentley rolling down the block. My shit would be played in luxury vehicles only.

When we landed in Barbados, the only thing that lived up to our expectation was the sun, the breeze, the trees, and the ocean. The rest of it was whack. The place the label booked for us was clean and decent, but it was mediocre, like a three-star. Fuck it, no problem. We had the water and the sound of the ocean outside the window, so everything was cool by me. I could see waves rolling in, I could smell the sea, and it was beautiful.

The staff were all black and they were really polite, asking us where we were from and bringing us everything we needed, like tooth-brushes, which both of us forgot. Ghost fell in love with the warmth of the staff the way I fell in love with the natural beauty of the island. We were going to be there awhile, so we got to know the people who worked there. We weren't too happy about it when we went down-stairs one morning and caught a manager, this white guy, screaming at one of the employees in a very degrading manner. We didn't say nothing and minded our business, but we were bothered. I can un-derstand correcting your employee if you're a manager, but it can be done with respect, which is not the way this asshole was doing it and it didn't sit right with us.

Over the next few days, the brothers on staff that we got to know told us that working in that hotel and in Barbados in general was some version of that every day. We could not stop talking about it, and we weren't getting any writing done because we were upset about giving our money to a racist hotel. The staff was nice and we tipped them generously, but in good conscience we couldn't stay someplace like that for two months. We didn't even want to see those interac-tions, so we just holed up in our room. Every time a new staffer came with our meals, we'd ask them in to talk and the stories just got worse.

We stayed a couple more days, vibing on the terrace and looking at that perfect still water, which was like a mirror at night reflecting the stars and the moon. In that environment, with RZA's beats on our radio, we got some shit done, but not much. We started working on "Rainy Dayz," going back and forth on the verses as the beat pulsed like the waves. That was a moment.

The next morning, when we caught one of the housekeepers crying in the hallway, that was it for us. She told us she'd been screamed at and just couldn't take it anymore and was going to quit. Ghost gave her some money and told her not to worry, because he was like that. He was the most 'hood motherfucker ever, but with a heart of gold.

We went down and cursed out the manager and everyone at the front desk until they asked us to leave by the next morning. We told the label we had to change locales, and when they asked us where we wanted to be, me and Ghost looked at each other at the same time and said, "Miami."

We landed in South Beach and checked into a boutique hotel called the Pelican, which was fine. It is a restored art deco hotel from the fifties with vintage-style furniture and music posters in the rooms, which was cool I guess. Even though it hadn't been that long since I'd been crashing in stash houses, I wasn't impressed with it. Back then there weren't really five-star spots on the beach, so it was fine for what we needed, and the water was right across the street. I couldn't complain about that. We got a nice big suite with two double beds, bunked up like we were on tour, and fell right into a groove.

We'd get some drinks and smoke and put on a beat and each go to our corner and start writing, handling it like we were studying for the SAT. We'd take a break for lunch, go down to the beach, maybe take a nap on a lounge chair, then we'd head back and write until we broke for dinner at eight o'clock. We'd compare verses, we'd go over each man's contribution line for line, working to perfect everything we were going to give the world.

Ghost was a very cautious and slow writer, sometimes working on one verse or just a few bars for an entire session. I was taking the process so seriously that to tell the truth, I got writer's block. It wasn't that I wasn't writing, I just wasn't satisfied with my rhymes. I'd write four or five bars, decide I didn't like the direction, and crumple up my piece of paper. It got to the point that Ghost started picking them up and saving the good ones, giving them back to me once I'd stopped trippin.'

I finally broke the fear that was holding me back when we started writing the song that would become "Knuckleheadz." I had been thinking about the neighborhood, thinking about the streets, still feeling overwhelmed with what we were trying to do when some lines came to me clear as day.

> Laying on the crime scene, sippin' fine wines,
> Pulling nines on UFOs, taking they fly clothes, they eyes closed.

I was sitting in Miami and I could feel that ocean breeze through our open doors, but in my mind I was back on the block, back in my hustling days, robbing and stealing. I should probably explain that UFO was our term for "unidentified flying ones," which were niggas we didn't know who we saw around our 'hood. We'd say, "Who's that UFO over there?" Back in the day we'd stay in front of this famous weed spot in our 'hood, waiting to stick up UFOs. If nobody knew you, you'd better hope you were quick enough to hop out your cab, get upstairs to get your weed, and get back in your cab before one of us saw you.

This was the moment that the entire record kicked off, because starting has always been the hardest part for me as a writer. With those lines under my belt, mentally I was in the right place, thinking about robbing dudes for their clothes when I was a young hooligan.

> We gettin' loot, no doubt, check the word of mouth,
> Unheard about, guns go off, now we're on the murder route.
> I'm out, my raps play the part like a *Get Smart* secret agent
> In a maze and style's blazing

It was tight, it was choppy, and Ghost loved what I was doing and came with some choppy lines of his own.

Who's the knucklehead wanting respect?
Chop his fingers in the drug game, money well-known.
Lead singer, humdinger, flash is the aftermath,
Here's his photograph.

It was the epitome of how we flowed together, which was always short and tight rhymes, not the loping style of somebody like Slick Rick. We drove each other forward, like with each rhyme our rhythm was saying to the other man, "check it, keep up with me." We called that "impressing the pen," and that is what drove us.

Some sessions we'd stop and look at each other and take a minute to say, "Yo man, our shit is so different!" What was really different was how each of us went at writing to get to the place where our shit came together. Ghost was so organized; he showed up with a hundred dollars' worth of nice composition books and pens, ready to go. He used to write in a graffiti style too, so when he'd hand me his pad it looked like it was all in script. I think I had two spiral notebooks at most and used whatever pen I could get my hands on. And I already told you how I write from the corner down and rip papers out of my pad as I go.

Each morning we'd get up and go down the street to this spot to have tuna melts on sourdough bread. Ghost is the pickiest eater alive, so he might get the tuna melt and a bunch of other stuff, not knowing which one he wanted. I'd always get on him asking if he was gonna eat it all.

"Hell yeah."

Whenever he didn't finish something, he'd save it. He's the only dude I ever met with composition books filled with dope-ass rhymes next to old sandwiches in his bag. Later in the day he'd pull the shit out, all full of mayonnaise, black pepper, and lettuce, and I'd be like, "Yo, that shit is six hours old, you gonna eat that?" He'd already be chewing it, like, "Yo, this shit is good." My brother Ghost is a very weird character.

We fell into a creative rhythm, having our drinks, our smoke—whatever we needed to charge our batteries—while we went through the beats and wrote the songs. We started to feel when it was time to switch books and share what we'd been writing to see if a song was coming together. We'd recite each other's rhymes to figure out how they should flow, and how they'd sit next to each other. Sometimes we might have nothing but eight lines good enough to keep, sometimes four verses and even the hook. Focused as I was, I was inspired and thankful to be doing this every day. Never in my life would I have dreamed I'd be a guy who went somewhere exotic to write an album.

I also learned to take the art of writing more seriously, and I have Ghost to thank for that. I'd only written moment to moment, tossing my rhyme papers out afterward. Ghost taught me to have patience and more respect for what I was doing. He made me realize that good shit might come fast, but incredible shit only came with dedication and time. We were on a mission to make a classic, and doing it brought us closer than we'd ever been. Every time Ghost or I didn't feel like the creativity was right, we'd close the session and watch some gangster movies for inspiration. Our regulars were our two favorite John Woo joints, *The Killer* and *A Better Tomorrow*; *Once Upon a Time in America*; *Miller's Crossing*; and of course *Scarface* and *The Godfather* 1 and 2.

One of the toughest tracks we wrote in Miami was "Rainy Dayz," which became one of my favorites on the album. The beat was something different and our rhymes were outside the box. We focused on that beat for three days before the song came together. We didn't get frustrated or move on because we knew it was going to be special. We spent an evening sitting on the balcony, taking in the ocean breeze, Ghost drinking beers, me smoking a blunt. When we went back in the room, Ghost came with the lines that set it off: "On rainy days I sit back and count ways on / How to get rich, son, show and prove, ask my bitch." It took Ghost a while to come up with the rest, but that didn't matter; he had set the tone, and the idea of the song began to take shape in our minds. Part of what we did regularly for inspiration was study the 120 Lessons, and there is some knowledge informing my verse in "Rainy Dayz."

> What brings rain, hail, snow and earthquakes?
> The beat breaks, cause all my niggas to break, son.
> Styles is similar to criminals locked up
> With gats, ghetto tabernacles is fucked up.
> I live once, though the mind stays infinite.

There is a question inside the lessons about what brings rain, hail, snow, and earthquakes, so that is where I started. And I let my mind go free, ranging over more philosophical ground. My verse represented more than the drug life; it was about everything black people go through. The hardest people who get treated badly are really kings and queens because of their struggles. If you can maintain yourself through hardship you can overcome your misery with mental harmony. I completed my verse and thought it was dope, but I didn't think it fit into the song. I was about to toss it when Ghost stopped me.

"Yo, you killin' it, keep going."

He was right. In that verse I connected the hardships of being black to what happens to blacks in the penal system. And most important, how a mind filled with knowledge will never break and always be free. I'm glad Ghost encouraged me, because this wasn't me just rapping, this was me breaking down words and elements of the rhyme. I was building my rhyme the way members of the Nation built knowledge when we got together. "Rainy Dayz" felt like something that hadn't been done before, and once we'd gotten all our rhymes down, it was one I couldn't wait to take back to RZA.

I stayed on the same type of mood with the song "Knowledge God," which I had a vision for and did by myself while Ghost worked on other things. This track was unique because I came up with the hook first, which never happens when I write a song. Most artists are the opposite, writing choruses or hooks before they create the verses. This one came to me as I was thinking about niggas in the 'hood getting money, and about how opportunities fly by motherfuckers because they're so lost in drugs, violence, and poverty that they don't see it in front of them. I was in the mind-state of wanting to help dudes through my music but knowing you can't help everybody, which is an ongoing problem in our communities. How can you help someone who don't want to help themselves?

"Knowledge God" comes from the number 17, knowledge being 1 and God being 7.

Yo, why my niggas always yelling that broke shit?
Let's get money son, now you wanna smoke shit
Chill, God, yo, the son don't chill, Allah
What's today's mathematics, son? Knowledge God.

The hook is about the mathematics, but it's also about brothers who don't know their own power, which I've seen too much of in the projects. I've seen too many trying to eat off of what other people got and jeopardizing themselves to get it rather than doing something to help themselves.

It wasn't all work and no play in Miami; Ghost and I definitely hit the clubs. DJ Tony Touch was out there and he was a friend of ours, and we hit the town quite a few nights. We also went shopping in South Beach, hitting up Versace to buy flashy shirts and clothes, dressing like the flyest drug dealers we knew to get in the spirit of the album we were writing. Ghost had some of his Wallabees sent down from New York so he could stay fly. He and I loved Wallabees so much that we did a skit about them on *Cuban Linx*. We had a rule that you had seventy-two hours on a new pair and after that, you couldn't wear them no more—they were hand-me-downs. Fresh Clarks meant the gum sole was clean, and once they started getting dirty, they didn't look the same. Ghost was so into the Wallabees, dude had a Chinese guy on Staten Island who would dye them for him. He had every color, two-tones, fades—all of it. The two of us set that trend off for sure.

We left Miami with about 80 percent of the verses and hooks written, and finished the rest in RZA's basement studio in Staten Island. We were proud of it, and RZA liked what he heard too. The record was different from any of the Wu-Tang albums the world had heard. Wu-Tang material was supreme lyricism filtered through our philosophy, which combined our love of karate flicks and the knowledge of the Five Percent Nation. My album was more personal, based on my life, Ghost's life, and real-life situations that 'hood nig-gas knew all too well. It was who we were and what we'd lived, fil-tered through all the shit that mattered to hustlers: gangster films, fly clothes, jewelry, cars, and a code of honor. Our shit was relatable; it was tales of the 'hood we knew, half Park Hill and half Stapleton. But those stories and characters could have come from any project community in America.

The way I saw it, making the album was like building a man-sion, brick by brick from the ground up. Ghost and I became best friends creating it too: once we got back we would be on the phone for hours talking about fine-tuning the album, talking about life. I'm a talker myself, but Ghost could outlast me on the phone every time. I realized I was his true confidant when he told me he'd gotten with Aaliyah like it was no big thing. My man Ghost was always a quiet lover boy.

At home, Ghost returned to running with his crew, doing what he was doing. I got back to my life as we started working on the next phase of the record with RZA. After another couple months, the music and lyrics were ready to be put down on tape, except for the fact that I had a hard time remembering my flows. This had never been an issue for me because I'd always written my rhymes and dropped them on the track almost as soon as I finished them. So there I was with a notebook full of verses, getting frustrated at myself every day in the vocal booth because nothing was flowing out of me the way I remembered it. When you're writing you keep saying a rhyme over and over again until you find the flow that matches your verse. I had just written a number of songs to different beats in a short period of time, so it made sense that I forgot a few flows. It wasn't a good place to be, but I was learning. I had never approached rhymes and songwriting the way I just had, so in a way, everything was new to me. I wished I had learned to use the type of shorthand RZA did in his lyric books: he'd put dashes next to a line or verse so he'd remember the rhythm. With the album deadline coming and RZA's schedule booked solid, the pressure was on.

Every time I got in the booth, I couldn't find the bounce I'd had in Miami and I didn't know what to do. With the clock ticking, we started skipping around, working on different songs, rather than seeing through one at a time, because I couldn't get my verses the way I wanted them. To relieve some of the pressure and to help get my groove back, I started partying a bit more than usual, sniffing coke. To tell the truth, I had a little bit of a habit, but I never let anyone know because I never wanted them to say I was falling off. I was taking bumps here and there all by myself but showed up to the studio looking fresh so that nobody caught on. I'd get to the studio a little high and then tell them to get me something to sniff, as if it was my first line of the day. My habit wasn't too crazy; I'd probably blow through half an ounce in three or four months, but still, that ain't dabblin'. It went with the *Scarface* theme of the record, and I started playing the part. During recording, more than a few times guys were like, "Okay, man, step off your own dick for a minute and come back down to earth."

I heard them, but by the same token, all I cared about was making the best record I could, no matter what. It had to be one for the real niggas, the ones I'd known who weren't here no more. The ones who paved the way, the stand-up niggas who'd gotten killed and the ones who went away and came home different. It was for the niggas who got rich, for the niggas who avenged their fallen soldiers, for the niggas the cops couldn't catch and the ones they did, for the ones who stacked until the feds came. My album was for all of them.

It hit home even more because Ghost had a couple of friends who went away that year to do real time. My right-hand man, Supreme, and another good friend, Tyree, went away too. Ghost and I realized we had a mutual friend who went away that year: C. Allah, the outlaw brother who educated me in the supreme knowledge of self when I was younger. It turned out that C. Allah was Ghost's cousin, which blew both of our minds when we realized it. It brought us even closer.

All of this was on my mind: my stories, Ghost's stories, and the tales of so many we knew as we got to finishing the album. Like I told you, I was stuck, having some problems tapping into the creativity I'd found in Miami. But it all came around for me the day I wrote "Incarcerated Scarfaces." This was another time the hook came to me first, because I was thinking about all my friends in prison doing hard time, and the fact that we called real hustlers Scarface niggas after the movie. Scarface niggas rose from nothing, got real money, and weren't afraid to bust a gun. Of course there's only two ways a Scarface nigga's story ends, one is in the title of my song, and the other is dead, shot to pieces like Tony Montana.

I was at RZA's house one morning and heard a beat he was making downstairs and caught a vibe. I grabbed a chair and sat down in a corner, and before I knew it, everything that was on my mind about my locked-up friends flowed out of me. After we got that song down, I felt like we had the heart of the record complete. I felt confident about finishing everything else and telling the stories that needed to be told.

This album was going to be a showcase for me and Ghost, but there was one guy coming up who I really wanted to feature, a dude from Queens named Nasty Nas. Tell you the truth, the first time someone told me his name, I thought they'd said Nasty Knives, so I pictured a ninja nigga throwing knives and thought, "He's gonna fit right in." I heard his track "Halftime" in the film *Zebrahead* and was like, "Damn, this guy's got it. He's a bad nigga."

I was with Ghost the first time I heard that song, hanging out with these two wild white girls from London that we knew. They were fans of ours, and when they came to New York they'd take us out. Both of us wanted to fuck them so bad. That English accent was so damn sexy, but they weren't giving it up. That was cool with us because they paid for everything and drove us around, and they always had dope mixtapes on them. And that's where we heard Nas for the first time. I loved his flow and his style because he wore the same hats I wore, and we had the same haircut. He was from the Queensbridge projects, and he was straight ill.

We met in person at a Wu show in L.A., and it felt like I'd known him for years, like he was a little brother. We bonded over the half-moon Caesar cut we were both rocking, and he'd had it since he was a kid just like me. I remember telling him I was going to come find his barber in Queens because I was always hunting for good barbers. I called Ghost over and we all started goofing around immediately. The love was flowing both ways, and Nas and I started hanging out as friends all the time back home. So when it came time to do my record, I knew he'd be down. We both showed each other our neighborhoods. At the time I had my blue Acura with the white seats, all custom with rims, and when Nas came to see me the first time he had the brand-new Lexus ES300 in gold, which was dope.

The night he dropped his verse I remember we first went to a Chinese restaurant on Staten Island from which some niggas I knew did sales. I would never have brought him anywhere that wasn't safe, but we ordered our chicken and fried rice watching niggas stacking money, with TEC-9s on them, dudes coming in and out, dropping off cash after making sales down the block. Nas had never really seen me like that, so he was like, "damn." But it was cool. We got our food and went over to RZA's place, which was in a more suburban area on the other side of town with no bad guys around. Then we got into it.

Ghost was there, and we had chosen a RZA beat for the track we wanted Nas on, so we thought that if the vibe was right we might get it done that night. I hadn't written anything, but Ghost had a verse in the making which he rapped to us. We hung out for about eight hours, just chillin', eating our Chinese food and rolling up blunts, sipping Hennessy, and listening to some of the tracks destined for *Cuban Linx*. I think we played him "Incarcerated Scarfaces," "Criminology," "Knowledge God," "Guillotines," and "Rainy Dayz." He was blown away by the production. After a while RZA threw on the beat that Ghost and I had set aside for the track with Nas.

"Oh, shit, that is serious!" Nas said.

"See?" I said. "I told you."

I figured we'd get some writing done and see where things went, but Nas was already feeling it.

"Yo, I'm ready to keep this going. I'm ready to fuck around," he said.

"Yo, go in there to the booth," RZA said. "Whenever you're ready, let's do it."

Nas was inspired, man. He had so many rhymes, throwing out multiple verses and multiple versions—just pure creation. *Illmatic* was out and he was getting hot, and I already knew Nas was special, but in that moment I saw the future and knew for sure he was the next golden child of hip-hop. At the time features on records were happening, but they weren't what they became by the late nineties. Wu-Tang didn't do highlights because we had so many dope and diverse rappers in our group already. But Nas was different and the only rapper in New York worth that shine.

After he laid all this down, he looked at us and said, "I don't really know which one I want to do, but this is the direction."

"Go through whatever you got to," I said. "Just fuck around for a minute and go with whichever verse you really feeling."

"All right, cool."

He went back in, did a verse, didn't like it, and started a new one. And that's when he came with this:

Through the lights, cameras and action, glamor, glitters, and gold
I unfold the scroll, plant seeds to stampede the globe

Ghost and I looked at each other and burst into grins because that shit was sick. Nothing he had said before came close to those bars. He saw us smiling at him in the booth, like, "yeah nigga!" and he stopped.

"Yo, is that it? Y'all like that?" He was trying to please us, and he had. RZA was nodding at him too.

"That is it my nigga! That's the one, keep goin'!" I shouted.

Nas's first take was perfect, but he spit it again comfortably. He fell right in with us too. He even came up with a mafioso-type alias, Nas Escobar, in keeping with what we were doing on the album. Once Nas's verse was done, there was no doubt that he was going first on the track, but it inspired me. So right then and there I wrote my own verse and got in the booth. And Ghost came after me and sealed it off. There is so much street poetry and knowledge on that track, all from dudes in their prime, all of us in our mid-twenties but speaking like much wiser, grown men. When the night was through I knew that track was going to be one of the highlights of the album.

Another great studio moment was putting the finishing touches on "Rainy Dayz." We loved our verses and we loved the beat, but we needed a skit and a hook to tie it all up. Like I told you, Ghost and I watched the John Woo flick *The Killer* a lot, and we were infatuated with the singer who gets blinded by the Killer by accident. RZA told us we couldn't use the sample of her singing in the song, and we did not want to hear that. So RZA called Blu Raspberry, who had sung hooks on our other projects, and told her to listen to the dialogue we'd recorded from the film and to vibe on it. Twenty-five minutes later Blue had it, perfect from the start: "It's raining, he's changing / My man is going insane, insane." We started jumping up and down when we heard it.

RZA thought we were done, but we weren't. "Yo, man, y'all mother-fuckers is crazy, man. What y'all missing now?"

"We need birds in the back or something," I said.

I went into the booth and started making bird noises, but thank God RZA didn't go with those. He found some dope bird sounds and mixed them in.

"All right we got that, now we need something like rain," Ghost said.

I thought RZA was gonna kill us, but he did it, and when it was all done, I think he saw the wisdom in our ways. We definitely pushed his patience to the limit, though, with the skits we put on the album. He gave us two days to do them all, because we were past our due date, and if we were any later we'd miss our release and fuck up all the shit the label had already set up to make the album pop off. RZA insisted that we didn't need so many, but Ghost and I didn't see it like that. We'd admired what Dre had done with skits on the N.W.A albums, *The Chronic*, and *Doggystyle*, which were some of the best albums of the era. The skits brought personality to an album, and we felt like that was missing from ours. We wanted our skits—with the movie quotes and all the slang—to elevate the record to the cinematic level we were aiming for. *Cuban Linx* was never going to be a collection of singles; it was going to be an experience. We wanted to take our listeners on a trip through the lives of the ultimate drug-dealing crooks and hustlers.

"Yo, y'all niggas is OD'ing with the fucking skits, bro," RZA said to us. Ghost had his love letter to Wallabees, we had the moody introductory skit of "Rainy Dayz," and a whole lot more.

"For sure, but it's all a part of what we stand for, RZA," I said. "Just let it be. C'mon man, this is how we want it."

But RZA wasn't having it when it came to one track. "I think it's all too much, but I'll do it. I'll do everything you want, but I am not letting y'all put no fucking voices over the beginning of 'Guillotine,' you hear me?"

Tell you the truth, we were planning on it. "Guillotine" is Wu-heavy (what we called a "Sesame Street" track because it had all the familiar characters), featuring Deck and GZA, and we were ready to come up with some good shit in the booth for that one. But I get why RZA put his foot down. He wanted it to link it up with the group by putting some Shaolin karate movie quotes on the front end, tying it all back to the origins. He even mixed the karate piece with a bit of Ghost talking about slappin' niggas that he had from an unused *36 Chambers* session, so it was a perfect compromise.

I wasn't there when Ghost did a lot of his final vocals on the record because he and I were on different schedules. Like I said, he dove right back into his old ways—doing shit like punching 'hood niggas in the mouth, so he came irregularly and at off-hours. Since he'd been away, motherfuckers were making him feel like he wasn't that nigga no more. Dudes get jealous and shit, and I remember him telling me every now and then, "You've got to come back to the neighborhood and punch niggas in they face to let niggas know." I hated to see him slip backwards, but he wasn't holding things up. He was getting his vocals done, just not at the same times as me. He was smoking wet, but he'd done it for so many years that he could control it. He thought it made his lyrical style stronger, the way Jimi Hendrix used acid to take his playing to another level. At the time Ghost's pen game was so strong I couldn't argue with his methods. Besides, I was in my *Scarface* chamber with my cocaine one-on-ones, so how was I gonna judge him?

The last important decision on the album I made by myself, and I had to fight for it. It had to do with the last song, "North Star (Jewels)," which is very different: it's slow, no drums, not a typical hip-hop track—and I loved it. RZA never really had an interest in it and didn't think it belonged on the album at all. To me it had a vibe like a slow-motion scene in a film where an innocent kid witnesses a murder while he's just sitting there eating a candy bar. It captured that feeling you get when you see a life-changing event like that, when time slows down and you take in every detail. RZA and I fought about this for an hour and a half until finally he gave in.

"Yo, man fuck it," he said. "That will be the outro of the album if that's what you want."

I wasn't giving up because this was my album, and he had to respect that. Everybody could make their albums the way they wanted, but this was mine—he had to let me make it the way I wanted. When we sequenced the album, we thought of it as sections of three songs that went together, each building on the next. We spent a long time debating those selections too.

I was super-passionate about everything because this album wasn't necessarily for fans of the Wu or other artists down with the Wu; it was for the real hustlers. It was for the few we knew that could relate to it because they'd lived that life. There were some other gangster-style rappers bubbling up in hip-hop at the time, like Mobb Deep, Biggie, Capone-N-Noreaga, Cam'ron, and Mase. They just made me competitive and determined to make the ultimate drug dealer album that nobody could touch. When we were done, I knew we'd done that.

I wanted the album to stand out in every way, so I went to Steve Rifkind and told him I wanted the cassette version to be brightly colored so it was easy to find among the pile of tapes people had in their homes and on the floor of their cars. CDs where one thing, because if there was art printed on them, you could still tell them apart from each other when they were out of the case. But tapes, which were still popular in '95, all looked the same: when they came out of their case, most of them were either clear or beige. I told Steve I wanted mine to be the color of money. The manufacturer didn't have that; they could only make it in clear, red, yellow, or purple. Now, you'd think that since the album cover was red that I'd choose red, but I didn't, I chose purple. Purple is the color of royalty, and to tell you the truth, I'd never seen a purple cassette tape, so I knew it would be different. Steve was there for me and believed in the album. He agreed when I pointed out that having a colored tape like this tied into the subject matter, because it echoed the way street dealers use special packaging to differentiate their product from their competitors. He did have to stay on budget though, so he offered to pay for a limited edition run of ten thousand purple cassettes. Once again his marketing mind was ahead of his time: by limiting the run to ten thousand, the "Purple Tape," as it came to be called, became a collector's item. Original copies of it go for over a thousand dollars today on eBay, and in 2012 we reissued a special edition of it that came in a luxury watch box (along with liner notes and a book of lyrics) to honor the twentieth anniversary of *Cuban Linx*.

What Ghost and I created was a hustler record that did more than talk about being fly and getting money. We were the first to be truthful about our feelings, and for all the bragging, we talked honestly about the hardship and pain that comes with the life of a hustler and life in the ghetto. In that way I felt we honored all the old-school artists who inspired us, while creating something new. Considering all the rappers that followed in our footsteps, from Jay-Z to Fat Joe to Biggie, I'd say we were the ones who set it off. I felt like I managed to represent every side of myself too. When I look at the album, I see Raekwon the MC, the scientist, the poet, the drug-dealing rapper, the scholar—I see myself as a fucking bag of vitamins giving rap an energy boost. But more than anything, this album was a success to me because it helped the dudes that inspired it. All the guys we reference on the record in one way or another—all our friends in prison—this album reached them. And whether we heard from them sooner or later, they all told us that it gave them and so many other brothers doing bids the strength to go on. They no longer felt forgotten, and that meant a lot to me. We heard about niggas getting into fights, cutting each other over copies of the Purple Tape. It became like a bible inside prisons across America. And to me, that was worth more than royalties, sold-out shows, or five mics in the *Source*.

CHAPTER 12

WHAT DO YOU BELIEVE IN, HEAVEN OR HELL?

I aimed to make a classic, and I did it. *Cuban Linx* was a masterpiece nobody could front on. It didn't sell out and try to make any dance records; it was all street. I was the guy from "C.R.E.A.M." and "Can It All Be So Simple," the one who hit ya with sixteen shots and more on "Protect Ya Neck." People knew what I was about and now they knew what I could do standing on my own.

"One thing I got to tell you," RZA said to me one day after we'd finished the album, "you and your man Ghost, out of all the music the group got right now, your album might be the most influential of them all. This album gonna make other niggas try to start sounding like y'all."

"You mean that?" I asked. "I feel that in my heart, but is that how you feel? You think this gonna mark a new era?"

RZA looked me dead in my face and said, "Yeah, y'all did something different. Y'all did something special here."

It felt so good knowing he believed in what we'd set out to do. This was my friend, the man who saw talent in me in the first place and called on me to help him make both of our dreams come true. RZA's praise gave me such pride. He made me feel like I could be an icon of a new era the way Rakim, Slick Rick, and Big Daddy Kane had been. I was on top of the world, and in terms of my status within the Clan, if we were the mob, I was a boss now. I was a made man.

We'd really hit the target musically, so even if the album didn't sell, I would have been happy with how I'd presented myself. Sales were important, but I wasn't worried about them as much as I was worried about respect. That's why there's an "only" in the title. My chamber might not be your chamber; this record was for the niggas who knew.

The thing was, the culture and the media agreed that we'd done something, and the sales reflected it too. We'd made a musical movie with me as the lead, Ghost as my supporting character, and RZA as the director of the whole masterpiece. We dropped August 1, 1995, and debuted at number four on the Billboard Top 200 Albums Chart and number two on the Billboard Hip Hop/R&B Chart. We moved 140,000 units our first week. Critics from newspapers like the *Los Angeles Times* to rock magazines like *Spin* understood what we were trying to do. Some of them compared me to legends like Kool G Rap and said that the *Linx* songs with my Wu-Tang brothers were as good or better than anything on *36 Chambers*. They said this was RZA at the top of his game and that Ghost and I brought out the best in each other. They said we'd dropped a full-blown album in a genre ruled by singles.

We were considered the new dons of something that came to be called mafioso rap, which was the East Coast version of West Coast gangsta rap. Generally, people think of Big Daddy Kane and Kool G Rap as starting it, but that fly, gritty, drug-dealing lyricism had died down until Ghost and I brought it back. One thing was for sure: our style was now on the rise. Nas's and Biggie's debuts had come out in 1994, Nas's boy AZ was coming up, and even Kool G Rap released a solo joint in 1995 in the same lane. A year later in 1996, Jay-Z got on with *Reasonable Doubt*, which took a page from our playbook in style and flow. On our own label, Steve Rifkind had signed Mobb Deep, who were right there too with *The Infamous* in 1995.

Ghost and I were real aware of this growing competition, particularly when it came to Brooklyn dudes like Biggie. When we started writing *Linx*, Meth had already been featured on Biggie's song "The What," on *Ready to Die*. I remember Meth playing that for us, and there's no denying the shit was dope. But at the same time, we were writing and recording, and I remember Ghost saying to me, "Man, fuck that shit. When our album is done that's gonna be the end of it." We knew we were about to crush the building, so everything else we heard was lukewarm to us. We had also heard what Biggie did with Super Cat back in '93 on "Dolly My Baby," but we weren't impressed with party records that were soft and commercial. We didn't care that by '95 that type of rap was starting to blow up the charts. We thought it was bullshit.

When Puff and Big were coming up and hanging with Super Cat, a guy we knew, we watched them change their style. They came out dressing regular at first, just sweatsuits and shit like everybody else, but then overnight they started wearing silk shirts and Versace suits, dressing the way Ghost and I already were. They definitely picked that up from Super Cat, because he's Jamaican and we'd picked up our style from the fly Jamaican hustlers. So we had our eye on them.

Now when we were doing our skits for the album, Ghost said some shit that definitely caused some waves amongst those in the know. Nas was our guy, and his debut *Illmatic* had come out in April 1994, featuring a picture of him as a little kid on the cover. Biggie's album *Ready to Die* came out in September 1994, featuring a picture of him as a little kid on the cover. Ghost was drunk and high, being real, and he said a bunch of shit that became the skit "Shark Niggas (Biters)": "Straight up, you got niggas biting off your album cover and shit," which raised some eyebrows in the studio and got us all smirking. Then he really went in, saying, "Niggas, niggas, niggas, niggas caught his little album cover, then done did a Nas for that shit."

If we had done our homework, we would have known that Nas and Biggie were friends. And if Meth had been in the studio that day, I'm sure he would have said, "Nah, I ain't gonna let you do that," or whatever because he and Big were close. The way we saw it was that Big was copying our boy Nas. When Ghost came out of the booth and we asked him if he wanted to keep it, he said, "Yeah, that's how I feel." So I backed him up and that's what it was.

Music is all about who did shit first, so Ghost was just trying to protect our little brother Nas's legacy, not knowing he might offend one of our Wu brother's people. It would have been a different scenario if we knew Biggie, but we had never met and really didn't give two shits about him right then. All we knew was that we were in competition because we'd grown up hearing about Brooklyn niggas. Brooklyn niggas will kill you, Brooklyn niggas will jab you, Brooklyn niggas is runnin' shit. It was always about Brooklyn and we were sick of it, definitely on some "fuck Brooklyn" shit out of jealousy. Growing up we constantly heard a saying: "Manhattan's making it, Brooklyn's taking it, Bronx creating it, Queens is faking it." That's every New York City borough but one, Staten Island, as if we didn't even exist. If you went to any hip-hop club in the city to see someone perform, it was only a matter of time until they shouted into the crowd, "Where Brooklyn at?" Ain't nobody ever asked where Staten Island at. That shit used to get to us so fucking mad.

People didn't have to ask where Staten Island was when the Clan started showing up to clubs with two hundred people behind us. And as for that skit "Shark Niggas," some people figured out that Ghost was opening on Big, but it never became a thing. Ghost and I never talked about it again, and since he didn't call anyone by name, the skit remained an item of speculation amongst hip-hop heads. Our group moved as a unit even when we didn't agree, so no one in the Clan ever said shit about it. If Meth had a mind to, he definitely could have. Meth was blowing up at the time. He was our pop star, and we used to call him our kid Michael Jackson, which he fucking hated.

"Yo, we know we're the Jackson Five and you're Michael, but get the fuck out of here with that shit, yo." We teased the shit out of him.

Meth might have been our pop star, but for the two first singles off my album, Ghost and I gave ourselves the pop star treatment. The first two singles were "Criminology" and "Glaciers of Ice," and we did a couple of videos that were legendary. I wanted to honor old-school gangsters like Vincent "the Chin" Gigante of the Genovese family, who I was a big fan of because he avoided prosecution for years by wandering around Greenwich Village in slippers, pajamas, and a bathrobe muttering to himself to support his lawyers' claim that he was insane. I told Ghost about him because I liked to gas Ghost up to do shit.

"Yo, nigga, you don't even need clothes on in our video," I said. "All you need to do is come out in a pair of Wallabees and a robe. That would be some gangsta shit."

"You right!"

So that's what he did, and Ghost has been wearing all sorts of extravagant robes since. I got myself a gold silk shirt, paid maybe four or five hundred dollars for it from an expensive Italian boutique down on Delancey Street, and we did our best to pay tribute to Rakim and his video for "I Ain't No Joke."

The album was successful in every way, but there was one moment above the rest that made me realize I had achieved something monumental. I had moved out to Inglewood, New Jersey, by then, into a condo near the George Washington Bridge. The location was perfect because in five minutes I could be in Harlem, and I'd just gotten myself a brand-new gold '95 Nissan Pathfinder to go with my Acura. Life was good—I was hearing my music on the radio every day. I remember waking up one morning at my new crib with my girl Candy. After I was shot, she and I were apart for a while, but once I got on with Wu-Tang and had a legitimate occupation away from the streets, she and I reconciled. We'd had a very loving relationship for years by this point. That morning I was happy, excited, and felt on top of the world, so I asked her nicely to make me breakfast.

"Yo, baby, I want some orange juice, turkey bacon, and grits, with an egg and cheese!"

Remember, she was African, so she didn't grow up with grits. In fact, she hated them and usually had oatmeal for breakfast.

"Baby, you just don't understand grits. I'm gonna show you," I said.

We went to the kitchen and I started showing her how to stir grits. You can't let them sit; you have to stay there stirring. She argued with me and I teased her, but at the same time, I didn't want my grits fucked up. All in all, it was a lovely scene and it felt like my birthday. Wendy Williams was live on the radio on Hot 97, and I remember telling my girl to keep stirring while I went to take a piss. So I'm in the bathroom, looking at myself in the mirror, admiring this little fly gold rope I had on, and that's when I heard Wendy talking about me before she played "Criminology."

"There's a new King of New York right now," she said. "And his name is Raekwon. This album *Only Built 4 Cuban Linx*, this is it. Raekwon is the new King of New York. He made this album with Ghostface Killah, and nobody has ever made an album of this magnitude and brought his boy along with him. This album is a classic."

I started bugging out. "Yo boo! They talking about me!"

My girl was still in her feelings over the grits, but what can I say? I like them a certain kind of way: cheese on the bottom, the grits over that, then black pepper and a sunny-side-up egg on top. Stir that all up, and there's no better way to eat grits. I learned it that way from my grandmother, and believe this, it's more habit-forming than crack.

Anyway, we ended up having a nice breakfast, and then I got dressed and went up to Loud Records to meet with RZA and Steve Rifkind to discuss what was coming next. I rolled in there so cocky.

"Yo, you hear the radio this morning?"

They were smirking at me. "Yeah we heard the fucking radio," RZA said. "You on some bullshit, motherfucking right, man."

I told Steve, "Yo, I got a feeling this album will go gold in six months." *Enter the Wu-Tang* went gold in four months and finally went platinum in May 1995.

That raised his eyebrow. "Six months?" he said. "You think it's going gold in six months?"

"Yeah I do, man," I said. "I bet you a hundred thousand dollars this shit go gold in six months."

At the time, we were in a serious Mercedes-Benz era. I'd always been infatuated with them, and they had come out with a new body type for the C-Class. The Benz I wanted for myself I still considered too expensive. I had other things to spend on first to get myself the kind of stable life I was after. But man did I want that new CL600 coupe with the V12 engine and 389 horsepower.

"Yo, Steve, but if I win you've got to buy me a brand-new silver Mercedes-Benz CL600."

The entire room was looking back and forth between me and Steve.

"All right Rae, I'll take that bet."

"Don't play no games, bro," I said. "Don't play no fucking games."

"I'm not, Rae. You are going to pay me one hundred thousand dollars if you lose."

We shook on it and that was that.

Three months later, in October, my record went gold and Steve came through and bought me my car.

Ghost and I were like twins by then, finishing each other's sentences and always into the same shit at the same time. Another thing we were entirely responsible for was the popularity of Cristal champagne in hip-hop. I don't care what anybody says, we were the dudes who referenced it first. And like so many other things with us at that moment in time, it just happened organically. I called it out on "Spot Rusherz," but we weren't trying to find some new expensive bottle nobody new about. We just experienced that shit one day and fucking loved it.

It happened when we had most of the album in the bag. The songs were done, we were sorting out the sequence with RZA, and we were about to dip into the skits. Like I told you, RZA gave us forty-eight hours to get those done because we were way past our deadline. The album was so complete that Steve Rifkind took the two of us out to dinner to celebrate it. We went to a place called City Crab on Park Avenue near Union Square because we like our seafood. Ghost and I wanted to pop some champagne because you ain't celebrating if you don't have champagne. We asked for Moët, and we wanted mad bottles because Moët was the shit. We were only into the rosé, by the way, not the White Star. The White Star was common, and we didn't do that shit.

"Get whatever you guys want," Steve said. "We're celebrating. Y'all just made a classic."

The waiter came back and told us that all they had was Moët White Star.

"Nah, son," Ghost said. "We don't want no fucking regular Moët, that shit taste like throw-up."

"What else you got?" I asked him.

"Well the only thing we have that is better than that in my opinion is Cristal."

"What?"

"Cristal."

"I never heard of that," I said. "Give us the most top-shelf expensive shit you got. We want the fly shit."

"I think you'll like Cristal. It's the best champagne we have."

We didn't believe it, and we were even getting ready to leave and shit. Ghost and I looked at each other across the table.

"So how much is it per bottle?" I asked him. "Is it really the best bottle you have? Because we don't even want to talk about it unless it is the best thing you got."

"I'm not lying, it's the best champagne I've ever had and it's the best we have here, without a doubt."

"Fuck it, give us four bottles," Ghost said.

When the bottles came, the first thing I saw was the gold wrap it comes in, which looked banging.

"Yo, son, this looks like money."

Two sips later and Ghost and I decided that it was our new shit. Moët was yesterday; we were drinking Cristal and nothing else, nigga. We had to pour it for everybody when we'd get it at a club because back then most niggas didn't know how to pour champagne. They'd tip it too quick and it would bubble up over the top of the glass, and then they'd act stupid and put their fingers in it to stop the bubbles. That was disgraceful. I never let anybody pour my bottle; I always did it for them. You have to treat fine champagne with respect. So the next day, when we hit the studio to finish the skits, we dropped those historic lines about Cristal. People in our culture had no idea what that shit was until we told them.

There was a downside to becoming the "King of New York" for a while: everyone I ever knew who needed something came at me. I've always been a generous and loyal guy, and I've always taken care of my friends and family. But things got a little out of control when my album popped. I was glad to be out in New Jersey where I was a little less accessible to dudes from the 'hood. Of course there were a couple of friends who needed support and help, and I didn't have a problem with helping them. But sometimes when dudes ask and receive several times, they don't ever feel like they've got to pay you back, and when situations like that continue too long, all manner of issues arise. And that's all I'm going to say about that.

Around the time that I moved out to Jersey, I also moved my mom out of the 'hood. Moms had never asked me for shit, even when she saw that I was making money. I took care of her and my siblings, made sure the holidays were good for them, and got them anything they needed—but around this time I decided they should get out of the community for good. I felt like I could make a difference in my siblings' lives by allowing them to grow up in a place that wasn't ruled by the influences that shaped me. I wanted my brothers and sisters to go to better schools and have the chance to finish their education. I had a little sister who was starting to run in the streets with the wrong set, and I was worried about her getting pregnant too young or experiencing all the other things that can happen to a girl in the 'hood.

I got my mom a condo in Fort Lee, where she lived for three years, but I wanted to do more. I took my time and built the family a brand-new house on the perfect lot in North Jersey, in Willingboro, in the Mount Holly area. I intended to buy myself a house, but when I thought about my mother and all that she'd done and struggled through to raise us, I had to buy her a house first. It felt good to do that as a young man still in his twenties. In my mind, I was balancing all of the running around and wiling out I was doing with my newfound celebrity and money by doing good things for my family. When the house was nearly complete, I picked up my mom one day and drove her out to see it. She was so grateful she started crying, and I wouldn't trade the smile I saw on her face that day for nothing. Aside from my sister, who unfortunately decided to stay in the 'hood, my other siblings couldn't wait to move in and start life somewhere else. When the construction was complete, it was a wonderful day. But what my mother didn't expect, and what wore on her, was that none of her friends came to visit once she'd moved in. The place was in South Jersey, closer to Philly than New York. It wasn't close but it wasn't very far from Staten Island, so it was pure jealousy. People started treating her like she had changed when all she was trying to do was move on up like the *Jeffersons* theme song. It weighed on my mom, as did living a different way, in a house that demanded more responsibility from her than an apartment ever had. I wanted something better for her, but putting her in that environment made her feel ways she didn't expect. When I'd check in, I began to notice that none of the trash was emptied and things were left a mess. Then I started to find that she wasn't there because she was staying back in the 'hood, hanging out with her friends. Soon my mom started dating a guy who was too proud to live in a house that his girlfriend's son had bought her. So for four years my mom barely lived in the house. Eventually we found her something smaller and closer to New York and I sold the other house. My intentions had been good, but I realized that my version of a better life for her wasn't what she wanted at all.

RIGHT when I was emerging as an artist and getting comfortable in my own skin, I had to contend with something I didn't see coming.

In 1994, before Ghost and I locked in and set about making *Cuban Linx*, the Wu did a tour that swung through the South. It was an eighteen-date run, and I spent it drinking, smoking, rapping, rhyming, fucking—all that shit. My God, we were hot. The Wu was in full effect and every crowd loved us. This shit was like hip-hop Beatlemania, especially down south. So there we were, in North Carolina, at a packed-out show, crowd going off, and the Wu at our best. Afterward at the club I met a young lady named Tabitha who was so beautiful, all I could think the first time I set eyes on her was that she looked like a miniature Toni Braxton. Toni was the hottest thing alive back in '94, and Tabitha had her haircut. She was wearing a hot black leather top, with long eyelashes and beautiful eyes like I'd never seen. On a similarity scale from one to ten, this female resembled Toni Braxton at about 8.3. Holy shit.

I went over and said hello, told her she looked beautiful, and said something like "If this was heaven then God blessed you." That might not have been my exact line, but I'm telling you it was slick enough to get her number. Soon after that we got together, and long story short, she came to see me in a few different cities on that tour. We had a very sexual relationship, a lot of unprotected sex and a lot of great times, but I wasn't trying to go long-term because after all, I had my girl Candy back home.

Some time went by, maybe seven months, and I was on the road again when she crossed my mind. I called her, wondering what she was up to, because damn she was fine.

"Hi, how you doing?" she said when she picked up.

"Yo, what's up? I'm chillin'. I just wanted to say hi. We ain't talked in months or whatever."

"I've been trying to get in touch with you," she said.

"Oh yeah?" I wasn't happy to hear this, because when a girl says that to a guy it means something is up.

"I've been wanting to get in touch with you to tell you that I'm pregnant."

"What?" I was twenty-five years old. This shit hit me in the head like thirty bricks dropped from the seventeenth floor. "You serious?"

"Yeah . . . I'm seven months pregnant."

I've got to be honest here, my knee-jerk reaction was real childish because I could not believe that she was seven months in and hadn't told me.

"Why you never reached out to me? Is this kid even mine?" I asked. "I ain't been around you. I don't know what you're doing."

I stumbled through all the shit that a young man in my situation would think and say. I felt like I might be getting played. Now that I was on, everyone else had been coming at me, so why should I believe that this girl was any different? We hung up and didn't speak for a while as I tried to get my head around things.

In the end, I didn't have a problem with the fact that I might have a child with Tabitha. I just didn't like how she'd gone about letting me know. She had a phone number to reach me at, so why did she wait so long to tell me? I was never going to skip out if the baby was mine, I'm not that kind of man. Since I wanted to make sure the child was mine, I asked her to come up to New York so that we could get a paternity test.

She agreed to that, but before we did the test she went to my 'hood—where I didn't even live anymore—and found out where my mother was living to tell her that she was pregnant with my child. She told everyone else that would listen the same thing, and in the 'hood word travels fast. That was a big blow to me because I was happy with Candy and didn't want to lose that. Judge me if you will, but I was trying to keep this shit on the low, at least until I found out if the child was mine or not. I did not want to break my lady's heart unless I had to.

Tabitha showing up real pregnant and talking about it all over the block was not a good look. My homeboys called me right away.

"Yo, there's some chick out here right now with a big belly saying she got your baby, son."

I didn't know what to do, so I denied it. "Yo, this girl is crazy. She's going to the neighborhood and showing the world even though it ain't mine. She's looking for a payday."

Her actions made me mad and arrogant, and relations between us got hostile. I was already upset because I'd fucked up, and I was worried about losing a happy and stable relationship with a woman I loved, and that was on me. I was all kinds of confused and angry.

To make matters worse, when she knocked on my mom's door, my mom took her in and believed her without ever talking to me. That made me mad, not only because she took this woman's side without question, but also because my mom knew my girlfriend well. I knew I wasn't being fair, but that caused me to push away from my mother for a while.

I took the paternity test and learned that the baby was mine, but I didn't set eyes on my beautiful daughter until she was six years old. After making a big show of it during the pregnancy, her mother decided to handle it all on her own, without me involved at all. I felt ashamed for the way I'd sworn up and down to everybody I knew that it wasn't mine and I apologized to my mother for being upset with her. I came clean to Candy, and that was the end of our relationship, something that makes me sad to this day because we loved each other very much. As a man who grew up without a father, I made it clear to Candy that I had made a mistake, but I would raise this child and not let her grow up the way I had. I intended to honor my responsibility as best I could, and she respected that. But she could no longer respect me, so we had to say goodbye. It was heartbreaking and we cried together. When she left, I made sure she was taken care of, with money, a Lexus, and all the furniture she'd need because I could never let someone I cared for leave with nothing.

I wasn't there when my daughter was born, which hurt me very much. Tabitha and I were not communicating well at all, both of us in our feelings, both of us still young at the time. She didn't want me there so I fulfilled my financial responsibilities and kept tabs on our girl, who we named Cori, after me, from afar. Over the next few years, Tabitha and I got through our issues because we had made a beautiful child together and wanted to see her raised right. She lived in North Carolina and I didn't, so that presented problems, but we grew together and learned to find a way. That being said, my life didn't stop, and time flew by, and by the time Tabitha and I got to some solid ground with each other, Cori was six years old. At that point, I came into her life properly, and I've been a constant presence in her life ever since. The circumstances that brought her into this world were not ideal, but I've done everything I can to make sure she has the best life she can, and I cherish every single moment we've spent together. These days my baby girl is in her late twenties, a college graduate leading a life of her own, and her mother and I, both of us now older and wiser, remain great friends who enjoy being her parents and love her with all our hearts.

CHAPTER 13

WU-TANG FOREVER

I didn't see the Wu much over the next two years. Everybody was off doing their solo projects, caught up in their own lives. Of course Ghost made *Ironman* in 1996, and I was there with him for that the way he had been for me, featuring on thirteen of the album's seventeen tracks. I even had a solo joint ("The Faster Blade") on his album like he had on mine ("Wisdom Body")—that's how inseparable we were.

It wasn't like that with the rest of the guys. Like I told you, we only came together when it was time for us to play shows and make some money. My solo success had me feeling a bit egotistical, so I spent those years being flashy, buying cars, living life the way I wanted to and doing my best to stay out of trouble. I got to networking in the business and became good friends with Fat Joe and AZ, who I spent more time with as friends than I did with anyone in the Wu besides Ghost. I didn't go back to the 'hood much either because I never wanted to make anyone feel worse about themselves by showing off. I hadn't changed as a person, but I felt a love-hate vibe from everyone out there, plus I was a conspicuous character in the 'hood now. Once

I drove my new Benz CL600 to see some friends and get some weed and nobody fucked with me, but the cops pulled me over immediately. I tossed the bags of weed out the window, but they found them, so I took the rap because I wasn't sending my homeboy who'd sold them to me to jail. He'd already done some time so this would have been real bad for him. That little visit home landed me behind bars for a day or two, nothing crazy, but enough to keep me from missing Park Hill too much.

When the group finally started talking about the next album, everyone was excited to get working. It was the follow-up to our debut, which from the start we planned as a double album. The record deal was bigger, which meant more money for everyone—about two hundred thousand dollars a piece—so we were happy. But a lot had changed. I was different: I had put out an album that critics and fans had declared a classic, and I had learned a lot about every level of the industry. Unlike the first round, I now knew how contracts are structured—what's fair and what's not—so I was far from the silent follower I had been back in '92. Unlike a lot of the other guys, I began to look at the infrastructure of the deal we were getting from Wu-Tang management and I didn't like what I saw. My success and the success of guys like Meth and Ghost weren't being rewarded and also caused some of the other members who hadn't gotten their solo moments yet to see us differently. And RZA, with his hand in all of our success, had a sense of his own power within the group. He looked at what had come about as the fulfillment of his prophecy, implying that we should listen to him without question and take what we were being offered on the business side of things.

On a creative level, one issue I saw right away when we got together to start writing was that the guys who had released solo records weren't as attentive when we got to working. Before, we used to get together and guys couldn't wait to show off their new rhymes. This time nobody was as hungry to create. More time was spent talking about how much money we were making and going to make than about any songs we were supposed to be working on. RZA saw that and decided that he had to take everybody out of their element to find their focus. So we went off to Los Angeles and checked into the Oakwood Apartments, each in our own place, and we got down to it. This was a far cry from my inspirational journey to Miami with Ghost.

Regardless of the other guys, my work ethic was strong, so if RZA said we had a session starting at 3 p.m., I'd be there. Most guys were late, some maybe an hour or more, but others really didn't give a fuck and would show up at eight or nine o'clock. And Dirty, he was pretty much MIA. This laziness and disregard made it hard for RZA to even get demos going, because he only had verses from a few of us. It really got to me. I told RZA that we should all be a part of watching the music grow because that's what we had gotten all of the money for. Instead we were letting him do everything on his own. On the one hand he liked that freedom, but the lack of enthusiasm he was witnessing did nothing for his ingenuity and imagination.

There were a lot of other things I wasn't happy about. There was a budget to make the album and to pay for our housing and our everyday expenses, which was normal, but none of us ever knew what that number was. RZA wasn't in charge of that—it was his brother Divine who handled the funds and our payments, which came in increments. Instead of giving us our entire two hundred thousand, we got fifty thousand up front with the promise of the other one hundred and fifty thousand once we'd finished the album. I understood that, but the way it all went down wasn't clear. We were led to believe that our expenses while recording came out of the recording budget, which is how it's usually done. At one point Divine's office even gave us American Express cards to use to cover our costs of living in L.A. But in the end, when it came time to pay the remainder of our promised advances, what we got was an itemized bill with every single thing we'd bought on those cards listed and subtracted from the money we were each owed. That was bullshit.

Like I said, RZA wasn't dealing with this, but what he did have to deal with was a bunch of guys who were no longer as creative when they got in a room together because there was no transparency on the management side. Considering that some of us had our own shit going on anyway—from Meth and his creative relationship with Redman, to Ghost and myself, and even GZA and Deck—being dealt with this way by Wu management made everyone just want to do their own thing. The Wu didn't feel like all for one no more.

Making that double album was a tough time for us. The camaraderie we shared on the road wasn't there even though we were all together living in the same apartment complex, like it was a hotel on tour. We never got dinner as a group or did anything together. Dudes would show up or not show up to the studio, and everyone had their own social schedules. Ghost and I were no better: we hung with each other and we'd go out, sometimes with RZA if he was down, but we didn't really try to fuck with the other members. That being said, Ghost and I did have one night out with a few of the dudes that turned out to be historic.

Since *Cuban Linx*, when Ghost had made his comments about Biggie, there had been this perceived Rae and Ghost beef with Biggie, even though there was no drama at all between the three of us. By the same token, we had never seen Big in person and given him love, which would put that shit to rest officially. If there's one good thing that came out of our time in L.A., it's the fact that we got to do that. It was the night the two of us went out with RZA and I think a few of the other guys, because it was the weekend of the Soul Train Awards in March of 1997. We were out at the Roxy and looked over and there was Biggie. At the time he had his issues with Pac, and all that anyone spoke about was the East Coast/West Coast feud going on. We didn't much care about it, want to know about it, or have anything to do with it. Wu-Tang was always our own thing, independent from all that.

Ghost and I were in a great mood that day so we decided we were going to say hi and tell him we had nothing but love for him—that we're all on the same side. After all, Ghost and I had a relationship with Bad Boy because we did a record with Jodeci, who were on their label, and Meth of course had done his record with Mary, so the Wu was down with Bad Boy. There was no animosity trip at all.

Big wasn't by himself, but he didn't have any bodyguards with him. Everybody was just being themselves in this particular club that night, so we went up and tapped him on the back. Ghost put his arm around him and Big was cool with it.

"Just want to let you know, man, we love you my nigga," Ghost said. "We ain't got no problems with you. We ain't on that. Yo, I hope you feel my sincerity and know that at the end of the day if I offended you in any kind of way, I apologize."

I followed right up behind him and said, "Big, you know what it is, my man. Nothing but love."

"Nah man, don't worry," he said. "Yo, I ain't thinking about that shit, man. Yo, man, whatever, we cool. Let's have a drink."

All of us got drunk and spent the night together and even made plans to do a track together. That was a special moment, because the Soul Train Awards were the next day, and by the same time the next night, Biggie was dead.

Biggie's murder made the air in L.A. tense; the East Coast/West Coast drama was at an all-time high. It felt like anyone in hip-hop from the East Coast was liable to get shot, and all the shit the hip-hop magazines were writing, speculating on who might have shot him and why, didn't help. Everyone from the East Coast left town as fast as they could, except us because we'd gotten everyone out there, which was a feat unto itself. We went back to the studio and tried to keep working, but every man was in his own world. Some dudes would come to the studio for a couple of days while other dudes just disappeared. Some came for an hour and left; some stayed all day every once in a while.

At the same time, RZA and his brother were making deals, signing him up to work with other artists and making moves to create other groups outside of the family. We had never written a rule book on that kind of thing, but it wasn't having a good effect on the group. And we was hot, so a lot of people came around RZA. He was like a rap shepherd, with all these different rap sheep circling him. Most of us didn't like the people Wu management started bringing around while we were out there. They were a distraction at a time when we were having enough trouble focusing. Beyond that, most of them just weren't our cup of tea, but that being said, maybe the people we brought around weren't RZA's cup of tea either, who knows.

We started hearing about these West Coast guys that Wu management had signed, who were out and about saying they were Wu-Tang, calling themselves the Wu-Tang Killa Beez, and the West Coast Wu-Tang. This was a group that RZA and Divine were developing, that he was going to produce and was already working with out there while he was working with us. I might not have had anything against them personally, but it was clear that this was infringing on our legacy. We had a streak going—just about every album we did with the Wu family was hot—so RZA acting like this side project was a Wu project was misleading. We were a very big group, but RZA wasn't separating the originals from his other projects and that was wrong on many levels. Wu-Tang will never be whatever he happens to be doing; Wu-Tang is all nine of us and that's facts. We can do whatever the hell else we want outside of that, but unless it's all of the original members working on something together, it ain't Wu-Tang.

Like I told you, we were already having issues, and dudes knowing what RZA was doing outside of the group didn't help matters. The family was upset watching our so-called leader out there using our flag to make opportunities for himself and for dudes we didn't know. And it's not like we were getting a cut of what they were doing, even though they were under our namesake. Even fans were confused when the Killa Beez album came out in 1998, thinking it was a Wu-Tang album since a few of us were featured here and there. That project and a number of other projects that would be released over the next few years were all being assembled while we were making *Wu-Tang Forever*.

We got our album done, but we got it done in the scrappiest way. To tell you the truth, for a group that had achieved all that we had, it just made me sad. If we had focused, it would have been an even better album. The chain we had shown the world on *Cuban Linx* was nearly broken just two years later. When we were in the studio, dudes were questioning each other's rhymes for personal reasons, not for the sake of the music no more. Dudes would just say another dude's rhyme was trash right to his face. It wasn't constructive, though I know I did it once or twice myself out of frustration. The energy between us just wasn't right. Like I said, we got it done, but we were divided on the result just as we were divided on all things at the time: half thought the album was dope, half thought it was trash, and there was no in between. RZA of course had a lot to say, especially to the guys who were critical of the album, since a lot of them hadn't shown up. And he was right: they had no business saying something wasn't it if they hadn't been there to make sure it was. He was in a tough place, because the album doesn't sound like anything else he'd done. The production was clean—he was going for a different vibe—and he just expected all of us to trust him on whatever he did. He didn't really want to hear our opinions at the end of the day. When we heard that finished product, there were a lot of fucking arguments, man.

That being said, when the album dropped on June 3, 1997, it debuted at number one on the Billboard Top 200 Albums Chart with a single, "Triumph," that is nearly six minutes of verses with no chorus.

The album went gold in its first week and went four times platinum by October. It is the best-selling album the group ever made. We even got nominated for a Grammy for Best Rap Album. Critics across the board liked it, probably more than most of our members did. From *Rolling Stone* to the *New York Times* to *USA Today* to *Entertainment Weekly*, and even *Melody Maker* in England, critics called *Forever* a classic and one of the best albums of the year.

We had a tour lined up for the entire summer with Rage Against the Machine, which was going to be huge even though some members didn't really get why we should tour with them. But we had another thing we were asked to do, which was headline Hot 97's Summer Jam that June. Now, for those who don't know, at all of these radio shows, artists perform for free, having to get themselves there and pay their crew and whoever else out of their own pocket. Nobody really talks about that. It's like payola or some shit that the radio stations do, flexing they power in the only way they can. It's an unspoken rule that if an artist is asked to do one of those shows and doesn't do it, they won't get as much radio play. We never got a lot of mainstream radio play as it was, because we aren't that kind of group, so a lot of members didn't want to do it. Steve Rifkind rightfully pushed us to do it because we had a brand-new album out. It had been five years since our debut, and we needed Hot 97's support, so we put emotions aside and decided to do it.

The show took place at Giants Stadium on June 7, 1997, four days after our album dropped, and it was all day in the heat with a lot of people on the bill: Jay-Z, Mary J., Bone Thugs-N-Harmony, Blackstreet, Diddy, Aaliyah, with us coming last, which we weren't told ahead of time. Nobody wanted to go on after us because they knew the Wu would take the room and never give it back. But by the end of the night people were tired; they weren't feeling us the way we expected. And the second we got onstage everything went wrong. Some of the mics weren't working, the sound system was off. They shuffle people through so quickly at those types of radio shows you don't get any time to make sure your stage sound is right. For us, with so many members, that kind of shit was always an issue and needed extra time to calibrate. Shit sounded terrible, so people started walking out, which was not the type of homecoming we were out to have, and especially not with us paying for the privilege.

We were all pissed off, so Ghost got up there on one of the good mics and said what we were all thinking. "Fuck Hot 97, we listen to Kiss FM!" he shouted, which got their attention. The now-defunct Kiss FM was Hot's rival hip-hop station, so this was a major dis. "Hot 97, where hip-hop dies!" he said, flipping Hot 97's tagline, "where hip-hop lives." Ghost kept going, shouting "Fuck Hot 97," then more of us joined in until we had the whole crowd yelling it and that was all you could hear.

I don't even remember what songs we ended up doing once they got the sound system working properly. All anyone remembered about our set was Wu-Tang and the entire audience shouting "Fuck Hot 97." In response, the station stopped playing our records for years. They even stopped playing our solo records for a while, which was definitely an issue for anyone launching they solo career. By 1997, the kind of innovative marketing that Steve Rifkind had cornered the market on had become standard. Without that edge, and with radio still a major force in breaking artists, this was bad for us, no matter how strong our fan base and Steve's marketing company still was. There were particular radio station personalities and certain labels who were in bed together, from Bad Boy to Def Jam, so artists on those labels were getting more exposure, plain and simple. It went beyond just paying your way in; these were strategic relationships and what we did that night hurt us for sure. In my mind, starting right there, the industry began to look at us as difficult people who didn't handle their business correctly. We didn't play the game according to the rules, so even if our label did, we were still getting left out. Steve and them were right to assume that Wu-Tang was a household name, but with a growing reputation, we were going to need more than that. Besides, by '97, there were quite a few rappers out there who had studied our blueprint and lifted from us as a group and as solo artists. So it's not like the type of fly, popular, drug-dealer rap that Ghost and I had pioneered would disappear from radio altogether if they didn't play us.

No one in the group was happy about this situation, because we are from New York and Hot '97 was our station. It was the station we helped make in a lot of ways, and now here we were five years later being told they'd never play us again. The thing about this blacklist that really hurt was that Hot was part of a national network, so other stations in their family followed their lead, and we got next to zero mainstream radio play. That experience at Summer Jam really turned a lot of the guys off of touring, so we did one more date in June, overseas at a big festival, then we canceled a month of dates with Rage Against the Machine. We took that time to get our act together, and we rejoined our tour with them in August.

We made a video for "Triumph" with one of Steve's friends, director Brett Ratner. Since that song was a true group record featuring verses from every single member, similar to "Protect Ya Neck," this was going to be a long video, so we knew the budget had to be half a million at least. I was excited about it because coming up with video concepts had become one of my strengths. I remember Meth coming to me personally and asking me to brainstorm.

I got with RZA and we came up with the bees concept, all of us guys turning into killer bees, breaking through the prison system, freeing our friends. I thought that each individual could have his own motif based on his verse. Deck referenced Spider-Man in his bars, so he'd have a Spider-Man vibe, running up a brick wall saving someone like a superhero. Method Man was calling himself Johnny Blaze, like the character in *Ghost Rider*, so his cameo would be something along those lines. Ghost and I would be incarcerated in a luxury jail like Pablo Escobar, and so on. There were going to be a lot of special effects and green screens and narratives that reflected the messages in the song. We wrote down all of our ideas, and Ratner loved them, but the scope of what we were thinking exceeded the budget. We dug our heels in, telling Steve that this was the second coming of Wu and pointing out how many people were doing real hype, big budget videos. We had to keep up. He fully agreed; Ratner revised the budget, and in the end what he needed to make the video was $960,000.

Aside from the Fugees in 1996, no one in hip-hop was doing million-dollar videos; just pop artists like Madonna and Michael Jackson were spending that much and more. But we knew the album was going to be big, and it was already critically acclaimed, so Loud went for it. And since we agreed to use Steve's guy Brett, RZA and I particularly were all over him during the making of the video. It was a lot of fun and a lot of work, and I've never seen so many cameras on a shoot in my life. I was all over the edit as well. Ultimately I'd give it an 86 out of 100. The other dudes thought it was perfect, but looking back I sill think there are things that could have been improved. There's a part where motorcycles come out from the sky at the transition into Method Man's verse that I think looks a little cheesy. But you know having a dude transform from bees into a gang of motorcycles wasn't an easy task given the computer technology in 1997. And of course, it's too bad Dirty isn't in the video, but he was nowhere in sight that day, even on a big day like that. The show had to go on, so we put Popa Wu, an older cousin of RZA's who had long been our affiliate and spiritual mentor, in his place. In the end the video was great for everyone: it was something crazy that made history, and Brett Ratner went on to become a big director and make movies like *Rush Hour*. Whenever I see him, I always remind him who gave him his start.

No matter how a record is received—and *Forever* did well commercially and critically—the true judge has to be the artist. I see a project as successful if there is some new ground broken, because that demands bravery. You have to take more risks than you did on your last one without losing a sense of who you are. On *Forever* I saw us getting stronger and braver artistically, even though the bonds between us were weaker. The music was different and so was our wordplay when we finally got it together. Considering all the ground we had covered since *36 Chambers*, I see *Forever* as another level for us. I think listeners did too, even though we were getting no support on the radio. It's too bad too, because alongside the gritty stuff *Forever* has a number of crossover records like "Reunited" that were aimed for radio. The production was different—because you can't keep a mad genius like RZA creating in the same science lab forever—and I was in the camp that liked it.

The one thing you can count on when it comes to the Wu is that when you talk to us as a whole, you will never get a hundred percent agreement on anything, even when you really need it. The egos in this group are out of control, so I had to learn at this phase in our history not to let it get under my skin. I had to be strong because if I wasn't, things would get gutter. It was fine if the mood was stormy between us, I figured, because it never rains forever. After all, we were always guys who loved the rain; rain never stopped none of us from going outside and having fun. Rain is just a different form of sunshine. The title of this album says it all to me: as disjointed as we were, we were still going to be us—the Wu-Tang Clan—forever.

WE got back on the road, linking up with Rage Against the Machine and a real edgy electronic group from Berlin called Atari Teenage Riot, for what we called the Evil Empire Tour. We focused on making our money and doing what we knew how to do. One thing about making money is that it takes your mind off of your problems. When we were out there moving around being Wu-Tang, none of us had time to think about the politics of the management company. None of that mattered on tour, just the show and the show money. Wu-Tang Productions used that to their advantage too. We were getting extra money on top of our tour salary; I remember one day an assistant from the office gave me a check for eighty thousand dollars. I was happy about it, but by the same token I said to myself, "Where is this coming from?" Other guys ran out of the room, smiling with their checks in hand, but I decided to stick around and ask some questions.

What I wanted to know was what the money was for and how much each man was getting. That question wasn't welcome, and it started greater friction between me and Divine. I never got an answer that satisfied me, so I kept demanding to know the source of every dollar we made and the method used to decide how it was split up. I talked to the other members about it. Some felt the way I did but didn't see the point in getting into it. All of us knew Wu-Tang Productions—which was essentially RZA, Divine, and their staff—made a lot of money off of our solo deals, our group deals, our shows, and our merchandise. There was a lot of money coming in but no transparency as to how it was dealt out, so this began a cold war between me—and other members too—and management. Each of us picked our battles on a case-by-case basis, but of course nothing really changed because we never went at it as a united front.

Despite those background concerns, a highlight of the tour was playing out in Big Mele, Hawaii, at the Kualoa Ranch in early August. We had a five-day break before the next date on the tour, out in Florida. All of us were excited because none of us had been to Hawaii before. We planned to make a video that combined the songs "It's Yourz" and "Older Gods," which is just me and Ghost, and RZA hired a crew to get some footage of us on that trip for a documentary.

We were out there wildin', having fun, doing all kinds of crazy shit. We rode three wheelers, and some guys rented cars and drove all over the place with the camera crew. There was a party around us

24-7. The ladies in Hawaii are beautiful, and since they didn't get a lot of big hip-hop groups coming around, they were all about us. We met some real bad bitches, and one time we had a few of them in a room, all of us getting down and shit. We were in there, everybody getting some, everybody fucking, and I can't put my brother on blast so I won't say who it was, but one Wu member popped in looking to get some pussy.

The girls were down to give it to him, but those of us already in there weren't about changing the rotation right then.

"Yo, nigga, you got to wait," one of us said. "You ain't jumping in this shit right now."

He pulled over for a minute, and when one of the girls was ready for him we looked at him pulling his shit out and every man said, almost at the same time, "Yo! Yo! You got to put a fuckin' condom on, son. Nobody raw doggin' in here!"

Now this nigga, who shall definitely remain nameless, he didn't have a condom, and none of us were going to give him one because we intended to use every last one of ours.

"Yo, baby, don't go nowhere," he said to the girl. "I'll be right back."

Dude left the room, and don't you know this nigga came back with some Saran Wrap? He wrapped up his dick in Saran Wrap, while the rest of us, still fucking, laughed our asses off watching him. The best part is that the girl went for it, and right in front of us, this nigga was up inside a bitch with his dick wrapped in plastic he probably got off a room service tray he found in the hallway. That was something I never thought I'd see, and something I never want to see again. It was too much, man; that was end of me running trains with my band-mates. At least he tried to protect himself and the girl. I'd never have guessed that Saran Wrap could work, but in his case I guess it did.

Being on the road was always fun, because no matter how separated we were offstage, we came together as one every night onstage. We are an ensemble group, a union that unites when it's time to build something. It was always amazing to create together, and in the best times on tour, to enjoy listening to music or challenging each other to a game of chess on the bus, the way we did in the beginning. On that tour we bonded over something new: GZA put us all on to UFC real early. We were all about watching that shit in '97 and have been ever since.

The thing was, it always took us a couple days to get used to each other again. I'd arrive on tour and see guys I hadn't talked to and think to myself, "Damn, is something wrong? Everybody okay?" But really it's just that dudes took time to loosen up. After a few days it was like no time had gone by. That being said, I'd never know what was on my brothers' minds. If dudes had unspoken issues with one another that had grown more serious during the time apart, there would be arguments. That happened a lot in those first few days, but it could happen at any given time with this group of men. The rest of us would hear the argument and then when we'd get on the bus, the whole vibe would be different. Everything would be quiet, nobody wanting to say shit. We were never going to allow physical fights, but arguments were fine. So there were tons of them, dudes saying shit you'd never think they'd say to each other. And everyone was a wordsmith, so shit got creative. But the next thing you'd know, three or four days later, those same two guys who'd been yelling at each other were back to being one again. And when it came to anybody fucking with us from the outside, in 2.3 seconds all of us would be there for each other no matter how we were all getting along. If conflict or disrespect came from the outside, our differences flew out the window and it was all for one, even at the worst of times.

Looking back, I'd say that tour was a victory lap for us. We flew Cathay Pacific, sipping champagne the whole way, all of it costing us half a million to fly the entire crew out. We were on top of the world, so it didn't matter. We did a couple of commercials, including one for St. Ides malt liquor, which made no one happier than Ol' Dirty

Bastard. That shit is like the cousin of Olde English 800, and he could not drink enough of it, getting blasted off that shit and mixing Bacardi rum drinks.

Dirty had been living that way for years, long before that sponsorship, and on this tour we saw him begin to unravel. By the time he got himself on the road with us, it was like being on tour with Richard Pryor and Jimi Hendrix in one. He was always next level, getting into everything, missing very important events and not really caring. He'd always been a bit like that, but he'd never taken it this far.

The one thing about Dirty was that he'd always run with maybe one or two guys that weren't part of the group, but they were his crew, and they were indulging in certain shit we all knew about. A lot of cocaine, because Dirty was a rock star like that, and a lot of alcohol. So when he came around, his energy was always hot. And nobody ever really bothered him when it came down to what he wanted to do because his name was Ol' Dirty Bastard. There's no father to his style or personality, and nobody could tell that motherfucker anything. Becoming famous allowed him to behave that way. He was a kindhearted dude, and that was his way of enjoying himself. He was indulgent, getting his nose wet out in Hawaii with dope and just absorbing the success of his career and our career as a group. If we were a basketball team, Dirty was our Dennis Rodman. He liked to tell me how he'd fucked on the flight, just all kinds of shit that always made whoever he was talking to laugh. Dirty always cheered everybody up, no matter how bad of a time they were going through. He was the class clown who did the unthinkable, and he did it so the rest of us could smile.

At the same time, he was in all kinds of trouble in his personal life. Dirty was crashing cars, getting into legal entanglements, and he hardly ever showed up for shows. With animosity in the air about payments, dudes who loved Dirty were still getting pissed at how little he did to earn his equal share. Each man rightfully looked at it like they'd never be allowed to do what Dirty did and still get paid. Some of us suggested real rules and docking pay when guys didn't fulfill their promises. Management applied that rule to the rest of us, but never did to Dirty no matter how much he stood us up. We could read the writing on the wall: Dirty was RZA and Divine's cousin, and everybody knew that was why he wasn't losing dollars over his work ethic.

This is the type of inconsistency that tears groups up. The rest of us questioned a lot of what Wu-Tang Productions did, but like I said, we never did so collectively, threatening to go on strike or whatever. It was a dumb error, because without us there was no Wu-Tang. All I could do was ask: Why are we not super-rich? Why are we not each making millions of dollars? Why isn't everyone treating this like a real job and showing up on time? Why are we missing this easy jump shot?

Aside from the money issues, I started to feel like our flag had holes in it because of all of the bullshit that RZA was creating outside of Wu-Tang. He and his brothers were out there making groups and taking record deals, focusing on nothing but money, making creative decisions based on what their cut of a deal was. And it was wearing on all of us. To make matters more complicated, every member now had his own lawyer, unlike before when all of that was handled under one roof, which had worked great for Wu-Tang Productions. The new circle of lawyers inspecting our deals was a deadly threat to them.

For one thing, we'd all invested in our clothing line Wu Wear in 1995. Each man put forty thousand dollars into it, and none of us have ever received any amount of money back to this day. We had stores in Staten Island, Virginia, and Philly, and we were in Macy's and a number of other department stores. In its best years, Wu Wear took in twenty-five million dollars annually. It was run by Power, a close associate of ours and friend of Divine's from Staten Island who we considered a brother. We never got residuals and we never saw annual profit-and-loss statements; we were just led to believe that at some point in the future we'd be given a check for a rainy day that would pay back our investment, with interest. Best-case scenario, down the road, we'd get a few million. The thing was even relaunched in 2017 in association with Live Nation, and we still haven't gotten anything. Too many other thunderstorms darkened our skies at the time for us to see what was really going on. Like I always say, people create their own storms, then get upset when it rains.

CHAPTER 14

REAL LIFE

I n 1999, I moved to Atlanta to record my next solo album, *Immobiliarity*, and I liked the city so much that I decided to stay for a while, until I permanently relocated in 2001. I even moved my mother down there, out of New Jersey, and away from Staten Island, which was a change that needed to be made. It was a struggle, because even though Park Hill wasn't the best environment for her, especially as she was getting older, she had trouble being comfortable anywhere else. In the end, her sister convinced her that a new start was a good idea, and since Moms didn't want to face it alone, I moved them both, buying each of them a house down there. It was the right idea, because my sister was on her way to college, which she could do down in Georgia, and my younger brother had two years left of high school, so he could finish up in Atlanta. I made sure to point out to my mom that the two of them had more opportunities to receive a balanced education from the black perspective down there. She saw the value in that, knowing that with the right education they could even be more successful than I was.

Atlanta was inspirational to me because it was full of motivated, professional black people who had made something of themselves. Musically, I found a community of artists my age and younger that recharged my battery. And to have my biological family relocated was great because I always cared about helping them live their best lives. If they weren't doing well, I didn't feel like a success. Like I had planned, my sister went to college and got her business degree, and my younger brother followed in her footsteps a few years later. If I hadn't moved them, I'm not sure what would have happened. The urban environment we grew up in would only allow them to go so far. With those restraints removed, they were free to make the most of themselves, and I'm proud of that. It's one thing to help your family out and make sure they have presents and meals on holidays, but it's another to enable them to have a real shot at life.

In a lot of ways, I was in the same position as my family. My situation with Wu-Tang was like still being in the 'hood—because with Wu-Tang, I could only get so far. Wu-Tang Productions had everything so tied up that even though we did great things when we came together, I couldn't rely on an operation that didn't have any transparency about their business and our money. I needed to figure out how to keep the lights on in my own house because I couldn't count on Wu. Everyone was in their own lane, which left me waiting for RZA to decide it was time for my sophomore effort. According to the rule book RZA had established back in '92, he was supposed to go around the dial, giving each man his own solo project, making ten albums in total. Seven years later, he wasn't even close, and he'd started making albums with his friends outside of the group. This was despite the fact that some of my brothers hadn't gotten their first solo albums yet. I began to question why any of us should be expected to honor the rule he'd broken himself? I went to him in '99 and told him I was ready for my next album, *Cuban Linx* being nearly five years old, but he didn't have the time for me.

So like it was for my moms, Atlanta was a new start for me. I went there to learn to be self-sufficient. Not out of ego, but out of necessity. As the Wu-Tang Clan, we built a beautiful house: it was clean with nice furniture, and people removed their shoes when they came inside. Seven years later, people I'd never met were up in there eating our food, their feet on our couch, leaving piss all over our toilet bowl and dirty plates everywhere. The only way this could have been avoided was through proper communication between the members, RZA, and Wu-Tang Productions, but we never got to that because transparency threatened their control. If they told us exactly how much money they were taking in, they would have had to justify the amounts they were not giving out to us. All I could do was adjust my attitude and reactions to the situation because I was never going to change it. I needed to pursue outlets that were all my own to make money because my family and my child were depending on me.

I decided to approach Power, our brother who was one of the original money men that helped found Wu-Tang Productions and now ran our clothing line, Wu Wear. He and I had become close friends by 1997, and I'd known him for years from the neighborhood before that. I'd confided in him about a lot of these feelings and my plans for the next two years. He really understood where I was coming from and was down to build something with me creatively and financially.

We set about making a budget to record, and I tried to figure out my perspective on this album. It was my follow-up to *Cuban Linx*, which I could not take lightly. I couldn't do the same album again, and it couldn't come off like I was still out there in the streets. I hadn't sold crack in damn near ten years, I wasn't posting up with guns, I wasn't dealing with crackheads and their bullshit. All that was a decade in my rearview. I was a totally different man.

For weeks I thought about how I should present myself, knowing full well that *Cuban Linx* was my brand. Was I going to play to that in whatever way felt natural or was I going to show my growth and do something different, even if it meant being somewhat unrecognizable? I wrestled with that until one day when I was at my crib in New Jersey making some chicken parmesan, *The Godfather: Part III* on TV in the background. I stopped everything I was doing when it got to the part where Al Pacino talks about taking the family legitimate and delivers the line about trying to get out and being dragged back in.

"Damn," I thought to myself, "that's it." My first album was about life in the streets and doing one last deal to get out of it alive, so this next one should be about what came next, and how my *Cuban Linx* character was trying to stay out of the streets. I decided to call the album *Immobilarity* as a tribute to *The Godfather* because in *Godfather III*, the entire play for the Corleone family to go legit was for them to take control of Immobiliare, a European real estate company partially owned by the Vatican and the largest landowner in the world. I made the title an acronym as well: I Move More Officially By Implementing Loyalty And Respect In The Youth.

Now, in my mind, this was a message to my brothers. I felt that we hadn't had those values instilled in us, which is maybe why the love between us had weakened so much. The love and respect between us was the bond, and the bond was the link, and that link was never supposed to break. Seven years later, where was the respect and loyalty? How could I give my respect if I wasn't being respected enough to be allowed to see if my business was being dealt with fairly? Wu-Tang had come to a "no honor among thieves" attitude, with each man wondering what the other was getting paid, and all of us wondering how much we weren't getting that we should be. This tension, mistrust, and dishonesty were putting our entire legacy at risk. It was one thing to beef when you're all millionaires, but most of us weren't millionaires yet.

Since I was determined to do my own thing, and RZA wasn't interested in working on my next solo album, I wanted to be free from Wu-Tang Productions. They had five-year production deals with each of us, which I chose not to renew, but I didn't want to make a big deal out of it because I didn't want to stir up drama.

Loud Records, which was now being distributed by Columbia, offered me a record deal for a million dollars, including the advance and recording budget. I entrusted the money to Power since I wasn't keen to take up the business side of things and have always been a trusting team player. That has sometimes been detrimental to me, because it's easy to love other people more than they love you. Power had known me since my crack-slinging days, and he felt the same kind of way I did about Wu-Tang Productions and the way they managed things. Even though he got money from them for his financial investment in the corporation, he wasn't part of the day-to-day. He and I had a trusting relationship with each other at the time, so I didn't think there was anything to worry about. And as far as the Wu family and Wu-Tang Productions went, working with Power seemed like a wise political move to me. They might think I was going against the grain by doing my record, but they'd have to admit that I wasn't stepping too far out of the box by working with someone within the box. They couldn't really call me a traitor.

P and I wanted to do more than just my next album; we wanted to set ourselves up with a new revenue stream and a new business venture. And we wanted to give back to our community musically by giving guys we knew a chance to make it in rap. Looking back, I'm not sure why I was down to create a management company and another group when I was having so much trouble with my own group and their management company, but I was. Maybe it was a competitive response to RZA and his Killa Beez; maybe it was just being caught up in the excitement and creativity that came from partnering with Power. I'm not sure, but that's what we decided to do.

We saw this as a chance to create something like Jay-Z had done with Roc-A-Fella. He was a member of his own rap family, which was like owning the team you played for. A situation like that would allow you to be an artist, have a dynasty, put some guys on, and be a company man, CEO type. Power and I hoped to get all of this done while making my album. We knew there was talent out there, plenty of guys who just needed a shot. I felt like I'd been paying my dues my entire career and was finally in the position to be a boss and a leader—one who wouldn't make the same mistakes I saw the Wu-Tang organization make.

We found a large penthouse in the Buckhead section of Atlanta, which is a pretty nice downtown section, and we moved the guys we had chosen back in New York down there to record an album at the same time I was working on mine. We planned to call them American Cream Team. We booked out a place called Patchwork Studio in order to make my album and what would become a compilation group album, the debut of American Cream Team. Patchwork was a low-key, small studio and we had the run of it, going in and out as we pleased.

There I was in a new environment, without RZA or my Wu brothers around to challenge me and push me when writing bars. It was an interesting project and one of the hardest that I have ever undertaken. I might not have had my brothers, but I did have my confidence and I wasn't going to drop the ball. I tried to keep from worrying what fans would think of an album from me without Ghostface on it, because I didn't have a choice. At the time, Ghost had gone to jail for four months after pleading guilty to a charge from 1995, so he was really in his own pocket. I felt like I had to have some of my brothers on the album, so I got features from Method Man and Masta Killa, but other than that there was no Wu influence at all. Other members probably would have contributed if I'd asked, but I didn't because I was determined to go somewhere else with this one.

I found my own producers, starting those creative relationships from scratch, while writing everything with only my own eye and ear as judge. It was a critical time. After I had my daughter with another woman, my relationship with my girlfriend had deteriorated and ended, which was another stress. So I didn't feel like my pen game was the best, and I didn't have my partner Ghost to push me. But I stayed positive and courageous going into the writing process.

I had met quite a few producers over the years, but I didn't want to do the obvious thing and hire a handful of hot, expensive dudes that everyone was after. A lot of times those guys settle into a sound because that's what they've become known for, and I didn't want my album to sound like everything else out there. It meant more to me to find up-and-coming talent, which I did, forming a little production team for both projects. Surrounding myself with the Cream Team was like having a new family, one that respected and believed in everything we were doing together. One of our rappers was a kid named Rhyme Recka from Staten Island who lived across the street from my building. His moms and my moms were real tight. He had such amazing energy on the mic, like a young Busta Rhymes. We had a guy from Queens named Lord Superb who was a full-blown character who could rhyme his ass off. He was a star who didn't know he was a star, which made me want to help him even more. The other two cats, Twiz and Chip Banks, were from Harlem, and I got to know them from going up there to buy weed. They always showed me love and used to spit little verses, so Power and I thought they'd be a good addition. We decided on the name Cream Team not because of the song but because we saw the team as a way to open up a new door to make money and put guys in a position to make money for themselves. It's always been about that cream, so the name was perfect. We figured we'd see which of the guys the fans liked best and let him be the first to do a solo album.

The guys were cool, and we were all friends. They knew their place as my extended family and never spoke against my Wu family. They'd ask me how things were going and if I was cool, but that was the extent of it. A lot of times I didn't know what was going on with the

Clan and I was fine with that; being in Atlanta gave me the space I'd been looking for.

We made a lot of music that year, and though a lot of my fans were not expecting what they got, *Immobilarity* still went gold and peaked in the Top 10 on the Billboard 200 Albums. The record was different, so I understood the people who wanted more Wu-Tang members on there, but I had to grow. I had to make something new, and I did. I give that album an 89 out of 100. I made something fun and personal—even including a song about my mom. Like I said, the music was different because I was a different man. There was no way I could make an album talking about cocaine every five seconds. I'm proud of the record, and of the fact that I made a full body of music entirely by myself. I listened through it and thought every song was hot, nothing boring at all. I took the criticism I got with a grain of salt and kept it moving, because most of the reviewers never said anything bad about the songs; they just weren't happy that my brothers weren't more involved.

I had intended to find out about management and business first-hand, and with Power and American Cream Team I did. Our guys had their issues, like any group, so Power and I had to alternate playing good cop/bad cop with them. It was eye-opening for me to understand how the corporate side of things worked, and I got a taste of what it was like for RZA to play the middle between Wu-Tang Productions and the rest of us. The one difference between the two situations was that P and I never played with anybody's money. If we promised them something, that's exactly what they got. For the most part I stayed involved with the creative, production side and left the administration to Power.

We went through all the typical shit that management and label people do with new artists. They'd need this or that, and we'd remind them that they had a production and management deal with us but they hadn't earned a dollar yet. Most new artists don't realize that when a record company starts spending money on you, it's not free; all of that money will be owed by you back to the record company when your record starts earning money. It ain't charity work: as an artist, until you recoup what you've spent, you don't make a dime. These guys took it personally, as if we didn't have the love for them that they had for us, which wasn't the truth at all. We got their track "It's Not a Game" on the soundtrack to the James Toback film *Black and White* and got them on some high-profile mixtapes. Things were happening, just not fast enough for them to feel like their lives had changed. Sometimes motherfuckers don't see that life changes forever when someone grabs you and takes you from point A to point B when you never would have gotten there on your own.

But all of the guys needed money to send back home. That was their reality, and they were not realizing that P and I were doing everything we could to keep their ship afloat. This tension tore us up. One mistake we made was telling them too much about the business and what we were doing for them, and that came from us not wanting to be anything like Wu-Tang Productions. But what happened reminded me of relationships with certain females I'd been with. If I gave too much too soon, they got too comfortable and stopped wanting to be who they were when we first met. When that happened to me I always felt taken advantage of, which is how Power and I started to see things. The Cream Team guys began to feel like everything would and should be easy. They lost the plot, forgetting that just because I made success seem easy didn't mean it was. They were talented, but it takes dedication and tireless hard work, and some guys just don't have what it takes to climb the ladder.

I gave the group as much as I could, all while trying to move to the next phase with my own project. It was too much for me to handle, and the stress of trying to handle them and my own career caused a deterioration in my relationship with Power. When the demands of trying to launch this group became frustrating, he backed off, spending more time on the clothing line. It got to the point that I stopped feeling like Power and his staff gave a fuck about Cream Team, about Wu-Tang, and about me. I still loved him, but I no longer loved him with a capital L. This was unfortunate but it was a familiar feeling, because that is how I regarded certain members of Wu-Tang and all of Wu-Tang Productions. I just didn't expect it to happen with my business partner in my own record label and management company. In the end, with the help of a man named Mel Carter, who became my manager for a while at this time, I discovered that Power had been using some of my money to pay for sizeable personal expenses. That did not fly with me. We had not been seeing eye to eye, but when I discovered that, I felt like an old wound had been ripped open. It felt like I was dealing with the same type of financial manipulation I'd tried to get away from at Wu-Tang Productions.

I didn't want to believe I was getting fucked over again by someone I'd known forever and thought I could trust, an ally who wanted to do business differently than the guys we didn't want to be like. When I approached him on it, he didn't seem to take me seriously. He didn't laugh in my face, but he acted like I'd get over it soon enough and everything would get back to normal. Not this time.

"Yo, you know what? I can't do this no more, man," I said. "I can't do it."

Fool me once, shame on you. Fool me twice, shame on me. Again, there wasn't enough transparency, and Power's temperament and lack of emotional control in business dealings made it impossible for me to keep going. He wasn't treating me like a best friend, a right-hand man, or a brother. He was acting like I was a nobody coming at him with an accusation. It was time for me to boogie and do my own dance. I had to create my own lane to do what I wanted to do and that was that. I had to stop loving motherfuckers more than they loved me. I wouldn't trust nobody no more.

The guys in Cream Team were very confused by our falling-out, wondering where it left them. My man Chip Banks had a meeting with me, hoping to get Power and me back on the same page.

"This shit don't feel right, man, I love both of y'all," he said. "Y'all got to fix this shit, I know y'all love each other. I know y'all love us. We won't win if y'all ain't together."

I explained to him why I just couldn't do it, and then he said something that has haunted me to this day.

"Yo, Chef, if you and P don't come back together, it's going to be fucked up for all of us, but for me, it's something more. Yo . . . I don't want to die out in those streets, and that's what's gonna happen to me. I need y'all to come back together."

This was a stand-up guy. He wasn't some little kid, and he couldn't conceive of success without his bosses being unified in their leadership. I promised him I would try, even though in my heart I knew that Power and I would reconcile our friendship but couldn't stay in business together. When it officially came apart, I kept working with Mel, who helped me get my personal goals in order, while Cream Team gravitated to Power and kept working with him. It was the end of things in Atlanta, so everyone, including me, returned to our lives in New York.

A few weeks later, Chip Banks got murdered in Harlem. It was over a dispute at one of those 'hood gambling spots that don't even get going until three or four in the morning. Power called me in the middle of the night to tell me, and we both started crying. Chip could get aggressive, and apparently he was bullying some kid he was gambling with to the point that they both got kicked out. The kid ran off, but they let Chip back in, and when he finally did leave, the kid was waiting for him with his gun. He popped out of a dark corner, started blasting, and chased Chip all around a parked car until my guy slipped and fell. Then the kid stood over him and did him in.

It broke my heart. I felt lost, blurry, thinking about my last conversation with him and blaming myself for his death. If Power and I had been on the same page, maybe he'd still be here. Power and I got together in person that day and cried on each other for hours like two little kids. We really loved Chip; he was the heart of that group and symbolized the future we were trying to make together for everyone involved. We were all held back by our own egos, impulses, and differences, and because we weren't able to grow beyond them and rise above, our friend was gone.

CHAPTER 15

HOLLOW BONES

D eveloping American Cream Team was like looking through a one-way mirror as the issues I saw
so clearly in the Wu-Tang corporation happened in
some way in my new business venture. I did not conduct my business
in the same way, but the same drama tripped us up in the end. The
experience made me all the more sensitive to what was wrong inside
the Wu family when we got together again in 2000 to record our next
album, *The W.*

We were always going to be brothers, because we came from nothing and turned it into something. As upset as we'd get, we'd never let
it destroy our friendship, and none of us would allow another to go
back to the street, no matter how much animosity there was between
us. But if we were going to be the best we could be, we needed guidance and counseling to help us get our shit together enough to record
a full-length album. I remember thinking to myself, "Damn, the issues we got are why white people do shit like therapy."

There was no way to get the group's undivided attention about
what was wrong with our communication, our business, and what

steps we should take to make it better. What upset me was that I believed a solution was possible, I just couldn't get everyone on board. We could have allowed ourselves to find a better method of dealing with each other if there was a more open-minded attitude amongst the members, if not management. It had gotten to the point that there was a black cloud in the room that nothing could clear. It was like we were crying from the inside out. There's a song I love by the seventies R&B group Blue Magic called "Three Ring Circus" that, to me, sums up the problems with Wu-Tang. The song is about a circus clown that makes everyone laugh while he's performing, but when he gets home and takes the clown suit off, he's miserable as shit. That's what was going on with us—we were that clown. When we got onstage, we made our fans and everybody else feel good, but when we got home, amongst ourselves, we were in hell.

When we were apart, it was easy to forget our problems, but when we got together, there they were all over again. I saw this more clearly than ever when we started the cycle for *The W* in 2000. There was no democracy amongst us and there hadn't been in a very long time. A few of us brought up the idea of having RZA spearhead the project, of course, but also use some outside producers because there were so many dope, talented dudes that wanted to work with us.

RZA didn't want anyone to participate like that on Wu-Tang albums, which we didn't understand. From the creative point of view RZA's sound was established. Outside producers weren't going to outshine him; they would just add to our legacy and development as a group. The family was in two camps about it: the vocal guys like me and Ghost and those that stood with us were pushing for including others, while the rest of the dudes who didn't want to go against RZA's wishes stayed quiet. They just saw the record as something that had to be done so we had a reason to get on tour and make our real money. RZA wasn't hearing shit about other producers or listening to us on anything else creatively either. He was real aggressive when it came to how he wanted to do things by this time, because from his perspective, he saw us as the guys who only came around to get their money, and himself as the one who did all the work. On this particular album, none of us were even excited to participate because we didn't like the beats or sound he was creating, and he wasn't accepting our input.

The music wasn't grabbing anybody in the room. It was too dark, but not in the way our older records had been: those were ominous but had a soul to them that came from his innovative use of samples and eccentric keyboard lines. His new shit was more one-dimensional, like a bad horror movie soundtrack. I kept trying to tell RZA this, to the point that he started looking at me different, like he no longer loved me with that capital L. RZA had come out with a string of gold and platinum albums with us and made tons of money and put our organization on the map. And he knew it, so it was hard to tell the motherfucker he ain't got it no more. But no matter what was going on with the group, RZA had a charisma to him. I could get angry thinking we couldn't see eye to eye, but then he'd take me aside and talk to me, talk circles around me, and keep talking until I agreed with him. The guy is very persuasive, like a cult leader. So no matter how little we were feeling his production on *The W*, we made the album, we did a tour, and everyone collected whatever money they had agreed to for the whole cycle. We kept it moving, but no one was happy.

Even Dirty didn't feel right about things at that point. When he was there at all he was only there for a good time, because Dirty could make a good time out of a bad one, regardless of his mood. Ghost told me about a conversation he had with Dirty where he told Ghost straight up that he was upset about how things were going with the crew. He said he didn't trust his cousins no more, and that they were messing with his money and fucking us all over. He told Ghost that was why he acted as outrageous as he did, because nobody saw what was really going on and he didn't know what else to do about it.

"Nobody see it, nobody know it. Everybody playing stupid," he told Ghost. "Well, motherfuckers gonna know it one day wh. not here. They gonna fucking know then."

Dirty was already foretelling his death from having to deal with the stress of the situation. Ghost told me that Dirty stared at him when he said that, and his pain was so real that Ghost felt like he could reach out and touch it. This was the start of Dirty talking like that. I heard him say shit to that effect too, about how those mother-fuckers were going to finally realize things was fucked up when he was gone. He knew no one else had his boisterousness, and Dirt was the first to tell RZA and anybody else when a track was bullshit. He'd never hold it in or whisper it in the corner to somebody else; he said it out front for all to hear. He'd make it funny and everyone would laugh, but they'd hear the truth behind the joke, and before you'd know it, his comment would move the room and change the direction, always for the better. That's why we always wished he showed up to the studio more.

There was no one like Dirty. When we did lose him in 2004, it was like our smile lost a front tooth and was never the same again. He had so much trouble in his life, from being shot by another rapper in the nineties and then again during a home invasion, and toward the end doing jail time more than once, being diagnosed bipolar (in 2003), and struggling with drugs and alcohol. I'll never forget when he went to jail for the longest time—two to four years in 2000 (he was released on parole in 2003). He was at Rikers Island and all of us went to per-form. The warden made a call to management and told them that he'd promised the inmates that if they behaved and there were no incidents for three months, he'd let Wu-Tang come and perform for them with their fellow inmate ODB at the end of his sentence. The inmates did it—there were no fistfights, no nothing. When we went up there, the COs told us they'd never seen a whole jail behave for so long.

I remember the moment we saw Dirty. He was in his green jump-suit eating a cheeseburger, cracking up like everything was normal.

already made. I didn't like it at all, because doing shows like that hurt our legacy. Worst of all, it hurt our fans.

There was a deterioration in the music, animosity within the group, and now there was backlash from fans because shows were sold as something they were not. The degree of perfection that we were known for was gone. I wanted to be there for those shows, but if I didn't stand for something, I'd fall for anything. And it confirmed for me that the money wasn't right when I asked the members if they got extra pay for the shows I didn't play, and they didn't. Management kept my money. They were playing a dirty fucking game and I proved it. I lost a couple hundred thousand in show money taking a stand.

At the end of the tour, when I caught up with the guys who had been upset with me for sitting out shows, they admitted that I was right. They felt my pain, and they understood why I'd done it. At the end of the day I don't think I taught anyone a lesson because no type of large group action was ever taken. With so many different minds, it was near impossible to come to a group decision, especially about a sticky situation like our management and money. All I know is that from that tour forward, whenever I saw him, Divine couldn't look me in the face. No "Yo, what's goin' on? Yo, you all right? Is me and you straight?" None of that. To me that meant I'd caught him out there. I don't know who made each and every decision, but at the end of the day he was in charge of management, so he had to be held accountable. That was the end of our friendship, because after that I could no longer be in the same room with the guy. RZA and I started looking at each other differently too.

Eventually I came to an understanding with management. When I came back, everything was cool; I acted like nothing had ever happened and it was back to business. I had a family to feed and I had a responsibility to my Wu family and our fans, so we compromised. I got about 85 percent of the number I asked for, they got me back in the group, and I returned to giving my all as I always had. But things were different. I'd come around and say "peace" to everyone, but I went to the show, did my job, and left. I didn't want to share the same bus, so I'd charter a van or pull up in a limo on my own. There were guys I didn't want to be in a room with longer than I had to, so I did my own thing.

One time after the initial drama had died down, I got into it for real with RZA about Divine. "Bro, listen," I said. "I understand that he's your brother and he helped create this situation here, but believe it or not, your brother is going to tear this group apart based on the way you dealing with things on the financial side. You're the man who anointed him with that position, so man-to-man you need to ask yourself, 'Do I save my billion-dollar franchise, or do I lose it because of my brother?' If I felt like my brother was destroying the business we created, I'd get him out."

I felt like he got it. After all, that is why teams hire and fire coaches. Things change and teams need change, and when I said this to RZA he knew I wasn't acting alone; a lot of other members wanted Divine out too. I made it clear to RZA that my opinion wasn't based on emotion. Divine was standing in the way of our growth, so we needed him to step down. We didn't want to cut him off. He'd still be making money from his piece of the corporation, he just wouldn't control anything no more.

If somebody told me to step down and was going to pay me for it, I'd take that deal. But this guy wasn't going for it. He would let the whole ship sink before he let somebody else be captain. There was even more to the situation; Divine was having all types of health problems from dealing with the stress. We heard all kinds of stories about his high blood pressure, how he didn't feel well. RZA would tell us we were killing his brother, driving him crazy, causing his condition, making him sick. Our thing was always: well, if he ain't well, he should step down. He didn't then and he still hasn't to this day.

RZA was stuck; his brother was his partner, but his partner was fucking up his organization. "You're a good leader, RZA," I told him. "But you're not a great one because there's no way a great leader would allow himself to feel himself losing and not make the moves to rebuild."

"You're wrong, Raekwon," he said, looking me dead in the eye. "It ain't the system, the system is fine. It's y'all."

I was speechless, just one thought in my mind: "Damn."

Wu-Tang wasn't going to be forever if that's how it was. In that moment I remembered that when Dirty passed I'd hoped his death would bring us together, but it had done the opposite. And then I remembered the show we'd done as a group on New Year's Eve back in 2004, the year Dirty died.

It was a time to party, a time to remember our lost brother, a time to look back, and a time to look to the future as a crew again. New Year's Eve is a time to celebrate and pop all the bottles you got. We were doing plenty of that as we got ready to go perform. As it came close to stage time, Ghost brought out a special bottle for us; I don't remember the brand but it was something real nice. But this bottle he'd been saving for us to share together wouldn't pop. No matter what he did, Ghost couldn't open it. He passed that shit all around the room, and not one of us motherfuckers could pop that fucking bottle. I don't care what God you believe in—that was a sign. We ain't the type of guys to get consumed by mysteries or superstition, but that night, in that room, all of us were bothered more than any man would say.

CHAPTER 16

RETURN OF THE NORTH STAR

When the next Wu album, *Iron Flag*, came out, in 2001, our record label, Loud, was on the verge of shutting down. That album was the most disjointed and low-energy we'd ever been. Dirty was on his downward spiral when we recorded it; he was in such a bad place that he's not on the album at all. The Wu was such a mess that all I could do was focus on my solo career.

Steve Rifkind was going to set up a new label, but that was a long way off, so I went to Universal Records and got a distribution deal for my third album, *The Lex Diamond Story*, which would be released on my own label, Ice H20 Records. I was going to do a drug-dealer storytelling album, so I took on the Lex Diamond alias to allow me to revisit those times in my life. This was a labor of love that I took two years to put together. I found a variety of artists to work with me on it, from Havoc of Mobb Deep to Fat Joe, Capone, and Wu brothers like Ghost, Masta Killa, Deck, Meth, and Cappadonna. I also brought in producers that I'd been wanting to work with, like Emile and DJ Khalil.

It was an interesting time in hip-hop to be on a major label, because they measured success by crossover hits, and I was pressured to move in that direction. The success of *Cuban Linx* had established my style and legacy. Then *Immobilarity* had shown my growth and creativity, but that album caused my stock to dip because it was different from what people expected of me. I had many talks with my guys at the label about the next move, and there was pressure for me to return to what I was known for—but to make a version of it that could also live on radio. To them that was the way to show growth and development. I didn't agree and didn't want to accept what I saw as a request to dumb down my creativity. This is the downside of working with a major label: they dictate what they feel you need to be.

I had to make an album that balanced what they wanted with who I was, so it had to be street but with nods to a more commercial sound. The first song I completed for the album set the tone. "The Hood" was a concept song where Lex Diamond writes a letter to the old neighborhood, speaking to it as if the 'hood were a person. The theme is how things have changed for me but how I haven't changed. The song allowed me to talk about things from my past that I couldn't forget.

At this time I brought my younger brother Kareem into my life and my business to give him some direction. He was getting into trouble in the streets, heading down the wrong path. Rather than leaving him for dead, which was where he was heading, I picked him up and kept him around me. Where I'm from that's what you do. I got him away from the cats his age who were hanging with guys my age. I knew them from the 'hood so I knew what was going on with him. I gave Kareem a focus and a goal; he started helping me when I did shows, and he saw from the inside how I conducted my business. I'm always looking for next moves, so I told him to be my talent scout in the 'hood. Even though I learned a hard lesson with

American Cream Team, I wasn't giving up on Staten Island. I knew there were talented artists there, and I wanted to find them and give them a shot. I wanted to lift them out of the life I'd escaped and give back to my community.

I'd been through it with Cream Team, but I kept telling myself that if I did it again and did it my way without compromise, there'd be no bullshit. I wouldn't have a deceitful partner like Power, and now I had my manager Mel Carter advising me. Plus my brother would be my number two. My record label was all set up, as was my distribution for my own record, and I made more connections in the industry with each passing month. When it came to business and creativity, I'd learned the value of networking, so there was no doubt that I was prepared this time.

I was going to write an album that revisited my roots, so I relocated briefly and booked a studio called Laughing Dogs out in Staten Island that was a small hole-in-the-wall spot on the outskirts of the 'hood. My brother knew the owners, so we got a deal and had our run of the place, which is how I like to dig in when I get to writing and recording. I started to perform here and there in Staten Island, and I got to working on new music. I wasn't hanging in the 'hood because I'd learned my lesson with that. But I was in the area, so I met a lot of local rappers—dudes my brother knew or had been checking out for a while. They'd come to Laughing Dogs and perform or play me their demos, and I got that same inspiration that I'd felt in Atlanta. I decided to make a group and record their album at the same time I did mine.

Things went well because I told them from the start that they had to let me drive and be willing to take the back seat and trust my vision and experience. In my mind I knew that this was a RZA-type attitude, but unlike him I wasn't going to be an egotistical dictator, just a strict guide. I would welcome their input always, but they had to understand that my experience qualified me to make the big decisions. Their job was to take this opportunity seriously. I am always doing shows, so I started bringing them on the road here and there to see what that was like. Then I put them in the studio for a couple of months. My brother was in charge of looking after them, and I planned to get them noticed with a look in the *Source* and other media outlets to jump-start their careers. We had a plan.

We named the group Ice Water, Inc., after the name of my label. We took a few years to build them up and put their album together, which we called *Polluted Water*. For those years while I recorded and released my album, I let them get a fly-on-the-wall perspective of what radio promotion and interviews are like. I decided to feature them on the Lex Diamond album, so it made sense to bring them on tour. I'd show them the ropes while putting money in they pockets. The first year or two of Ice Water was real cool, but as time wore on the guys had issues with each other. I saw it the minute we got on the road, and it reminded me of the shit that pulled Cream Team and Wu-Tang apart. This time I made sure they knew it wasn't gonna be a short, easy ride. It seemed like they got it, but they didn't. They were bickering and causing bullshit amongst themselves the minute they got a taste of tour life and the spoils of success. The egos flared up and they got at each other. This can be normal, because dudes got to go through their shit and beef and argue or whatever, but this was extra. They'd get it under control when shit was important, like recording, but the teamwork never stuck. It's too bad, because I called in a lot of friends to make sure their album was dope. They got features from Meth, Busta, DJ Paul of Three 6 Mafia, Rick Ross, Pimp C, and Jagged Edge. I felt they deserved it because they really wanted it and were putting in the work. We found an independent record company, Babygrande, to put them out, so things were looking good. But once their album was released, the bullshit and craziness took over.

My brother handled a lot of their day-to-day needs and I was more executive, but regardless, I started feeling like a two-time loser when it came to putting a group together because these guys could not handle the hard work that came with starting at the bottom. How the fuck were they going to handle real career demands? I gave them the platform, but I wasn't gonna hold their hand. These guys felt like I should. They expected me to be out there doing everything, knocking down all the doors for them, making it easy. I stuck with them as long as I could, but it became clear as day that they weren't willing to work as hard as I was. I found myself sounding like RZA when he complained about us, and at least from the creative perspective I had sympathy for him and the pressure he's under leading our group. No matter what business you're in, if your partners aren't willing to work as hard as you are, get the fuck out. These guys had all the advantages I was capable of giving them, but they weren't willing to use them to network and find their own opportunities. I needed them to contribute equally to the enterprise for it to work and that just wasn't happening. They made a dope album, but that's all they thought they needed to do. It went to their heads and they didn't step up. These days, with so many acts out there and so much music being released, a new artist especially has to constantly push themselves to even get noticed. I dissolved the company and realized that no matter how hard I tried, I couldn't save everybody.

Lex Diamond wasn't a flop—none of my solo records have been—but it didn't sell the way I hoped it would. And it made me think harder about who I was making music for and what kind of music I wanted to make. My manager told me that my last two records I had made for myself, not for the business. I was following my own path regardless of the trends, so I was bound to be disappointed in their commercial performance. I didn't think I was doing that, but I saw that he was right. I wasn't making radio-friendly tracks to dominate the airwaves, and when I tried to go in that direction they didn't come out right. I no longer had contacts in radio and didn't know any of the new-school executives at labels, so I was getting no support there.

And all of that was discouraging to me. I had to find a way to get visible again in the industry. If I found a way to build new relationships, I'd get more support when I came out with a new project.

What I had to do was what I'd told Ice Water to do: I had to make connections. I turned to the elements of the industry that inspired me the most—all of the artists who had become friends over the years. I observed what they were doing, judged what would work for me and what wouldn't, and searched for inspiration. I tried to work smarter, and harder. At the time I was successful, pulling in four hundred thousand dollars each year doing shows, but I was operating in my own lane, outside of the hip-hop industry at large, and I had to change that. I still knew how to hustle, but I hadn't kept up with how the music hustle had changed.

The problem was, and I can only say this now, I'd become too Hollywood. I expected everybody in the business to kiss my ass, and it was a brand-new day where that shit wasn't happening. I took a hard look in the mirror and saw a guy who had dug himself into a hole with his last two albums. I was out on my own without a crew of any kind: the Wu Family was basically dismantled for the time being, and both my efforts to start my own rap family had gone wrong before they ever got going. I had lost my fire: I only came around the Wu to make money, and played my solo shows to pay the bills.

To make matters worse, my domestic life wasn't smooth sailing either. I had begun a serious romantic relationship with a wonderful and strong-minded woman named Liz, which caused a lot of friction in my relationship with Tabitha. I met Liz one day while I was driving through Harlem, on St. Nicholas Avenue near 155th Street. I was with my brother Donperrion in my brand-new BMW X5 that I'd just picked up that week, and I saw this beautiful woman on the corner wearing a full-length goose down coat. We rolled by and my brother and I were speechless.

"Yo," I said, "she's bad."

Candy and I had broken up and I was a single man, so I had nothing to lose by trying to talk to her. I went around the corner and she was still there, waiting at the bus stop, so I pulled up to the curb and rolled down the window and said: "Excuse me, I think you're a beautiful lady. Do you know where I could get one of you from?"

Liz laughed but wasn't impressed and kept her distance. "I see you there, with your little BMW," she said. "If you want to talk to me, get out the car."

I said something about my leg injuries and not wanting to get out, and before I could get another word in, she said: "Well, if your leg broke, motherfucker, then you missed out. Keep it movin.'"

When you're in a fly car, you never want to get out and give a girl her points. The entire reason you're in a fly car is so that she'll run up to the car and come to you. Liz was slick and wasn't that type of chick, so what else could I do but park and go talk to her? We conversed and I found out that she was Dominican; when we talked about our astrological signs, I found out that she was born March 14, the same day as my grandmother, who was always close to my heart. Liz lived with her grandparents at the time and was very close with them, which impressed me. She was family oriented when so many girls in their twenties were out running around getting into trouble. With every passing minute, I grew more attracted to her feisty and cute personality. I got her number, called her, and we started dating. We had instant chemistry: on top of the attraction, we were two great friends with similar interests. Liz is a hip-hop head who also loves slow soul music and R&B as much as I do. When we were first dating, we'd drive around listening to songs, rapping to each other and making each other laugh constantly. It was nice to find a partner who understood my life, my industry, and how much music means to me.

At the time, Tabitha was struggling in her personal life, and the contrast of me being happy and serious with someone didn't sit well with her. To give Tabitha the space to handle her business, we agreed that Cori should come live with me. My daughter was seven then and I was thrilled to start making up for the years I'd missed. That put pressure on my life and my new relationship, but Liz rolled with it and we got through our growing pains.

You have to remember, I was just thirty-one years old. I came from the 'hood, and all I knew of home life was various degrees of abandonment. What I'd witnessed and what I knew of male-female relationships up to that point was not refined or enlightened. With Liz, I learned all of these things, but it wasn't easy. It never is when you are growing out of years of deep-rooted behavior. Me being naturally stubborn, and also unhappy creatively, definitely made me tough to deal with. With Liz I learned the true nature of what a relationship should be and could be. I credit her with teaching me how to properly respect a woman, and through being with her, I unlearned years of immature and incorrect behavior. She taught me how to be a good partner, the importance of experiencing the world with your other half through travel, and the simple things that keep your romance alive when you become parents, like going out on dates. Liz and I have two beautiful children together, our son Jaibari and daughter Sekai, and she is a great mom to them. I have a very healthy relationship with her family and we all love each other very much. Liz and I lived together and raised our children for a few years out in New Jersey, but we started to drift apart when I relocated the family to Atlanta. Liz wanted to be closer to home and her family in the Bronx, so eventually we split up, but we still have a wonderful friendship and relationship today.

WHEN I think back on this period in my life, I refer to myself as being in a "spin cycle," stress coming from all sides, as I went in circles, getting wrung out. I had done a lot of good and made my own way, but I'd never addressed the mistakes and hardship of the past.

All of those issues were mixed up inside me, coloring all my victories with pain. It left me not knowing heads from tails. I felt a bit lost and needed time, and calm, to find the strength to evolve and rebuild. At this stage, it just felt like I was being pulled in a million directions. My home life was up and down and very demanding, I had problems with my crew, and problems with certain people in the business who I didn't trust. I felt alone, and I didn't know where to turn. Any sense of creativity or purpose that I had was poisoned. I was heading to a dark place where nothing seemed worth the huge fucking effort it was gonna take.

I had friends and advisors, but no one who could really tell it to me like it was and shake me out of it. My pen had always been my savior, but I didn't feel inspired to pick it up. I started hanging around rap cats who I knew well because that was the next best thing. If I wasn't inspired to make music, I wanted to be near guys who were.

Busta Rhymes had always treated me like one of the Greek gods of rap, and the respect and love were mutual. We'd known each other for years and always had a good time on a friend level, so when I ran into him one day and he invited me to his studio, I went. He was working on the album that became *The Big Bang*, which ended up being Busta's first number one and a highlight in his incredible career. Bus is a ball of energy, and always makes me laugh, so being around him was a great escape from my home life and stress. There was no pressure when we were together because I was there as a friend, not on some rap shit. The first time I went to see him I showed up in my brand-new Mercedes 500.

"Yo, I see you're still doing your thing," Busta said when he saw it, cracking up and flashing that huge smile of his. To tell the truth I was struggling financially, but I'd never let nobody see it because I had to look good in the streets.

Busta had a penthouse in New York City and was doing most of his recording and all of his writing there. He was on Aftermath and fucking with Dr. Dre, and everything I heard that he'd already done seemed destined for greatness. It was cool, because Dre didn't fuck with too many dudes from the East Coast, but everyone loves Busta. My man was focused; he didn't have many people around. He had a stack of about three hundred CDs on the counter, all beats and tracks for him to choose from. Every day he and his engineer who lived there too would get to it. Bus would sip some Hennessy, smoke a blunt, and just make music. And I got to be there chilling and vibing with him.

All I kept thinking was how phenomenal he was. I loved being around his energy, and it lifted my mood, but I wasn't inspired to pick up my pen. I was gun-shy and, for the moment, content just to do my shows and make my money.

"Yo God, I need you on this album," Bus said to me one day after I'd been coming by for a few weeks. "I need your ears and I need your pen because you made one of the most impeccable albums on the planet. Your ears mean a lot to me."

I was happy to listen and give an opinion, because hanging out with Busta was giving me life. So I became Busta's advisor, listening to all the tracks he was thinking of using and weighing in on the songs as they came together. We hit the clubs together too, which was cool for me because Busta was up on all the Manhattan spots. We did it all: we'd hit the clubs, get drunk, hang out with other artists, head back to his spot, and get working on a track if that was the feeling. Busta's energy is like no other person I've ever met. He's loud as hell, to the point that when he's speaking to you it sounds like he's screaming. We would drink, smoke, and bug out, and all the while he was making a classic.

He was also making mixtapes, which was a big thing that everyone in hip-hop was doing at the time. That format is perfect for Busta because when he's in the zone, he's got more verses coming out of him than any man knows what to do with. He was going heavy on the mixtapes, throwing down freestyles as a warm-up and training ground for song ideas for *The Big Bang*. I was definitely getting my battery charged, but I wasn't ready to write. Busta wasn't having that, though.

"Yo, you got to get on this joint for this mixtape with me, God," he said one night. "It's me, Q-Tip, and Lil Wayne."

I had to give in, so I dropped a freestyle and was surprised at how good it felt. He could see that spark, so next thing I knew my phone was blowing up at all hours with him talking about all the other joints he wanted me to drop verses on. The guy was bringing me into his universe, putting me on tracks and giving me exposure, whether I liked it or not. Busta was always a good networker; he knows a ton of producers and had beats from all of them. Right in his house, he and his engineer could create however and whenever he pleased.

"Yo Rae, I got a track for my album you need to be on," he told me on the phone one day. "It's a Dre track and it's called 'Goldmine.' The brother is a big fan of yours and would love for you to be on this one official."

"A Dre track?" I asked. That was an honor because Dre didn't fuck with just anyone. He had a small circle of dudes he'd allow on his tracks. "For real? When you want me to do that?"

"Come over tonight and get on and do what you do!"

Spending all that time with Busta got my groove back, and we both heard it when I dropped my verse on "Goldmine." It came easy, naturally, and Busta went crazy for it. Hanging with him was like getting in shape with an athlete you know is gonna win a ring that year, and when I got on that track I felt the difference. I saw Busta as a mentor for many reasons. He'd been in the game longer than me, he'd done everything right in terms of networking within the industry on both the artist and business side, and he had a work ethic like no other. When I asked him about it, he just said, "Lord, this is what I do every day. This is my life, you know what I'm saying? I can't see myself doing anything less than what I love to do. And you're programmed to do it just like this if you want to."

Bus gave me a lot to think about. I started to wonder how much my life would have been different if I hadn't put so much time and energy into making group dynamics work, both with Wu-Tang and the two groups I tried to start. Busta had been in a group early in his career, Leaders of the New School, but when that energy shifted, he left and struck out on his own. He'd had ups and downs, and I'm sure he felt the same frustrations that I had over the years, but he stayed true to his love of the music and kept making it. He had success financially and creatively and was happy as hell leading the life he chose.

"Yo, Rae," he said when we were hanging one day. "I think it's time."

"What's goin on? Time for what?"

"It's about time, Lord. You got to come back with another *Cuban Linx*. It's been over ten years. That's too long. We need Part Two."

Man, *Cuban Linx* wasn't even on my radar. In fact, in light of all this new-era type shit I was getting into with Busta, I felt like the album had almost been haunting my career, hanging over me like a shadow because I'd set the bar so high right out of the gate.

"You been doing good shit," Busta said, "but that album inspired me. I was scared of y'all because of that album. You motivated me to be better, to be who I am today."

I was honored to hear that from a king like Busta, and tell the truth, my confidence needed it. I'd learned so much from him when it came to mixtapes and the joy of making music, plus Busta was a master at picking fire beats. He'd play you fifty songs he'd made that wouldn't even end up on his album; he was that dedicated to the craft. I heard what he was saying but immediately saw the many obstacles in the way of creating *Cuban Linx Pt. II*. There were too many gripes and grudges in Wu world at that time for us to even get in the same room. And I didn't know what Ghost was up to. He was doing his own thing, trying to find his lane, and I never took that personally. That being said, there could never be a *Cuban Linx Pt. II* without Ghost.

"Lord," I told Busta, "the energy ain't where it's at right now. I hear what you're saying, but it can't go down that road right now."

"Listen to me, don't worry about none of that!" he said. "Once you do it, the brothers will come back. They gonna embrace you, Lord. Trust me. They gonna come to you. Let me help you. Can I help you with this album?"

"Yo, you sure you want to do that? We starting from nothing, man."

"It would be an honor for me to be involved with you and do this album with you and give you the energy that you bring when you come and work with me, Lord."

At that moment, talking to my brother Busta, knowing this was no easy task, something clicked. "You know what, Bus? Fuck it, I'm going to try."

After that we did another freestyle record together for a mixtape that I dropped two verses on, and Busta, who didn't even do a verse, got on the hook and at the end of the song shouted, "*Cuban Linx II*, motherfucker!" Next thing you know, Star and Buckwild on Hot 97 got their hands on it and started playing it—just that shout-out— every single morning when they started the show: "*Cuban Linx II*, motherfucker!" They played it for a few weeks straight, which got all kinds of people asking questions and getting excited.

It was going to be a test to get it done, but with Busta's support, I felt like I could succeed. First step was talking to RZA, because it wouldn't be *Cuban Linx* without RZA beats. I called him and he was real nonchalant about it, but he said if that's what I was going to do, he was in. I was glad, but I was also worried based on RZA's production style at the time, which had become real slick and uninspired to my ears. I was going to have to tell him to pull out some old shit. RZA is always trying to bring his new shit, even when he's asked for old shit. It's a process with that dude, and in the end he might not give you the original style you want.

When it comes to getting beats from him, it's always best to hang out with RZA. He prefers to play his shit for you rather than just send it to you. So I went to his place, which at the time was way out in Jersey, about an hour from Newark Airport. We had a good meeting and he felt where I was coming from and what I wanted the album to be. He pulled out some old shit, promising to give me even more new beats in the same style.

That was a green light for me. But I wasn't quite ready to jump in, because this sequel had to be a classic. So I put myself in training, following Busta's lead, and got into my own mixtape madness. I had to get my mind prepared to enter the zone of *Cuban Linx*, so I spent a year and a half making three different mixtapes. The process strengthened my game as I met different producers and got traction with fans and journalists. People were bumping my shit, talking about my new freestyles, and I got good reviews in the press. It felt like something was happening for me again. Busta noticed it too and started telling me I was getting stronger.

I rented my own small, private studio space for the first time ever. It was out in New Brunswick, New Jersey, in a compound called Black Studios that had soundproofed rooms for rent as either recording studios or practice spaces for bands, and I spent nearly every day out there creating. For what I'd pay at an established commercial studio for a week of time, I paid monthly for my own private room. It felt good to invest in myself. I fixed the place up to my specifications because I need the energy to be right for me to write my best. I painted it, pulled out the rugs, bought new speakers and an entire recording setup, and made my spot just what I wanted. I found a local kid to be my engineer; he'd been making beats for years, and he introduced me to a friend of his, a guy who goes by Frank G, and the two of them did most of the work on my mixtapes.

I finally had my own situation: my own studio, my own recording team, and the freedom to rediscover my love for making music. As

I knocked out freestyle records, I began picking beats for the next Purple Tape, getting my weight back up in music on every level. RZA gave me a beat that became the song "State of Grace," and Busta did the hook. Busta did a number of hooks for me; he was real supportive like that, making sure I did not lose focus on making the album. "State of Grace" was my way of testing the waters, and it was the track I wanted to use to get other people interested in working on the record. It was the worm on the hook. In my mind, if I had a good RZA track to play for anybody I wanted on the album, they would see that this shit was happening and they'd get excited.

Next I talked to Ghost. He was down, but I knew he wasn't going to be there like he'd been back in the day. He and I hadn't been in the studio together for years, and though we'd never had a falling-out, Ghost had spent quite a few years going through shit and trying to make changes in his life. So when he agreed to be on the record, I knew he wasn't going to be at my side every day, picking beats and discussing skit ideas the way he'd been the first time. He'd come in, represent and do his thing, but that was it, and that was fine by me.

When I put the call out, I got so many dope producers to fuck with me. The legendary Pete Rock came hard on "Sonny's Missing," the incredible J Dilla gave me three tracks, my hero Erick Sermon gave me one, RZA brought his A-game, and I got two tracks from none other than Dr. Dre. My features were equally strong. My Wu brothers Deck, Killa, GZA, Meth, and Ghost got what I was doing and elevated the proceedings beyond my expectations. Even RZA dropped fire bars on "Black Mozart." Jadakiss and Styles P kept it real on "Broken Safety," Beanie Sigel got down on "Have Mercy," and Busta did his thing on "About Me." One of the things I'm happiest about when I look at the record is that I got to know and work with J Dilla a bit before he passed in 2006 from a rare blood disease, far too soon at the age of thirty-two. Busta introduced us. I hadn't heard his shit before that, which is my bad, but damn, he was so talented. He loved the Wu and understood my shit, and he already had the beat to what became "House of Flying Daggers." It was something he'd put together years before because he'd wanted to do a Wu-Tang group track like "Triumph." He could think of no better home for it than on *Cuban Linx Pt. II.* That beat is so hard and banging, it begged for the entire Clan, and I think we captured that vibe in the end. It definitely put me in the mindset to go and find beats that reflected the times and tones of *Cuban Linx* but were modern and new at the same time.

I took over three years to get the album right, which was the longest a project has ever taken me. I've never worked harder on anything and I'm as proud of Part II as I am of Part I. By the time the album was in motion, I was in a good place with my Wu brothers, and even me and Divine were talking. I was able to forgive, but I would never forget. At the time Divine was opening a new recording studio in Manhattan called Wu-Tang Studios, and he told me to come up there and do some work on my record. I knew that if I was around, I could get the guys to be on my album; I also realized he was inviting me to work there so he could get the guys to come around for another Wu album at the same time. I was nervous about engaging with him again, but I hoped, yet again, that all of us being together like old times would rekindle the best in us.

Divine and RZA used me as the bait to get guys to come down and do some verses that RZA ended up using on *8 Diagrams*, so there was a give-and-take. It worked for a while, but it was just a matter of time until Divine and I had another falling-out over money and I decided that I needed to keep my album separate. No one else was a problem, just Divine, so I decided to continue work somewhere else. I told Busta about all of it, of course, and he told me to keep going and not to worry about the timeline.

"You are killing it," he said. "Stay in your pocket and don't let nobody tear you down. You are your own boss. Move like a boss, do what you do and don't get caught up in everybody else's wind."

I thought about those words a lot throughout the many years of making the album, whenever I found myself feeling down and out. No matter how low I got, I promised myself I wasn't going to let no one steal my joy.

This album was four years in the making from the time I started brainstorming with Busta to its release in fall 2009. There was a time when Busta went back to L.A. to get in the studio with Dre to record *The Big Bang*. That's when he played Dre some of my under-construction *Cuban Linx II* joints, which started the next chapter of the journey.

Busta told me Dre went bananas when he heard the tracks, and he must have, because he asked for a meeting with me. I couldn't believe what I was hearing.

"Yo, Bus, you telling me Dr. Dre want to have a meeting with the Chef?"

"That's what I'm saying, God. I'm setting the whole thing up."

All I kept thinking about was that an album with Dre and RZA on it was some Frankenstein shit of the highest order. Some crazy historic hip-hop shit.

A few months later I went to L.A. and met the Doc in the flesh while he and Busta were working. I brought three more tracks that Busta hadn't heard, and Dre went crazy for those. He told me the shit was fire and pointed at a studio room across the hall in his compound. "You see that room, there? If you want it, that's yours. Yo, take the room."

When Dre stepped out for a minute, Busta said, "Yo, I think you could get a deal with Dre."

I was acting cool as a cucumber, but my mind was going wild. Dre invited me back to the studio the next day, real casual, but Busta told me on the side that Doc planned to play me some beats. I couldn't even believe what I was hearing, but that's what happened: Dre cued up a bunch of beats he'd picked for me.

Everything he played was banging, but I stayed focused on what was right for the album. He played a track with a sample of the Stevie Wonder song "Village Ghetto Land" on the hook that went, "Would you like to go with me down my dead end street?" I loved it, and when I looked over at Busta, I knew he loved it too. Busta is a facial expression nigga, so if a beat hits and he stops making facial expressions, you know it's serious. I was like, put that track in the bag. Next he played more of a 50 Cent–style club banger and I was about to start pinching myself; this shit was so crispy.

"You like this shit?" Dre asked. "You could go work on it right now if you want to."

Busta dropped a hook on that one that night and it was dope, but in the end I didn't put that song on the album because I had Bus on so many other hooks I didn't want him to only serve that purpose.

We spent the rest of that day fucking with these beats while Dre jumped between studios the way he does, making magic. He came back to check on us and played us this beat that he didn't really like that much. It was an experiment to him. But Busta and I loved it. It was perfect for Purple Tape II.

"Y'all like this shit for real?" he asked. "Yo, this don't sound like something I've ever made before."

That track became "Catalina," which I named that night because it sounded like a beat you'd play on a yacht while you were hanging out with a bunch of your friends. Dre was down because he knew the beat wasn't weak, it was just totally different from his sound. I took that beat into the other studio and fucked around for about two hours until I had some verses. They weren't what ended up on the final version, but that didn't matter. In seventy-two hours I ended up getting four tracks out of Dre. It was an inspirational trip.

"I think Dre wants to take on your project," Busta told me the next day.

"You serious? You think I could be down with y'all on some Aftermath shit?"

"Yo, Lord, listen, on a scale of one to ten, you at a nine-point-six. I talked to Dre myself, he wants to fuck with you."

This was a dream come true. When I went back to the East Coast, I talked to RZA about it, because he was the musical author of *Cuban Linx* and I felt like I had to have his blessing. I wanted him and Dre to coproduce the project, which alone would make it legendary because they'd never collaborated before. It was all Busta and I could talk about, and by then I'd asked Busta to executive produce the album with me because if it wasn't for him, there wouldn't be an album at all.

A few months later RZA was in L.A., so I flew out and we met with Dre. Everything went great; they were both comfortable and fans of each other's, so in that meeting it got to the point where Dre brought up finances and asked me how much I wanted for the album. We had never talked about that, so I respectfully asked him for a few minutes to think it over. When he left the room, I turned to RZA and told him that I wanted three million dollars for the album.

"You want to tell him you want three million?" he asked.

"Yeah," I said. "You think that's kind of high?"

"Hell yeah I do."

"Listen, trust me, I got this."

"All right, talk to me," Dre said when he came back in the room. "What are we doing? Where are we going?"

"All right Dre, this is it, this is what I want to do. I need three million."

Dre looked up, looked me in the eye, and said, "All right, cool. I'm down for that. It makes sense."

Then he hopped out the room to go into different sessions, eating that three million like it was nothing. I felt like he understood the worth, knowing it was him and RZA and so many dope features that it would be a good look on his label. He did make one thing clear though.

"When we close this deal, RZA, I respect you so much that I want to tell you now before this goes any further that I'm not doing any other deals with other members of the group. I ain't trying to be funny, I just don't want to have another discussion about signing anybody else from the Wu. I want to fuck with Chef. We have a great relationship and I want this to be an opportunity where I work with you and him on this particular project and that's it."

"I respect that," RZA said.

I could tell RZA wasn't expecting that, and I think he heard it but didn't hear it because he didn't want to. It made sense: Dre is very particular with who he decides to work with, so he was letting his door policy be known. Dre also said something to the effect that he was the type of person that became a dictator when he took on a project, and the last thing he wanted to do was mess up our friendship over something like this.

"If things don't feel like they are falling comfortably in your corner," he said, "then it may not be good for us to do business because I'd rather keep friendships than have business cause controversy between us."

The Doc knew his mind and was a real diplomat about it. In a nutshell he was saying that if he was paying, it was his show, so if either of us weren't down with that, we should remain friends and not do business. I got it: he wasn't going to put anything out until he was ready, and he was going to be in control of the whole thing. You can't argue with that; at the end of the day, it's his fucking yacht. RZA and I both agreed, so at the end of the meeting we shook hands on a three-million-dollar deal for *Cuban Linx Pt. II* to be released by Interscope/Aftermath. It was going to have Dre as executive producer and RZA as co-executive with Busta getting a coproducer credit, and it was going to be historic.

I was living in Atlanta, so I flew home. I was on top of the world, waiting on the contracts to come from Dre's office. RZA had agreed to everything, but in the next few weeks he got real distant. I didn't think much of it, but as time went on and I didn't get paperwork from Dre I started to worry. A month or so went by. I heard from Busta that Dre was busy finishing up other projects before he could chop into anything new, so I kept working on the album. At some point word got around the industry that I was going to sign with Dre, which must have come from someone on Dre's side. I knew better than to say a word before the ink was dry.

I didn't get a chance to speak to Dre again until three months later. He told me that he couldn't close any new deals at the time because he was stuck in a situation that he had to get out of business-wise. He still wanted to do the record, but he told me straight up that it was going to be a minute before he could focus on it. He had obligations to Interscope and all of the complications that come with being involved with a major label, even being Dr. Dre. He told me that if I didn't want to hold up and wait for him to get to the project, he would invest in it one way or another because he believed in it. It was a tough decision because I wanted to work with Dre more than anything, but at this point, I was nearly four years into the project. I felt like it might be another two years or more waiting for the Doc. I was disappointed of course but that is how it is if you even get the one-in-a-million chance to work with an icon as busy and in-demand as Dr. Dre.

In the end, rather than take money as an investment, I agreed to take the four tracks he'd given me for free. Let me remind you: at that time, Dre tracks, if you could get them, cost $250,000 each. His only request was to retain the right to mix them.

"Of course, Doc," I said, laughing. "What you think, I'm gonna get a local to mix a fucking Dre track?"

Even though I didn't sign with Aftermath or get that advance, Dre was a big help to me beyond those four beats. We talked about the best way for me to finish the album and get it distributed. He encouraged me to finish it independently, making it exactly the way I wanted to before letting a label or anyone else get their hands on it. In the end it was the best outcome because if I'd signed with Aftermath, not only would I have been locked into Dre's availability, but I'd also have been controlled by Interscope's release schedule. Who knows when the album would have seen the light of day? In the end I did it all myself and put it out on my own label, and it was distributed by EMI. Most important, I kept full ownership of my masters and made a friend in Dre.

The day I played the final mix of the album for Busta, four years after he told me I had to do it, we both cried. "You outdid yourself with this Purple Tape II, Lord," he said. "The shit is fucking amazing!"

"I'll never forget this time or the light you gave me, Bus."

I've never worked harder or smarter on anything, and I wouldn't take a minute of it back. Without this album, I wouldn't be the artist I am today. I fucked with legendary producers and I got amazing shit out of my Wu brothers, and getting their verses wasn't easy. When I finally got to the end of this journey and released it, the result was like a breath of fresh air in my lungs.

I wasn't the only one that felt relieved. My manager Mel told me that I'd killed it, and he was always a very harsh critic. And critics themselves loved it too, which was a win for me because they hadn't felt the same way about my last two albums. I was voted MC of the Year by *HipHopDX*, and the record made so many critics' best album lists that year in the hip-hop press as well as publications like the *New York Times* and *Pitchfork*. *Cuban Linx Pt. II* debuted at number four on the Billboard Top 200 Albums Chart and number two on the Hip Hop/R&B Chart, which is exactly where the first *Cuban Linx* landed fourteen years before. If that ain't proof that history repeats itself, I don't know what is.

CHAPTER 17

SHAOLIN VS. WU-TANG

Cuban Linx Pt. II was the moment I proved I still got it and that nobody should ever count me out. I'm the kind of artist who works best under pressure, and with all the advance hype and the time I took to complete the record, the pressure was on. But I knew I was going to do it, because when you practice, work hard, and go for it, you can't lose. I'd put in the work and didn't stop: the year I released the album, I featured on upward of thirty tracks and remixes. I say that if you work for yourself and you work like a slave, eventually you'll eat like a king.

My successful return didn't help my attitude when it came to the Wu-Tang Clan. I had distanced myself and was definitely considered the cocky, outspoken, problematic guy by management, especially the pair in control, RZA and his brother Divine. Everybody knew that I was loyal to the organization but would stand up for what I thought was fair and refuse to do what I didn't think was right. Divine and I had a brief reunion when I recorded at the new Wu-Tang

Studios for a minute, but when Divine and I got into it over money, things got worse than ever between us. After that he really had it out for me. This was a problem because he's a very emotional person, the kind who lets his feelings interfere with his business.

I was in a cold war with Wu-Tang leadership when we did the *8 Diagrams* album, which was recorded in 2007, toward the end of the four years I was worked on *Cuban Linx Pt. II*. The other members knew I was unhappy with the guys in control even though I never let it be known directly. Those issues aside, what angered me most was that the music was not where it needed to be. I watched my friends in the group bust their asses, trying to believe in a record that wasn't right. The guys would say things to me like "I know the album is fucked up, but I don't want that to fuck up my relationship with RZA because he's a great man." The truth is, RZA may have cared about the record to a degree, but he was involved in so many other projects. Those seemed to matter to him more, particularly his film career. He didn't give the album as much time or effort, and it shows. Besides that, he was no longer the musical maestro he'd once been, but he refused to let go of the reins. The record didn't stand a chance of matching the greatness the MCs in the group were capable of.

I was happy that RZA had found a film career, doing music scores and appearing in movies and television, but that success went to his head. He'd forgotten where he came from, and it wasn't good for the organization as a whole. I used to tell RZA, "You not in the streets listening to music no more. You're not checking out new styles of production." He was very arrogant whenever anyone criticized him and had been that way for years. His long list of accomplishments had him believing everything he did was solid gold, which wasn't the case. He was going to do it his way and that was it—and whoever didn't like it, so be it. Business issues aside, RZA and I didn't talk for a while because I couldn't stand his egotistical, dismissive attitude. I'd come to him on a creative level to discuss the problems with the album—but he'd try to flip it around and make me feel like I was buggin' when the majority of the crew felt the same way as I did. RZA and I are both prideful men so of course we went at it. He was thick-headed, but I don't fault him entirely for that. He never had people around him to tell him how it was when he needed to hear that. After my attempts to start my own rap family I understood his position more than ever, but I still think he should have treated us differently. I always treated the guys I was developing with respect and made them feel their opinion mattered, even when I knew I'd be leading them in another direction. The reason being that I had experience and success that those guys didn't have. When it came to Wu-Tang, even though we'd been on the journey with RZA from the start, he made us feel like we knew nothing and he knew it all. It was like we didn't even have the right to question him.

The situation had me so frustrated that I started writing an album of my own. I named it before I even began writing: *Shaolin vs. Wu-Tang*. I would always be Wu-Tang, but at that time I was Shaolin. In the mythology of the martial arts movies we love, Shaolin is the original temple, home to monks who are great listeners and wise students of philosophy in addition to being karate masters. The founders of Wu-Tang were originally part of the Shaolin brotherhood, but they became arrogant and stubborn and caused so much trouble that they ended up being kicked out. Karate movies are so dope because they're all about brotherhood, revenge, discipline, and mastering an art form to stay on top. This was the perfect title for the album because it captured everything going on with Wu at the time. It was also a reference to me choosing myself and my roots in Staten Island, which we called Shaolin, over what Wu-Tang represented at the time.

RZA heard the message loud and clear when the album came out, and he called me one time to get into it. We started arguing, cursing each other out. In the middle of it he said something that made me laugh even though he was dead serious.

"I'm more Shaolin than you," he said.

He'd been to the Shaolin Temple in China, he'd shared a meal with the monks and done some other things. And he had an ego about it, thinking he was more annointed with the philosophy of Wu-Tang and Shaolin than the rest of us. He saw himself as our wise, spiritual leader that we should all follow without question. He had the idea for the group and he executed it, but he could never have done it without the rest of us contributing. The dude needed to stop thinking he did everything all by himself.

I did some interviews at the time, letting it be known that as much as I respected RZA, I wanted to do an album with other producers. The idea was a return to an updated version of the signature Wu-Tang sound. Some of the other members didn't like that either and saw me as a traitor who had gone and aired the family's dirty laundry. A lot of them seemed to think I was acting like a kid born with a silver spoon in his mouth because of my solo success. Of course that wasn't the case, but I took notice of which members had never come to me and said, "Yo, I'm proud of you," when I did my own thing. Even if they had been featured on one of my records, hearing words of congratulations from a brother's mouth would have meant so much more.

The ones that felt the same as I did about the last Wu albums showed up on *Shaolin vs. Wu-Tang*: GZA, Deck, Meth, and Ghost. I also got features from Busta, Black Thought, Nas, Lloyd Banks, and Rick Ross, with production by a bunch of dudes like Scram Jones, DJ Khalil, Alchemist, and Havoc. I was able to make the type of album I'd been pushing the group to make for years, featuring new producers and outside artists. RZA never allowed any of the artists and producers who loved us to contribute to our group albums. The rest of us wanted the world to hear all of Wu-Tang on a DJ Premier track or a Dr. Dre track, but he was totally against it. He'd front and say he wasn't against it, but we all knew he was. He never wanted to engage with other producers. If he did, he'd have to share splits and royalties and lose that money. It's the same reason he stopped wanting to use beats with samples: if there were no samples to clear, he could take home more of the publishing cash. Mind you, none of us were insisting on using samples, we just wanted dope music. When it came to samples, Ghost and I always said that if the record had a sample that worked, just clear it and keep it moving. It was the quality of the beat as a whole that was going to elevate you to success; no sample alone was going to do that.

Making *Shaolin vs. Wu-Tang* was important to me. It came out in March 2011 and debuted at number twelve on the Billboard Charts. From a sales perspective, it didn't do as well as my other albums, but it was critically acclaimed, and it brought the original Wu sound back to the fans. It would have done better if the guys who featured on it had supported it more, but that was a sticky situation because of how vocal I'd been against RZA in the press. When it came to promotion the guys weren't there 100 percent because they didn't want to be associated with or dragged into that, so it changed the way the album was embraced by the fans. The album did let the public know my perspective on what was best for the team.

In response, RZA did some interviews denouncing me to the point where I almost made a dis record. I was going to give it to him, call him out, disrespect his whole world, because that's how his public comments made me feel. But I'm the type of guy who never forgets his roots, and even in my darkest moment I still looked up to RZA. I just didn't respect him as much as I used to because he had an excuse for everything and never thought he was wrong. What made me angry was that he never once took a look in the mirror and considered that what he was doing might be hurting his reputation as well as the organization. He was too caught up in his own thing to register all the bickering going on within the family.

When RZA wasn't there, dudes had a lot to say about him. When he came around, dudes kept it quiet, but you could feel the energy.

They never wanted to confront him, but when it came to me, they had no problem with that. If a man thought I was being difficult, or I was fucking with the well-being of the group by standing up for myself, or if they didn't agree with something I said on *Shaolin vs. Wu-Tang* or in an interview, you better believe I heard about it from them. At the worst times I woke up in the middle of the night in a cold sweat, so tired of it all. I'd sit up in my bed thinking that I had to announce my departure from Wu-Tang first thing in the morning. The next day I'd wake up, have breakfast, and say to myself, "How the fuck can I leave my family? They are the most important thing I got."

From the Jackson 5 to the Isley Brothers to the Temptations, groups have broken up over less than what was going on with us. Our chain links had weakened, but I didn't want to see them break. None of us wanted to say that Wu-Tang was dismantled, even though we felt like it was. Everyone had left their Wu-Tang productions contracts long ago and had their own managers wrestling with Wu-Tang on every project. I hated all of the issues; my motto was "Let's get rich and argue later." The problem was that only some of us were getting rich, not all of us. I wanted to see everyone comfortable, and I knew what it took to get there. But we were so brainwashed by RZA and his brother, and it seemed like that was the plan all along: to keep guys at a lower level so we were beholden to Wu-Tang for a career. I am one of the lucky ones with an established career outside of the group. I can only imagine how the guys who never got their RZA-produced solo album felt.

There was a Wu tour booked after my solo joint came out. I didn't want to go, but I did because I'd never keep money out of my brothers' pockets. Then there was talk of another album, which was a major event since there hadn't been a Wu-Tang Clan release in seven years. RZA and Divine started arranging for that in 2011 and finally got it released in 2014, and it was called *A Better Tomorrow*. For everything I did with them at that point, I wanted to know exact numbers when it came to the money—amounts being paid per man on tour, percentage points on publishing, splits on merchandise—all of which they refused to tell me. I had a number I wanted to be paid for my time and hard work for both albums and tours, which was always a tense negotiation. When and if we compromised, I'd end up with something I was never happy about but could live with. The problem they had with me was that by negotiating my value, I inspired the others to do the same. All of this pointed toward the organization needing a new leader on the business side. Since that wasn't happening, everyone kept going around in circles, haggling once again, fighting for every penny when it came time to come together for a tour or album.

Like I told you, RZA's cockiness and focus on his movie career didn't help. It started with him appearing as an actor as early as 2005, before he worked on the soundtracks for the *Kill Bill* movies. Later, in 2012, right when this next Wu album was starting up, *The Man with the Iron Fists*, a movie he wrote, starred in, and directed, was about to be released. The rest of us were happy for him, but we would laugh about his egotistical attitude. Sometimes me and Ghost would fuck with him by asking if he knew certain people in the film business. We would make up names of people who did not exist, and every single time, RZA said he knew them, which was fucking hilarious to us. We still loved him, but Hollywood had created a monster: *Attack of the Fifty-Foot Ego.*

On *A Better Tomorrow*, I'd say 85 percent of the crew straight up told him he didn't have this one in pocket when it came to the production. This amounted to more bad reviews internally than he'd ever gotten before. If anything this brought us together: guys were calling each other, there were side conversations, and if we were all somewhere for whatever reason, it was the topic of conversation. It got to the point that we huddled up and decided as a group that before it went any further we had to very seriously, in a unified fashion this time, float the idea of bringing in other producers. We did that, as a group, and once again, RZA shot the idea down. He insisted that he had to be the head honcho of all Wu-Tang projects including album production. His logic was that since he'd released everyone from their management contracts without a fight, we were expected to comply with all things Wu-Tang in return. That wasn't agreed upon in any way when we terminated those agreements, but eventually each man cut his deal with RZA and Divine and work began on the album.

I was the last member to sign his deal and contribute. Wu-Tang Productions and I only communicated through representatives, and I didn't even go to the studio or hang around RZA for this one. The music was sent to me and I dropped in all my verses in my own studio. I only did it because I didn't want my fellow members to suffer, and the group didn't want to make the album without everyone involved. So much of our turmoil had gone public that it would look bad if I wasn't on the album. The other guys hadn't been my everyday dudes in years, so all I could do was scratch my head when we didn't get our way as far as the production went, because I couldn't understand why they'd agree to make anything but a crazy great album after a seven-year hiatus. Then again, I was coming from a place where more money was appreciated but not needed. Unfortunately, not all of the other brothers were in that same place. They were looking for that live-show money, and I couldn't fault them for that or stand in the way.

In the end, after the entire group lobbied for change, the only concession RZA made was having Rick Rubin coproduce one song, "Ruckus in B Minor," which is a "Triumph"-style full-group joint that was released as a single before the album dropped. In my opinion, doing so did more damage because that song, which was called out in reviews and by fans as the best moment on a very disappointing record, sounds nothing like the rest of *A Better Tomorrow*. If anything, that track got people's hopes up, only to be let down by an album full of music that sounds nothing like it. The other tracks were all produced by RZA, Mathematics, and guys who had been working with RZA for years and it is all pretty lifeless. Not even my brothers spitting fire like they always do could save the day.

In any case, I kept my mouth shut and did my part, including attending a big press conference to announce the album release and upcoming tour. It was a public show of unity so that everybody could see that we were reunited and standing as one after all of our well-publicized infighting. It seems RZA and Divine had sold the album to Warner Bros. under the pretense that we were all involved and that the Clan was unified again. That's why they chose the title *A Better Tomorrow*, which the rest of us hated. Our today wasn't better, our tomorrow wasn't better, nothing was better—not our group dynamic, not the production, nothing.

Everyone was at the press conference. It had been sold to us as routine, but there were other things going on. Attending this event was a condition of our deal, and without telling us, RZA and Divine used the opportunity to shoot photos that were intended for the album cover. They did something else too. We had each agreed to our deal terms, but none of us had finalized contracts in our possession at that point. They'd apparently closed the deal with Warner Bros. without closing their deals with us, because RZA was always the type do that kind of cold-blooded shit. He figured he could talk any of us into what he needed after the fact. He'd say whatever to get the money from a label or promoter and worry about the rest later. The press conference happened on a hot day in L.A. All the members were there in a big conference room, sitting at a long-ass table with microphones on it, answering questions about the record and about coming together again after seven years. We had the worst energy. All of us kept it cool, but we looked like the Bad News Bears after they lost the championship. Afterward, each of us went to different areas of the room to do one-on-one interviews. During that time, someone from Divine's office handed each of us a piece of paper and a pen and told us to sign—while we were doing interviews. It was the fucking contract. Those two literally tried to get us to sign our fucking contracts for the album while we were doing press. All of us were blown away at this underhanded shit, and no one signed it. I damn near threw mine in the guy's face. We were shocked, but RZA was in a bad position: he had convinced the label to sign their contract with Wu-Tang Productions and probably got them to release the album advance without having gotten us to legally agree to be on the album. I never did end up signing that paper, and I wasn't the only one. I know for a fact that a few high-level label executives lost their jobs over this shit.

After that episode it was time for our photos. None of us thought they were for the album cover, so we weren't dressed appropriately. I was wearing shorts, thinking this was just a press conference. In the end they didn't use the group shot for the album cover because it wasn't very good. They went with some hokey cover art, but they did use those photos in promotion. If you look them up, you'll see a real casual photo of the Wu-Tang Clan, everyone looking like we're going to a barbecue. Except for RZA, who is wearing a slick shirt, sunglasses, and nice tailored jeans.

Looking back, *A Better Tomorrow* became our worst yesterday. The tours supporting the album weren't any better—I'd come in the tour dressing room backstage and see nobody smiling. It would be quiet with no energy at all. Everyone in Wu-Tang is such a good MC and performer, though, that when we hit the stage it was like throwing a power switch. As a group, we'd go from lifeless to giving the audience the greatest show on earth in a matter of seconds. We're all good showmen.

Sometimes you have to swallow your pride because you've been given a gift. Our gift was to be loved by the world. The way we see it, our fans are innocent. They know we're dysfunctional, but they don't know the half, and they shouldn't have to. Our fans come to relive their memories and experiences with our music, to get wild on some live Wu-Tang shit once again—or maybe for the first time. We give our best onstage because our audiences ain't got nothing to do with our drama. Like I say, we were given the gift of love, and our responsibility is to give it right back.

That album cycle was my last real interface with the group beyond showing up for gigs. When it came time to perform tracks from *A Better Tomorrow*, I'd sit them out even if I was on them—that's how strongly I felt about the record and the handling of the business surrounding it. Some of the fans caught on and called me out on social media, but I don't think it bothered them too much because *A Better Tomorrow* is our least liked album. Fans love the albums they came up with—the classics—and generally they're happy to hear those records over and over. The energy when we perform the older shit is beautiful. Everybody rocks out together, and we've never had a problem rocking a crowd. In fact, we've never gotten booed in our entire career. One time when I was doing a private corporate gig, I asked the crowd to boo me just so I could see what it felt like.

"Yo, yo, yo, you know in my twenty plus years in the game I never got booed before," I told them. "I never got booed, Wu-Tang never got booed. Can I ask you something? Y'all think you could boo me one time on the count of three?"

On the count of three they started booing, and I came to the front of the stage, lifted my head up, and raised my arms to the sky. Even though the boos weren't real, the sound was, and I let my mind imagine what it would be like to give your best to a crowd and get that in return. A wave of humility washed over me from my head to my toes.

"Thank you, thank you," I said. "I needed that balance."

THERE have been two more Wu-Tang records since *A Better Tomorrow*, and I ain't got much to say about either of them. I'm only on two songs on *The Saga Continues* (2017), but I thought Mathematics did a good job on the production, bringing it back to some street shit. And *Once Upon a Time in Shaolin* (2015) wasn't something any of us besides RZA was a part of. That album was made from preexisting verses that RZA and the other producer, Cilvaringz, had collected over the years. RZA had signed Cilvaringz to Wu-Tang management years ago and we all worked with from time to time, both as the group and on some of our solo albums. He would give guys beats and not charge them, in exchange for verses. So between shit he'd collected from most of us over the years and the many extra verses RZA had, the two of them had enough material for this concept record. He and RZA took it a step further and came up with the idea of hiring an artist to make a custom silver box and pressing just one copy of this Frankenstein album. They took all these vocals that were done in other situations, created the shit, and auctioned it off for two million dollars to that Pharma Bro guy and convicted felon Martin Shkreli.

It's some of the dirtiest shit I've ever heard of. But I can't say more about it because I'm still involved in a lawsuit related to the album. The artist who built the very intricate and beautiful silver box sued everyone in the Clan for damages because he never got paid. He'd done the deal with Cilvaringz, who is Dutch-Moroccan, not a US citizen, and lives in Morocco now. He can't be tracked down, so this artist is suing those of us he can find. I don't know the terms of his deal because I wasn't involved, but he went after all of us. He claimed that we promoted the album, which I know I never did. RZA settled, and I think most of the other guys have settled by now too, but I haven't. I have a lot of thoughts on it, but I've been deposed for the case and can't say any more because it's ongoing.

I never met Martin Shkreli. I was never down with that deal, and I didn't get money out of it. In fact, I got nothing except a lawsuit. I know that thirteen minutes of the album were played for a crowd of about a hundred before they did the auction, but I don't have the slightest clue what the songs are or what any of it sounds like. That's whatever, but to then allow it to be sold to the guy who hiked the price on a life-saving HIV drug 5,000 percent? That's fucking disgraceful. I don't care if he won the auction, RZA should not have allowed him to get the album.

The story got even weirder when Shkreli threatened Ghostface. Ghost had called him a shithead for raising the price of the drug. Shkreli demanded an apology in a YouTube video with these masked goons behind him. Ghost got him back with a video featuring some girls scolding the guy and all kinds of hilarious digs. That shit was funny, but the rest of this fiasco was despicable. That Shkreli guy is not only a criminal and a villain; he's also really crazy.

That album just goes to show there will never be a group with a story like ours, man. We made the impossible possible. When we were all together in the streets, I didn't know where we were going. I never imagined we'd be here twenty-five years later, still sticking it out. We are doing the best we can, coming from an environment that taught us nothing but survival. It's been the illest experience of my whole life, loving something that I also can't fucking stand.

The latest adventure we've taken together has been in the world of film and television, with the release of our documentary *Of Mics and Men* on Showtime as well as our scripted bio-series on Hulu, *Wu-Tang: An American Saga*. RZA had been talking about a Wu-Tang movie ever since he got involved in Hollywood. In his usual way, when he got serious about it he started having conversations with groups of us—one-on-one, three-on-one, whatever—but never to the entire team as one. As usual he said, "I think I can get X amount of dollars for each member. You don't have to do nothing. All you got to do is say you want to do it."

To me, a TV series sounded dope, but I was driven to see our story on the big screen. When the N.W.A movie *Straight Outta Compton* came out and was a huge success in every way, talk began circulating about our story being told in that format. For years, people had called us the East Coast N.W.A. I brought that up to RZA, telling him we should stay on the movie side of things, but he was already out there building his relationships with a certain company that I guess convinced him a series was the better way to go. RZA in turn convinced some of the guys to do it and told others that they didn't have to be involved if they didn't want to.

I was against the deal because I didn't like the terms, the money, any of it. I kept telling RZA to look at *Straight Outta Compton*, which made two hundred million dollars worldwide and was the highest grossing movie by a black director in history. It made no sense to me to sell our story for a TV series where nobody would walk away with real money. Everybody except RZA, that is, because he was getting more on the deal—as an executive producer, writer, creator, composer, and I'm sure a few other ways we'll never know about. He insisted that our story was too complicated for a two-hour movie and that it had to be a series. Plus, he said we could keep extending the series into more seasons so guys would ultimately make more. I was skeptical because there is no guarantee that a series won't be canceled after the initial run of episodes is ordered. If it didn't connect or if the executives who bought it left the network, it could be axed at any time. When it came to a movie, I knew we could get back-end money, which would amount to a lot more for each of us if the movie was a hit. We could only sell our story once, so I told the other guys to think hard about it.

The guys saw my logic enough so that RZA went out and shopped for a movie deal. He allegedly received a production offer of ten million dollars, which he insisted wasn't enough to make an official movie about us. Maybe, but I couldn't understand how he thought that wasn't a lot of money as a starting point. Production companies team up all the time to raise the fortunes it costs to make a Hollywood movie—just think of how many company logos you see at the beginning of a film. If we got ten million off the bat, that was a good sign that we could turn that into twenty if we kept going. But RZA wasn't having that, and tried to use what he considered a small number to justify his preference to go with a scripted series. I told him before we made that decision final to let me try to get a better film deal because I had some connections too. I'm sure RZA and his brother wanted to drop poison in my chocolate milk, but they let me give it a shot.

First thing I did was call my brother Q-Tip, who told me he'd get me in touch with Leonardo DiCaprio, who is a real close friend of his and a big Wu fan. Next time Leo came to town, me and Tip met Leo and his then girlfriend out in Brooklyn at an old mafioso-looking pizza spot near Sunset Park that Leo loves. As a gift, I let my brother come along as a fly on the wall because Leo is his favorite actor. We had a great time, eating pizza, telling stories, laughing and shit. Then we started talking about the possibility of a Wu-Tang movie and I told Leo I'd love to see him play a role in it, anything he wanted to do. He talked about his production company and all the directors he thought might do a great job—and these were big names and people he'd worked with. He was super open to the idea, and after that meal, he had his production company executives reach out to me. We took it to the next level with them. They were very interested, so we got the ball rolling, talking real numbers, with the goal of an even bigger release than *Straight Outta Compton*.

"Yo, how'd it go?" Tip asked me after my meeting with Leo's people.

"Yo . . . Tip, I think we found the big fish. Thank you, man. I appreciate you."

"That's incredible, man. I'm glad to hear it."

A lot of other cats would have said they'd make that call and maybe never get around to it. In entertainment, people are always gassing you up while making themselves look important. But Tip is such a humble and genuine person that when he tells you he's going to do something, he does it. He was truly excited to see this happen. The next step was to sit down with RZA. He'd let me go do my thing, but I know he didn't expect me to come back to the table with one of the most in-demand, influential, and highest paid actors alive. I couldn't wait to blow his mind.

I got back with RZA and told him Leo's production company was ready to raise all the money needed to make a major motion picture. They just needed assurance that all the guys wanted to be a part of it. I got a typical nonchalant response, but RZA agreed to take a meeting in Beverly Hills with the top executives of Leo's company. The day of the meeting, we all sat down at a rooftop spot and got into the details of what they were ready to bring to the table, which was pretty much everything. It was the perfect situation for Wu-Tang, but I looked over and saw that RZA wasn't comfortable. I've known the guy for years and seen him act all kinds of ways, and in that moment, I saw him playing a role. He sat there, taking it in, watching to see how far I could get. At the end of the meeting, without emotion, he just said, "Okay, I'll get back to you," and Leo's people left. I sat there with my index finger to my temple, elbow on my armrest, leaning back in the chair, staring at him.

"What's goin' on, RZA?" I asked him.

"Yo, that's big shit right there," he said.

"Yeah, it is. Listen, let me tell you something. You told me to go out there and fish, see what I could find. I came back and brought a fucking whale to the table. You need to think about the logistics of what this could be as a movie on that level compared to a damn cable TV series. You can't look at up-front money, because a movie like this will gross so much money for us that we have an opportunity to take home more from it than we have made in our entire music careers. This could be our big payback."

"I agree, Raekwon, I agree," he said. We kept talking, and I left feeling good about the conversation.

It seemed like he was cool with it, so I set up another meeting with the same players. It would be the most important one—the third meeting is when you close the deal. We met somewhere in the Valley, and the minute he got there, RZA's energy was entirely different. He barely said anything and seemed to be going through the motions, nothing more. I could tell he wasn't going to agree to do it, and my instincts told me why: my guess is that he was already in bed with a production company, deep into developing the scripted series for TV, even though none of us had signed off on it.

It was clear that something was very different, so after a respectable amount of time, Leo's people ended the meeting and got up to leave.

"Thanks," RZA said. "We'll call you."

"You son of a bitch," I thought to myself. "You had something in your pocket the whole time and knew you'd never close this fucking deal. You didn't think I could put something together that was better than what you got. You ain't about us. You about you, motherfucker."

I kept my cool and didn't spaz out on him, but in my heart I knew more than ever that his relationships in Hollywood mattered more to him than his relationship with us. He was burying a dream deal over pride.

The two of us sat there for the next hour as he tried to justify it, saying that a series was a better way to tell the story, that people streamed more than they went to the movies, that a series would be around for more years than a movie. I'd agree with him if we were looking at an indie, small budget movie, but that wasn't the case. We were looking at something produced and backed and probably featuring Leonardo DiCaprio. That's a whole other level. No matter what he said, nothing was going to change my mind or the fact that the series wasn't making us real money. When he tried to convince me that we were going to get the biggest actors and actresses in the business attached to the series, I'd heard enough.

"Yo, stop frontin', RZA," I said. "Stop frontin'. There ain't no way Hollywood's biggest talent going to sign up for a Wu-Tang TV show."

But a major motion picture produced by Leo with a top-tier director? Yeah, that they might do. So stop frontin'."

This bullshit hurt my feelings because it proved to me that he'd already counted me out before I began. He didn't think I could bring that kind of power to the table, but I'd gotten them there, all ready to rock 'n' roll. They were excited and connected, so with the snap of a finger they could have gotten the ball rolling for real. Not to mention that even if he had signed some preliminary agreement to develop a series, deals get called off and bought out all the time, so if RZA were honest about it and admitted to me that he'd signed something already, it could have been worked out. But the dude wouldn't cop to that. He just kept insisting the scripted series deal he had found was better than the major motion picture deal I had found. As I left him that day I had tears in my eyes.

Right away, RZA went around to all the other guys, convincing them to do his little series. If you'll notice, Meth is the only one named co–executive producer, which means more pay. That didn't surprise me. Meth has been in movies and knows his way around Hollywood, so RZA wasn't going to get one over on him. My guess is that Meth got the title and extra money in exchange for helping RZA convince the other guys to sign up. If so, that would be some cold-blooded shit right there. Not only did the rest of us not get the right money, but we didn't even get equal billing. It wouldn't have cost them anything to give us all credits as producers after we agreed to be paid what we were paid—people get credits like those all the time as a courtesy. The other guys, minus me, are listed as "consulting producers," which doesn't mean shit. RZA has multiple credits per episode and Meth is his co–executive producer, and I'm sure they're actually getting paid for those.

When it came down to it, I refused to sign off on the production deal. That didn't stop RZA. He went ahead without me and tried to write the history of the Wu-Tang Clan without Raekwon. They got deep into the making of this thing, to the point that they even had a trailer featuring "C.R.E.A.M." but no episodes featuring the guy who made the song. How the fuck was that going to work?

I had my business partner and lawyer get in touch with the production company because I was too emotional about all of it to have a civil conversation. I was ready to get on the phone and tell these people I'd never spoken to before to fuck themselves and get ready for a lawsuit. My partners did it right and pointed out that they were trying to tell a story without one of the group's top-tier, most outspoken and respected members. If they intended to use my likeness in any form they needed to negotiate or face litigation. They thought about it overnight and came back conceding that they needed to make me a better financial offer and get me involved in the storytelling process. Even at this point, my so-called brother RZA didn't have my back. He didn't want me to be part of it because he knew how I felt about the project. He'd been telling them they didn't need me to tell the story. My reaching out was a big wakeup call for the production company, so they went back and told RZA they had to get me involved. They were already deep into writing the episodes, which none of the other members had reviewed, by the way. The show was a picture painted by RZA and no one else. Maybe 35 percent of the content was inspired by interviews with the guys and 65 percent was straight from RZA.

I was steaming hot, but I played it cool. There was a television series being made of my life whether I liked it or not. How could I not engage and at least try to make sure I had a hand in it? Because I stayed true to myself, my people were able to negotiate a better deal for me than what I'd been offered by RZA. In exchange for that, I agreed to get involved, consulting with the writers and meeting with Shameik Moore, the actor playing me, to make the story more accurate. For what it is, I think the show has done a good job with the story so far. Let's see what they do with the second season. I'm happy to have Shameik play me, he's a really talented kid, they definitely made the right choice there.

After my agreement was finalized, I got a call from RZA. "Congratulations," he said. "I hear you're on board."

I had a lot of things to say to him. He had tried to write me out of the history of the group and didn't reach out to make peace. He'd let me negotiate my own deal, which was fine, but didn't get involved in that and weigh in on my behalf to help move it along. And that hurt me the most. He was after a good look for himself and it seemed to me only brought the crew along to sell us out. Most of the dudes don't see it that way, maybe because they don't understand the film and TV business or don't care, or are just happy we have a TV show.

So many things rolled through my mind, but they weren't worth saying to RZA. Our friendship and brotherhood were over. I'd been there from the start, weathering all the storms with him and trying to keep the group together. I'd sat next to him at his mother's funeral, crying like I'd lost my own. All that was done. It was strictly business from now on.

"Yeah," I said. "I'm on board. It's all good. Peace." I hung up the phone with tears in my eyes once more.

When RZA and his brother read these words, they are going to say I'm frontin' on how they handled the film offer and the TV show. They'll say it's all bullshit. To that I say, "You know damn well I'm not lying."

The pilot episode of *Wu-Tang: An American Saga* begins with my story, so I guess it turns out I'm important. I'll never look at RZA the same way again, and the saddest part is that we both have families and children who know each other well and are friends. They're entirely innocent in all of this. It bothered me that our feud might make them see me differently. So one day I had to say something to RZA's lady, and I'm glad I did.

"Please don't ever look at me a different way," I said. "We're men and we're going to go through things. But I want you to know I have the utmost respect for you, your family, and your children. I want you to know that no matter what, I respect who you are." She smiled and thanked me for saying so and that is all I needed to hear.

I've been through so much with all of these guys, even more than what is written in this book. We are bound by our history, like brothers, like a real family. You may have a brother that puts you in jeopardy, the type who tells you to jump off a cliff or put your hand in a fire. My Wu-Tang brothers like to throw me in the water knowing I can't swim, but then they dive in to save me. The story of Wu-Tang is the tale from the 'hood. It's a comment on urban America. When you're born in the 'hood, you're caught between love and hate. When your story starts there, often enough that's exactly where it ends too.

CHAPTER 18

INTO THE WILD

When I set out upon the journey that became this book, I promised to tell my story. The whole truth in all its glory—the good, the bad, and the ugly. The way I see it, we've spent enough time on the bad and the ugly. Let's get back to the good.

Life is a cycle. Everything that goes dark can become light again. I'm living proof that you can turn a negative into a positive, and so are all of my brothers. My mission here has been nothing but that. Hear me when I say this: if you don't want to turn bad things into good in your life, you never will. It must come from within and you must want it with all of your heart. The most beautiful and most difficult thing about being human is that you manifest what you want in your time on earth, so be careful what you wish for.

One of the most important changes I've ever made was my decision to convert to Islam. Being a Five Percenter had been the right thing for me as a boy. The Five Percent Nation was a gift to me when I really needed one; the knowledge and the brothers who served it to me were the fathers I never had. I took that wisdom into my life in what I would like to consider the correct way. But I began to get disillusioned, not by the teachings but by some of my fellow followers. I found myself around dudes who used the knowledge as a shield and a filter for their reality rather than applying the lessons to their lives. They were more into being identified as a Five Percenter than learning and living the lessons.

I saw myself apart from them, I identified as someone who was willing to die for what I believed in, like loyalty and family and for what I knew in my heart to be real, like a higher power. The more popular it became in hip-hop culture, the more I encountered too many loose interpretations of the knowledge that didn't jibe with my point of view. I decided to leave the half-truths behind so I could get serious about my religion. As I grew into manhood, I realized that becoming a Muslim was where I needed to be.

I converted in 2009, at the age of thirty-nine. Becoming a Muslim, having that faith and the desire to give back and grow, was a yearning I couldn't deny. Following that instinct is one of the most important things I've ever done. As I see it, the fundamental difference is this: the Five Percent Nation preaches that every black man is God, while Islam preaches that there is only one god, Allah, and he accepts everyone.

I worried about what my Five Percent and Wu brothers might say. But the guy who put my mind at ease was Popa Wu. He was RZA's older cousin, an honorary member of the group, and a very active Five Percenter all his life, until his death at sixty-four in 2019. He was one of the most spiritual men I'd ever known. He made appearances on a number of our records, from *Cuban Linx* ("North Star [Jewels]") to *Wu-Tang Forever* ("Wu Revolution") and was always there to guide us with some wisdom through the years. When I told him about my change of heart and leaving the Nation behind, he wasn't upset at all.

"That's beautiful," he said. "When you look at religion it boils down to: Who is the most high, who do you love, who do you give your attention to? Five Percenters are gods . . . to the ones we provide for. The ones we bring food, clothing, shelter, and peace to. If you are giving that love to the one who allows you to do that for your own, then it's a part of the same belief, God."

Popa Wu devoted his life to serving the Nation until his dying day in 2019. To get his wisdom and acceptance meant so much to me. All I ever wanted was to look at the most high in my life as the entity that gave me the blessing to be the man I am today. This has been a journey, and I've made mistakes, always striving to be better. I feel I've finally arrived at the image of self I've always held in my mind. The most high walks alone, and making my transition to that understanding has been a beautiful thing.

This clarity came to me the day a childhood friend of mine came home from jail. His name is Tyrese, and I've shouted him out on my records over the years. Growing up, this guy was a terror—on a different plane, unlike anyone I've ever known. It's no surprise that he did real time, for many years. When he got back, he was somebody else because he'd converted to Islam. I saw such a transformation that I helped get him a job and get rehabilitated back into society and onto the path of reclaiming his life. While I did that for him, he enlightened me with the true teachings of Allah. We'd pray together, go to the mosque, and share the teachings. I'm proud to be a member of the largest religion in the world, one that doesn't discriminate. We are all brothers and sisters under Allah. The day I took my Shahadah I felt like I was glowing from within. It felt like years of darkness were lifted from me and I was shining in the way I was always wanted to.

Since that moment in 2008, the blessings have come faster and stronger than ever. I've taken my time learning the Quran. One thing I know to be true is that if you take one step toward Allah, he takes ten steps toward you. I have felt that, and it's been the best thing I've ever done with my life.

As a man in his fifth decade on earth I can say this: all of the best elements of my character originated in my household, as troubled as it was. My mother taught me to treat people the way I want to be treated, and though I haven't always done so, I've grown to realize that she was right. If there is one lesson I hope to pass on to my children, that is it. My mother also had a sense of humor, a sense of community, a true heart and a concern for others—and I'd like to think I have a piece of those things, too.

I love the life I've been allowed to live. I love that my ability as a rapper has given me so many gifts. But it hasn't been easy on my three children, because this life hasn't allowed me to be an everyday dad. When they were young, it was tough to explain to them why I couldn't be there all the time and why I was constantly coming or going. Now that I'm established, nothing is more important than keeping a balance and being the best father I can be. My kids all have different personalities: Cori is outspoken, Jaibari is an introvert, and Sekai is both. She's sweet as cotton candy and it takes a lot for her to go off, but when she does, it's on. I love the challenges I face getting myself on each of their levels.

My children are going to create another generation from what I created, and that means something to me. I try to instill in them the wisdom I've learned, knowing that they will soon be even wiser than I am now. It's taken me years to form relationships with them, but I think we are all at a place where they understand the demands of my life and why I wasn't around as much as I'd like to have been. I'm happiest to be able to give my children the comfort to go out into the world and be whoever they want to be. All that my kids need to do is figure out what makes sense for them, and I hope I am the one they come to when they need guidance. If there is one thing I know, it's that the most important thing in this world is family.

All of my kids now live in the South, in Georgia and Texas, in well-to-do suburbs where it's relatively safe. They're sheltered, and when I see that in them, I'm glad. One time I was walking with my son Jaibari and we saw a homeless man. I laid a hundred-dollar bill on the guy and kept it moving, but the man got up and started following us. I could see my son getting nervous because he didn't know where the situation was going, even though the guy just wanted to say thank you. I wasn't going to make a big deal, but I did tell the guy to do something productive with it, like getting some food rather than getting drunk or high. It made my son uncomfortable, and I understood why. I love that there are those differences between us because I've worked very hard so that he and his siblings will not face the struggles I have. My son isn't interested in sports the way I was at his age, but if you asked him, he could tell you everything you need to know about the political situation in China right now. I'm glad he's got a brain like that, it's amazing to me.

I intend to give all my children what they need, not necessarily what they want. I will give them the ability to go out into the world and earn money for themselves, to make their own lives on their own terms, always with their heads held high. I stress confidence, integrity, and loyalty. If you have those, no matter what life throws your way, you'll come out on top.

I feel such freedom in my life now, as a man, a father, and as an artist. I may not have satisfaction, but I have found a type of peace in my relationship with the Wu-Tang Clan; it simply is what it is. I've found happiness as an independent artist, able to create the way I like with whoever I like. I make and release records that satisfy my vision, all on my own label. I felt the permanence of this change when I made my sixth album, *F.I.L.A.*, in 2012. I wanted to come up with a concept record, because I've always looked at my music as pieces of art. The acronym in the title stands for *Fly Luxurious International Art*, which says it all: these songs, these pieces of our existence, are like paintings and should be treated as such.

On that record I wanted to twist it up, so I found a group of new producers whose music moved me. I've always been the type to look for up-and-coming talent, so that was my focus. I gave my man Frank G his moment, among others, and I looked at the project in a new way. I also stopped trying to dictate things. I now see my role as bringing together a group of smart people so that we can make something together that is bigger than all of us. It's a side effect of getting older, of calming down and getting to know myself better. I've found happiness with my children, their mothers, my extended family, and in my spiritual life. All of that growth and change I've made within has changed my world without.

Keeping myself open has allowed me to make connections I'd never have made earlier in my career. On that album I worked with the producer Jerry "Wonda" Duplessis, who is Wyclef Jean's cousin, and he really changed my perspective. Jerry is a musician who plays multiple instruments, so having him at my side was very different than working with guys who only push buttons when they make beats. Jerry became a new creative element in my arsenal and opened up my writing process. I finally felt like I'd arrived at a place where I could enjoy everything I'd worked so hard for. During the years I wrote that album I was traveling a lot, playing shows in the most exotic locales that would have me. I tell people all the time that the greatest privilege I've earned is the ability to travel internationally. More than anything else, seeing the world has opened my eyes and my mind to other cultures and ways of living. I've gained an appreciation for art and foreign food that I never had growing up. Experiencing life outside of your comfort zone makes you rich in ways that money cannot buy.

This kind of freedom and receptiveness led me to even greater heights on my album *The Wild*, which I put together over two years starting in 2015. I was able to pull in artists of all generations, from Snoop Dogg and A$AP Rocky to 2 Chainz. I wanted to challenge myself to interact with the younger era while still feeling relevant, and I did that. This ain't news, but I got to say, Snoop Dogg can fucking smoke. I've smoked weed plenty, but that brother made me feel like it was my first time. At some point in our working together, I just couldn't hang with him like that. Snoop smokes these fat, thick blunts, and after passing two of them back and forth with him I was comatose. When we got in the studio there was no way I could be alert at the production board, so I'd have to let it pass by me. Snoop was one of the first people who showed up for me on the album. He made me realize how many friends I have in this business after all these years.

I've also made new friends and connections as I've branched out into new enterprises. I've got a luxury barbershop and boutique called 611 Purple Factory in Toronto that carries the collaborations I've done over the years, from sneakers, boots, and clothing to skateboards and bikes. I have my own wine, Licataa, which is a Lambrusco named for a town in Sicily, and that journey took me to all parts of Italy that I fell in love with. This isn't just a product I'm putting my name to, it's something I spent time developing with the wine producers, Cantine Ceci, and from what's inside to the glamorous blue mirrored bottle, I'm proud of it. I'm excited to bring this style of sparkling red wine to America because most people here have probably never tried it. I hope it is around for fifty or a hundred years and is something my children can inherit and continue to be a part of. I also have a film company, Third Eye Films. I'm busy making a documentary on the making of the Purple Tape and that is just the start of my plans. The way I've painted pictures in lyrics, I intend to do on the big screen. All of these entrepreneurial pursuits have taught me so much and I'm ready to learn more.

Being true to the higher power continually sends unexpected blessings my way. Consider this: I met 2 Chainz before he got famous, when I first moved to Atlanta. I had a Maybach at the time and I was getting it washed when this guy came up to me, shouting, "Chef, what's good?" At the time he was still calling himself Tity Boi.

He showed me love and said he appreciated how I'd been moving. To tell you the truth, I needed to hear it. What's more, he told me he got that smoke. I took his number, and just like that, Tity Boi became my weed dealer. I used to meet him out back of a Wendy's to pick up a couple hundred dollars' worth of weed.

"Yo, Chef, you fucking crazy," he said, laughing. "You out here by yourself, driving your own shit through the 'hood?"

"Yo, man, I'm a real nigga," I said. "This ain't nothing new to me."

I really liked the guy, so one thing led to another and he invited me to his studio. This was when I realized that the dude is a dope fucking rapper. We became cool on a whole other level because he never pressured me when it came to music or the industry. He didn't ask me for favors; the friendship was all real, so I willingly gave him advice about working with labels and talked to him about the business the way a big brother would. And next thing you know, he did a record with Lil Wayne. I remember the day he told me he had changed his name.

"Yo . . . you ain't got one—you got two chains?" I said, laughing. "I love it, man!"

I'm so proud of that guy. He really did it, and he's fresh to death. He brought all that energy to my album, and I hope we continue to work together. I think it's important for the future of hip-hop to have the generations mix it up. That's the only way this art form can evolve. Hip-hop is just as important today as it was when I was a kid. It is the most honest expression of urban life that we have, and it continues to be. No new style can be discounted, and the true artist knows how to bring every era into their creative process. When I made *The Wild*, I worked out of a studio where all generations of hip-hop artists were doing their thing, and that gave me energy. Creativity has no limits.

And neither does the potential of the Wu-Tang Clan. There's no reason we can't return to ourselves, reclaim our throne, and celebrate our legacy with our legions of fans around the world. We just need to tap into the hunger that once bound us. It's been long enough if you ask me. I think we're ready and I think the world is too. I would love to see us do an album the right way, we can't have that last effort end the story. I'd love to tour a new set of songs as powerful as the classics and bring the ruckus to the fullest. Whatever you put into the universe comes back to you, so anything that went away can reappear.

I keep that in mind a lot lately. I have a degree of prestige that numbers can't touch, so I no longer work based on what dollar amount my art can get me. I will only make music that I feel in my heart. That is the only way I'll be able to carry the respect I've earned in the game. It's the only way I'll be able to respect myself. I've achieved heights that a kid from Park Hill never expected to see. All I keep thinking about, as I look ahead to the days to come, is what adventure awaits me, just one level up?

ACKNOWLEDGMENTS

I want to begin by saying all praises due to Allah, and may Allah make us bearers of light and not the darkness.

Creating this book has been an amazing experience, so I want to give a special thanks to everybody who worked so hard preparing it for all of my fans. Thank you always to my management team: Rashida Watler, Supreme, Don P, and the entire Wu-Tang Clan alliance.

Anthony Bozza, you are one hell of a writer. Thank you to my literary agent, Lisa Gallagher, and the entire Simon & Schuster team for the love: Maggie Loughran, Jeremie Ruby-Strauss, Jen Bergstrom, Aimee Bell, Ian Marshall, Jen Long, Sally Marvin, Jessica Roth, John Vairo, Lisa Litwack, Caroline Pallotta, and Bianca Salvant. I want to personally thank Thomas Hopke and Christian Pascale. To my photo team, Erik Sasso and Chad Griffin, thank you for blessing me with the dope portraits for the book.

To my entire household family, I love you all! My kids, Sekai, Jaibari, Cori, mothers Ashley, Liz, and Marte, you are always in my heart, as well as my sister, Simone, and my brothers Kareem and Don P. I send shouts to my love Jas Brenton and family, to the Canty family, to the Jaime Zekofsky family, and to the Trini family. Also to Samont "Skip" Washington, Pop "Khadil," the entire Haney family, and the Loud family. Love to all of my cousins: Dorinda, Brenda, Ricco, Born, and Dorrie, as well as the Shaw family and the Carter family.

To my 611 team, Licataa team, Hashstoria, CitizenGrown, to my accountants Bruce and K., to all of hip-hop culture and my outstanding peers that give me the strength to prevail and elevate the game, I say stay real! So many have helped me become the man and artist I am today, so if I forgot to mention you, please know I've got nothing but love for you! To all my home teams on the block, God bless your souls. Stay striving for perfection.

Peace,

"Parkhillians"